Faulkingham

Negotiating the past

Negotiating the past:
The making of memory
in South Africa

Edited by Sarah Nuttall and
Carli Coetzee

OXFORD
UNIVERSITY PRESS

OXFORD
UNIVERSITY PRESS

Great Clarendon Street, Oxford OX2 6DP

Oxford University Press is a department of the University of Oxford.
It furthers the University's objective of excellence in research, scholarship,
and education by publishing worldwide in

Oxford New York

Athens Auckland Bangkok Bogotá Buenos Aires Calcutta
Cape Town Chennai Dar es Salaam Delhi Florence Hong Kong Istanbul
Karachi Kuala Lumpur Madrid Melbourne Mexico City Mumbai
Nairobi Paris São Paulo Singapore Taipei Tokyo Toronto Warsaw

and associated companies in Berlin Ibadan

Oxford is a registered trademark of Oxford University Press
in the UK and certain other countries

Negotiating the Past: The Making of Memory in South Africa

ISBN 0 19 571503 9

First published 1998
Second impression 1999

Copy Editor: Mary Starkey
Designer: Mark Standley

Published by Oxford University Press Southern Africa,
PO Box 12119, N1 City, 7463, Cape Town, South Africa

Set in Dante by Castle Graphics, Cape Town
Printed and bound by ABC Press Limited

Contents

PART IV: Inscribing the past

Notes on the contributors

EVE BERTELSEN teaches literature and media studies at the University of Cape Town. She has edited a collection of essays on Doris Lessing for McGraw Hill (1985) and has published numerous articles on the novel, film, and South African media.

ANDRÉ BRINK is the author of eleven novels, his most recent being *The First Life of Adamastor* (1993), *On the Contrary* (1993), and *Imaginings of Sand* (1996). He has won the CNA Prize three times, and his novels have twice been shortlisted for the Booker Prize. He is professor of English at the University of Cape Town.

CARLI COETZEE teaches in the department of English language and literature at the University of Cape Town and works in the area of southern African studies. She has published a number of articles on South African literary and historical topics.

PATRICIA DAVISON is deputy director (public programmes) of the South African Museum in Cape Town. She holds a doctorate from the University of Cape Town and her research is primarily concerned with material culture and museum practice.

HARRIET DEACON did her Ph.D. in history, on Robben Island medical institutions in the nineteenth century, at Cambridge University, and then held a junior research fellowship at The Queen's College, Oxford, where she worked on the history of medicine at the Cape. She is editor of *The Island: A History of Robben Island, 1488–1992* (1996) and is currently a lecturer attached to the multimedia education group at the University of Cape Town.

EDUARD FAGAN is a senior lecturer in the department of public law at the University of Cape Town. He has published a number of articles on aspects of South African law and is an associate academic member of the Cape Bar.

MICHAEL GODBY is professor of history of art at the University of Cape Town. He has lectured and published on fourteenth- and fifteenth-century Italian art, eighteenth-century English painting, especially Hogarth, nineteenth- and twentieth-century South African art, and the history of photography.

MARTIN HALL is professor of historical archaeology at the University of Cape Town. He is currently researching the archaeology of colonial Cape Town. His books include *Archaeology Africa* (1996), an introduction to the practice of archaeology in Africa, and *Slaves, Rings and Rubbish* (1996), a historical novel which fictionalizes the archaeology of the early colonial city for young adult readers.

ANTHONY HOLIDAY is a senior lecturer in philosophy at the University of the Western Cape's school of government and a contributing editor to the opinion columns of the *Cape Times*. His book *Moral Powers: Normative Necessity in Language and History* (1988) deals with the relationship between Marxist and Wittgensteinian thought and political morality. His more recent papers include discussions of Wittgensteinian exegesis, colonial discourse theory, and the meaning of slavery.

INGRID DE KOK is director of extra-mural studies in the department of adult education and extra-mural studies at the University of Cape Town. Her first collection of poems was *Familiar Ground* (1988); a second collection will appear in October. She has co-edited *Spring Is Rebellious: Arguments about Cultural Freedom* (1990) and was the advisory editor of the Winter 1996 issue of *World Literature Today: South African Literature in Transition*.

SINFREE MAKONI holds a Ph.D. in applied linguistics from the University of Edinburgh. He has published locally and internationally in the areas of second-language acquisition, language in education, and language among the elderly. He is chairperson of the board of the National Language Project and of the Southern African Applied Linguistics Association. He teaches in the English department at the University of Cape Town.

GARY MINKLEY is a senior lecturer in history at the University of the Western Cape. His Ph.D. research was on industrialization in East London 1945–57, and he has written numerous articles on South African historiography and oral history, as well as on public history and memory. He is currently involved in a research project on 'The history of history teaching at southern African universities' with Ciraj Rassool.

NJABULO NDEBELE is the vice-chancellor of the University of the North. He is the author of a collection of short stories, *Fools* (1983), and has published influential essays in *Rediscovery of the Ordinary* (1991).

SARAH NUTTALL is a lecturer in the department of English at the University of Stellenbosch. She is co-editor of *Text, Theory, Space: Land, Literature and History in South Africa and Australia* (1996) and writes about South African literature and culture.

CIRAJ RASSOOL lectures in history at the University of the Western Cape. His doctoral research on I. B. Tabata is a critique of South African resistance historiography. Since then, he has published in different areas of public history and culture. He is a member of the board of trustees of the District Six Museum.

STEVEN ROBINS lectures in the department of anthropology and sociology at the University of the Western Cape. He has published on land and identity issues in Zimbabwe and South Africa, as well as critical literacy studies and South African-Jewish identity. He is currently working with urban planners and architects on memoryscapes of the city and the politics of development in Cape Town's informal settlements.

KERRY WARD is studying South-East Asian–Cape forced migration in the eighteenth century at the University of Michigan. Her previous work in South Africa has included an oral history project, a study of identity and migration at Mamre, and co-organization of the Sheikh Yusuf Tercentenary Exhibition at the Cape Town Castle.

NIGEL WORDEN is associate professor of history at the University of Cape Town. He is the author of *Slavery in Dutch South Africa* (1985) and *The Making of Modern South Africa: Conquest, Segregation and Apartheid* (1994), as well as articles on South African public history.

Negotiating the past

Introduction

THE MOST IMPORTANT EVENT that has taken place since the first democratic elections were held in South Africa in April 1994 has been the drafting of the final constitution. Forward-looking, the constitution represents the vision of South Africa's future as one of freedom and equality. However, the ongoing event that has most captured South Africa's imagination has been the work of the Truth and Reconciliation Commission (TRC). The task of the TRC has been to delve into South Africa's grim past; the records of the hearings of the TRC are the repository of South African memory.

It is therefore an appropriate time for the publication of a book of this kind, a book which investigates the ways in which memory is being negotiated in South Africa, at a time when many are urging their fellow South Africans to forget the past and to look to a new future. It is not presented as the final word on memory, nor does it aim to define or theorize memory in one particular way. Instead it is intended as a contribution to an ongoing debate about the processes of memory, and about how memory is created and inscribed. We are as yet unable to judge which memories and ways of remembering will come to dominate in South Africa in the future. The questions addressed by the chapters in this collection centre on how it happens that certain versions of the past get to be remembered, which memories are privileged, and what the loci are for the production of memory.

The first section of this book consists of a number of responses to the TRC and the questions raised by this public forum for the production of memory. The status and task of the TRC has been the subject of major disputes, given voice through public debate and through the media. Which deeds should be brought to light, and what the reaction of the TRC should be to evidence, have been

sources of conflict between a number of factions. Perhaps predictably, the National Party (NP) has wanted to argue that actions
performed on behalf of the previous government should be
pardoned because they were executed in the name of what was
then seen as the general good. Related to this is the argument that
past acts of 'terrorism' by those resisting the NP government
receive equal treatment with misdeeds perpetrated by the armed
forces and secret police units loyal to the NP government. This
version of 'equal wrongs' has been a powerful force in the
discourse of retribution and reconciliation.

The most significant counter-arguments to this position have
come from Kader Asmal, minister of water affairs, in a book
called *Reconciliation through Truth: A Reckoning of Apartheid's
Criminal Governance* (1996; co-written with Louise Asmal and
Ronald Suresh Roberts). As the title indicates, the aim of the
book is to characterize the NP government as 'evil', and to insist
that its deeds be remembered and that retribution be made for the
actions of those who acted as agents of the NP. The book is a
defence of a particular role for the TRC, namely that it should act
as a vehicle that will allow South Africans to move to 'reconciliation' through 'truth', by 'reckoning' with apartheid's actors.
The book uses psychologized metaphors to talk about the
'healing' of a nation, assuming that – if psychoanalysis is taken as
an appropriate way of achieving healing for the individual –
nations' healing resembles that of individuals.

This approach is perhaps necessarily attracted to representative
individuals, one of whom has been Mark Behr. Behr was a
member of the white student left at Stellenbosch University, and
recently (as the keynote speaker at a conference in Cape Town)
confessed that he had been a police informant all along. Reactions
to his confession ranged from anger and dismay (from former
comrades and friends) to praise for the fact that he had made this
admission, and thereby turned himself into a victim-hero: his bad
consciousness as a student and his subsequent silence is denied,

and he enters history as one of the 'good' white South Africans, entitled to membership of the new nation by means of his confession and the performance of a purge.

The first two chapters in this book, those by Njabulo Ndebele and André Brink, form a fascinating pair. Ndebele and Brink are both interested in the wider significance of the TRC's work, but use the process to very different ends. Ndebele wants to insist on the need for the production of 'truth', to counter the lies that were associated with and produced by apartheid. Brink, on the other hand, finds it more useful to write about the TRC as a representation of healing through narrative. For both of these writers the effect is transformation; the nature of the process is theorized differently.

Ndebele's argument develops some of the concerns of his previous work, most significantly the essays collected in his *Rediscovery of the Ordinary* (1991). He wants in his work to insist on the need for a South African realist mode of fiction, and to this end he contrasts a metaphoric mode of writing with a mode that is grounded in 'validated mass experience'. This version of the TRC sees it as the means by which the reality of the past in South Africa can be resuscitated and brought into the open. Through this process of piecing together the 'real' lives of South Africans, through memory, Ndebele argues, the 'moral desert' in which we live will be turned into another kind of landscape.

Brink's chapter, like Ndebele's, can also be read as a theorization of his own recent creative writing. Always concerned with history and memory, Brink's latest novels have taken a more explicit turn towards narrativizing the past. For Brink the lacunae in the archives are most usefully filled through magical realism, metaphor, and fantasy, modes that allow for a large degree of affective and symbolic interpretation of the ways in which the past can be remembered and used. So Brink talks of the TRC as a 'patchwork', thereby emphasizing the fragmentary nature of the work of memory, as well as the ways in which old scraps are put to new use in larger wholes.

Anthony Holiday's chapter adopts a different approach to the TRC. Unlike the previous two authors he does not try to interpret the significance of the TRC, but instead focuses on the contradictions in the way it has been conceived and is being managed. Holiday points out that the TRC's project is explicitly one of healing and of contrition. This is indeed how the TRC is set up in the National Unity and Reconciliation Act 34 of 1995. However, according to Holiday, contrition is a private matter, and allowing contrition to be performed in a public sphere opens the process up to abuse and cynical manipulation. Public confession, he reminds us, is no guarantee of contrition or of any transformation within the confessor. Thus the question of amnesty and pardons, the second part of the TRC's work, becomes a highly vexed issue.

This issue is central to a recent case brought to the Constitutional Court by, amongst others, the family of murdered activist Steve Biko *(Azanian People's Organization* (AZAPO) *and Others v President of the Republic of South Africa and Others*, heard in the Constitutional Court). One of the three committees set up for achieving the purposes of the National Unity and Reconciliation Act was a committee on amnesty, which has the power to grant amnesty to anyone who makes full disclosure of any acts committed with an expressed political motive before 6 December 1993. The applicants in this case argued, unsuccessfully, that that section of the Act which grants amnesty be declared unconstitutional. Instead of seeing amnesty given to such as the murderers of Steve Biko, the applicants argued, they wanted to exercise their right to have the matter settled by a court of law or another independent and impartial tribunal. The question of amnesty is still unresolved; and the way in which the TRC will finally deal with the matter of amnesty for actors on the two sides of the historical divide still remains to be seen.

Ingrid de Kok's chapter raises another set of concerns around the drive to reconciliation and unity, arguing that the TRC runs the risk of promoting amnesia. De Kok points to the important and complex connections between the TRC and nation building, and the silences imposed in the name of the reconciled nation. The TRC is criticized for silencing the institutional effects of apartheid and for narrowing down the notion of victimhood. In place of this potentially silencing version of memory, De Kok develops the notion of the TRC as elegy: a way of remembering which allows the bereaved to reassemble life, but always with the acknowledgement of the destruction and contradictions that caused the bereavement.

So her chapter title refers to a 'cracked heirloom' in wanting to find a metaphor for the processes of memory in South Africa. The chapter cautions against the construction of a unified and sanitized past, arguing instead that contradictory voices should be heard. The task of memory should therefore not be to reconstitute and make whole, a whole which needs to lie about the fracture; instead the task of memory is to reconstitute turbulence and fragmentation, including these painful reminders of what we were, and what we are.

In the second part of the book, the relation between individual testimony and collective memory is examined from another perspective. The chapters in this part are concerned with narratives of the self, and the often complex relations between autobiographical identity and collective identity. The contributors in this section concern themselves with what could be called the distortions of memory, necessary to the narration of the self in autobiography. In particular, the focus is on the structuring metaphors that shape personal and collective memory, including the evolving metaphor of the rainbow nation, and the discourse of 'reconciliation'.

Sarah Nuttall looks at the differences between what is often regarded as the 'freeing' of memory on the one hand, and the intervention in the lives of others by means of an autobiographical narrative, on the other. The autobiographies written (and ghost-written) by the heroes of the struggle, as well as the many books on prisoners' memories of Robben Island, are examples of the latter kind. Nuttall argues that autobiographical narratives written in response to what is seen as the new, more inclusive, political moment also reveal the pressure to tell a 'redemptive' story. She looks at memoirs which attempt to deal with and perhaps work through the past by telling intelligible stories about it. She contrasts this recent work with examples of earlier South African autobiography, in which the impetus was towards exile, and even death, rather than reconciliation and healing. Nuttall thus sees a shift away from what could be called 'cause' writing, associated with and reflective of the political struggle. What is emerging in its stead is an autobiographical mode of writing which is conventional in another way, concerned as it is with offering stories of redemption and healing.

One typical mode of autobiographical writing practised in South Africa at the moment is to write life stories that proclaim one's liberation from the bonds of the past. Another, perhaps produced more often by white writers, is the adoption of the mode of the confessional. The first mode, with which Nuttall deals, relies on a constructed wholeness, through the healing effected by moving away from the past; the second is constructed around the narration of a self which is in some ways 'split'. The narrating self in these texts typically aims to effect a distance from an earlier, politically less enlightened or in other ways unacceptable, version of the self.

Michael Godby looks at artist William Kentridge's short film *The History of the Main Complaint*, which can be read as a commentary on the drive to the confessional as a mode of relating to the South African context. The body of Kentridge's protagonist resembles the artist's in some ways; thus the viewer is invited to read the piece as self-reflective. Kentridge uses metaphors of disease and the visual vocabulary of the body to meditate on the role of art as / and social diagnosis. His work has provided a consistently critical perspective on the excessive life-styles of many white

South Africans, and the theme recurs in this film. The ending remains ambiguous, and seems to question the extent to which the healed South African body – or at least the white body with which he is concerned here – is different now from before. The final frames show his cartoon protagonist return to his office, and once again surround himself with the accessories of capital.

Minkley and Rassool's chapter intervenes in the debates around the practice of oral history in South Africa. They argue that oral historians have too often constructed a master-narrative of resistance from the individual memories collected in interviews. As has been suggested about the work of many ethnographers, Minkley and Rassool also imply that oral historians' autobiographical eagerness to write revolutionary narratives may have shaped their reading of their informants' words. Their chapter offers a critical reading of that school of historiography that has been known as 'history from below', suggesting that the complexities of memory have been glossed over by this approach. Central to their argument is their reading of Charles Van Onselen's *The Seed Is Mine: The Life of Kas Maine, a South African Sharecropper 1894–1985* (1996), a monumental biography by one of South Africa's foremost historians of 'a man who, if one went by the official record alone, never was'.

Thus Minkley and Rassool look at how personal memory, especially of black South Africans, has been used in apartheid's dying decade to counter the official memory which desired to obliterate them. Carli Coetzee's chapter examines an example of another kind of counter-memory which is being produced at the moment, this time by white Afrikaans-speaking South Africans in search of ways of inscribing themselves into the new chapters of the country's history. She comments on the recent cultural appropriations of a seventeenth-century KhoiSan woman named Krotoä, and baptized Eva, known to us through the official journal kept by the employees of the Dutch East India Company. How is it, she asks, that a woman whose genetic and cultural contribution to white South African, and especially Afrikaner, identity has been disclaimed for three centuries is coming to be remembered as 'our mother' by white Afrikaners? Here is another example, then, of biography as fantasized autobiography.

Krotoä is not the only remembered woman whose life is being used as a template for a perceived lost wholeness. Steven Robins looks at how the body of Saartje Baartman (a Khoi woman who was displayed to the public in London and New York between 1810 and her death from neglect in 1815) is being used as a vehicle in nationalist claims for land and recognition made by some groupings in the Coloured community.

The call for Baartman's return is an attempt, many have pointed out, at appropriating KhoiSan memory to serve the political project of a contemporary KhoiSan and Coloured ethnic nationalism. KhoiSan and Coloured nationalists have challenged what they claim is the marginalization of the KhoiSan past and the privileging of black (African) historical experience of the recent apartheid past. The call for the return of the remains of Baartman's body to South Africa for burial is part of a wider national interest in reburial and return. Although apparently an issue that has to do with the past, it also requires stark interpretation in contemporary terms: who will receive the body that is to be returned? Who have become the guardians of a community's, or the nation's, memory in the present? On another level, burial may be an uncomfortably appropriate representation of the call to forget, and to become reconciled.

Robins' discussion of Baartman forms part of a wider discussion in his chapter about the symbolic potency of links between the corporeal body and the body politic. 'Miscast: Negotiating the Presence of the Bushmen', a controversial exhibition in Cape Town's National Gallery in April 1996, displayed photographs of charts and instruments for measuring and classifying KhoiSan bodies, as well as resin casts of some bodies and body parts, with the aim of challenging conventional portrayals of the 'Bushman' past.

The exhibition opening became the public space for a volatile

KhoiSan politics which exploded in anger at the 'voyeurism' of the curator and of visitors to the exhibition. Robins examines in some detail the politics of memory at work around this event. At the opening of the exhibition, and at a colloquium held the next day, members of the KhoiSan community were invited to be present, and to speak. While many of these representatives wanted to talk about the restitution of land, the exhibition's purpose was to comment on modes of representation, and none of those involved in the exhibition had any power to make a direct political intervention. Many argued that the exhibition, purportedly exposing practices and representations of the KhoiSan, unwittingly mimicked some of the very gestures it intended to criticize.

Robins also offers a more autobiographical response, through the comparison he finds with how the Jewish body was measured, photographed, and categorized in order to develop Nazi racial theories of Aryan supremacy. His observations are drawn not from some loose historical analogy, but from his own history as a Jewish South African. During the apartheid years, Robins writes, he found it impossible to engage either with his Jewishness or to confront Holocaust memory, including the death of his grandparents in Auschwitz, since to be Jewish in South Africa was to be inextricably bound up within apartheid's categories and constructions of whiteness.

Sceptical of the explicitly autobiographical impulse in his work, Robins is also careful not to draw simplistic parallels between South Africa and Nazi Germany. He does not use the often-too-easy metaphor of the Holocaust for South Africa and apartheid, such as is found in *Reconciliation through Truth: A Reckoning of Apartheid's Criminal Governance*. Instead his chapter draws on the sophisticated literature that has been produced around questions of testimony and remembrance.

In part III, the focus is on some examples of projects that have attempted to intervene in the reshaping of public memory in South Africa. The 'Miscast' exhibition and the range of responses it elicited recur in a number of the contributions. Robins makes the point that public responses to the exhibition reveal that many (white) visitors viewed it as a type of Truth Commission: they experienced it as a confessional space that forced them to confront European colonial violence in ways similar to the TRC's interrogation of apartheid's past. But the exhibition also clearly raised a more theoretical set of issues about the representation and the appropriation of voices and images, concerns central to museum practice.

Patricia Davison and Harriet Deacon each write about how state-funded national museums are responding to new political imperatives. Davison looks at ways in which the South African Museum is attempting to show that identities, including national identities, are not fixed, but shift over time, and assesses public responses to this. So the South African Museum is increasingly making use of contextualizing labels and information boards, in an attempt at giving museum-goers a sense of the shifting nature of representation. Deacon discusses the rehabilitation of Robben Island and its transformation into a national symbol of hope and victory. She highlights the tensions between the island's symbolic role and the memories of individual activists and ex-prisoners, and argues that it is necessary to create a space that allows the diversity of accounts of the past to be articulated.

What both chapters point to is the increasing commodification of what has come to be known as the heritage industry, and to the fact that the struggle against apartheid is being seen as the most significant and attractive lens through which to view the past. The result for museum practice is that narratives of resistance are often foregrounded, with exhibitions thereby serving the aims of nation building. But, as both chapters indicate, marks of dissonance and conflict over which versions of memory to exhibit and to use as framing devices are not hard to find. On the Robben Island tour, which is permanently sold out to local and foreign visitors, the discourse is that of hope and the overcoming of adversity.

When African-American comedian Bill Cosby visited South Africa recently to attend a banquet on the island, national television and newspapers carried images of him sitting with Nelson Mandela (whom he called 'Nelson', one of the very rare occasions when anyone has publicly used his first name) in his former cell. To many it seemed inappropriate that this space become the source and space of humour. South African visitors, both black and white, have expressed discomfort about this and other examples of too light a tone being adopted towards the island and the prison, insisting that the meanings of the island still, for the moment at least, need to be primarily those of conflict and suffering.

The next chapter in this part reminds us that when we are looking at – and writing about – museums and heritage sites, the found objects or images with which we are presented may resist containment within the narratives of 'memory' that we use. Objects, Martin Hall writes, have a 'polyvalency of meaning', and it is this quality that gives them their potency in the construction of memory. But memory is not always textual; it may bring into circulation elements of the everyday world in ways which cannot be reduced to language alone. Hall attempts to construct an 'archaeology of memory' through imagining a possible discussion between the nineteenth-century philologist William Bleek and his Khoi interlocutor and source, //Kabbo. In a subtle and evocative analysis, he reflects on the different qualities of the object and the text, the statue and the book, for capturing memory.

Kerry Ward and Nigel Worden's chapter examines another example of clusters of memory which fade and reform in other ways, in response to the demands of the present. They show how slavery and its legacy at the Cape has appeared, and disappeared, from official and popular memory at particular historical moments. In the nineteenth century, following the emancipation of slaves on 1 December 1838, celebrations were held yearly in Cape Town to commemorate the day. By the early twentieth century, memories of the slave past began to be suppressed, until it became almost completely silenced during the apartheid years. In 1996, following the ending of official apartheid and the 1994 elections, the 'December 1 Movement' was launched by middle-class Coloureds in Cape Town. Added to this are attempts by local tour operators to establish a Western Cape 'slave route'. Ward and Worden track the political shifts that have taken place in order to explain this fascinating 'recuperation' of memory.

In the final part, Eve Bertelsen and Sinfree Makoni's chapters also focus on the shortness of memory. Many have commented on the fact that young people in South Africa know very little of our recent history, and that children entering school this year have not known a time when Nelson Mandela was still in prison. Steven Robins' chapter ends by asking how we will remember, and cause others to remember, the conflict of the South African past. Soon after the elections, the collective amnesia of Coloured voters in the Western Cape was the subject of much commentary. The Western Cape was the only new province to elect a National Party government, thanks largely to the Coloured vote, proof of what some might regard as almost incredible political amnesia.

Eve Bertelsen's chapter examines recent trends in South African advertising during the period around and after the national elections. She shows how the language of the political struggle has been emptied of its original significance and used as part of consumer discourse. The use of revolutionary terminology in this new context, she shows, erases the logic and context of terms and signifiers that had particular historical meanings. Thus what one sees in advertising, in particular advertising aimed at black consumers, is the obliteration of the desire for a social good by the desire for material goods.

Sinfree Makoni's chapter is a commentary on an aspect of the new constitution, namely the new language policy. His chapter can be read as a cautionary tale that we should not take too seriously the seeming diversity heralded by the new South African language policy. This policy has been presented popularly as all-inclusive because eleven, rather than the previous two, languages are regarded as 'national' languages. Much scholarship has been devoted to the systematization and orthography of African languages, and the missionaries' contribution to this process, often regarded ambivalently by contemporary scholars, is a staple of such discussions. Makoni's arguments question a language policy based on the idea of languages as neatly divided and hermetically sealed units. This, he cautions, risks distorting the richness and variety of South Africans' languages; and is a form of collective amnesia.

In the final chapter Eduard Fagan argues that the South African constitution, unlike other constitutions which are typically forward looking, carries within it the traces of an attempt to keep the significance of the past alive and active. Fagan's argument has wider significance, pointing as it does to the effects of what has sometimes been called South Africa's negotiated revolution. Because the ANC and the NP (as the most powerful political groupings) together drafted the constitution, what one reads is not merely an updated version of the 1955 Kliptown Freedom Charter, a document based on the views of ordinary South Africans about the kind of society they would like to see in South Africa, drawn up by the opposition movements. Yet it explicitly frames future relations between South Africans through reference to the past. In this text, the most important document to have been produced on behalf of the 'new' South Africa, the aim is to inscribe the memory of the past in its vision of the future.

Which versions of the South African past will come to dominate, and come to harden into history, is as yet unclear. What will certainly be central to the resolution of these questions is the way in which issues of land ownership and land restitution are dealt with. Already it seems clear that, for political and symbolic reasons, certain periods of misappropriation are regarded as more significant than others. So the 1913 Land Act has come to function very powerfully as a moment that needs to be reversed, while some other land claims are given less prominence.

South African literature is obsessively concerned with land and the emotional and proprietal relations one can have with it. In white South African writing, as J. M. Coetzee (1988) has shown, a tension exists between versions of the land as something one can divide and own on the one hand, and on the other the view of land as something that denies the viewer (and owner) access – perhaps because of the guilt associated with the position of the white viewer. In the poetry of urbanization by black South African writers, mining is sometimes described as a process that empties the land of meaning, and disturbs one's proper relationship with the ancestors. Once one is forced to leave the land where one's ancestors are buried, the link is severed. Even if land restitution can be made, there is a sense in which particular kinds of relationships with land cannot be remembered and reconstituted.

In her preface to Sol Plaatje's *Native Life in South Africa* (1982) South African writer Bessie Head writes of the book as a 'missing link in black South Africans' sense of history'. Some will indeed want to argue that memory is a key way in which a sense of continuity and unity can be restored in South Africa. But in many cases the mnemonic devices to be found in landscapes and built structures have been destroyed, and it is hard to imagine how these links can be made again. It also remains as a challenge to all who are, in some way, involved in memorializing the past, to keep multiple versions of the past alive and not to privilege, as has so often been done, a few master narratives that offer a sense of unity at the cost of ignoring the fracture and dissonance.

In its interim version, the constitution is described as 'a historic bridge between the past of a deeply divided society characterized by strife, conflict, untold suffering and injustice, and a future founded on the recognition of human rights, democracy and peaceful co-existence and development opportunities for all South Africans, irrespective of colour, race, class, belief or sex'. This view of the future, according to the document, can only be realized by means of the pursuit of national unity and reconciliation, the transcendence of the divisions and strife of the past. Thus the constitution is described as 'a new chapter in the history of our country'. The chapters in this book examine the 'newness' of South Africa since the elections; but also insist on the significance of keeping older chapters unclosed and simultaneously present.

SARAH NUTTALL
CARLI COETZEE

PART I

Truth, memory, and narrative

I

NJABULO NDEBELE

Memory, metaphor, and the triumph of narrative

WHEN IT WAS ANNOUNCED RECENTLY that a group of former police generals of the old South African Police were going to apply for amnesty, I thought to myself that a new chapter had opened in the work of the Truth and Reconciliation Commission (TRC). No sooner had I registered this thought than I was struck by the irony contained in it. The stories of the generals would be more than simply the next event in the activities of the TRC. They would, indeed, be a new chapter in the narratives being told at the hearings of the TRC throughout the country.

I remembered that at the end of the historic first round of the TRC hearings which took place in East London, Archbishop Tutu, TRC chairman, was quoted as having said: 'The country has taken the right course in the process of healing to hear these stories. Very few of us can be the same today as we were on Monday' (the day on which the testimonies began). This was one of the first pronouncements I remember in which the TRC testimonies were referred to as stories.

Is it not that we often think of stories as imaginary events which we may call tales, fiction, fables, or legends: stories as narratives of one kind or another? Yet, the testimonies we continue to hear at TRC hearings are the recall of memory. What is being remembered actually happened. If today they sound like imaginary events it is because, as we shall recall, the horror of day-to-day life under apartheid often outdid the efforts of the imagination to reduce it to metaphor.

But time seems to have rescued the imagination. Time has given the recall of memory the power of reflection associated with narrative. Isn't it that there is something inherently reflective about memory, as there is about narrative? If so, narratives of memory, in which real events are recalled, stand to guarantee us occasions for some serious moments of reflection. Hopefully it is this reflective capacity, experienced as a shared social consciousness, that will be that lasting legacy of the stories of the TRC. Possibly this is what the archbishop implies about the capacity of these stories to change us.

What seems to have happened is that the passage of time which brought forth our freedom has given legitimacy and authority to previously silenced voices. It has lifted the veil of secrecy and state-induced blindness. Where the state sought to hide what it did, it compelled those who were able to see what was happening not to admit the testimony of their own eyes. In this connection, the stories of the TRC represent a ritualistic lifting of the veil and the validation of what was actually seen. They are an additional confirmation of the movement of our society from repression to expression. Where in the past the state attempted to compel the oppressed to deny the testimony of their own experience, today that experience is one of the essential conditions for the emergence of a new national consciousness. These stories may very well be some of the first steps in the rewriting of South African history on the basis of validated mass experience.

And so it is that we are privileged to experience social change as the incremental exposure of an elaborately constructed intrigue of immense size and complexity. The narrative of apartheid, which can now be told, has reached that part of the plot where vital facts leading to the emergence of understanding are in the process of being revealed. While some key elements of the intrigue are emerging, I believe we have yet to find meaning. In fact, it is going to be the search for meanings that may trigger off more narratives.

If and when that happens, the imagination, having been rescued by time, will be the chief beneficiary. The resulting narratives may have less and less to do with facts themselves and with their recall than with the revelation of meaning through the imaginative combination of those facts. At that point, facts will be the building blocks of metaphor.

This point is worth emphasizing. One of my favourite quotations is the observation made by T. T. Moyana (1976, 95), in which he speculates why it was often so difficult for artists and writers to extract metaphor from the day-to-day horror of apartheid. He writes:

An additional difficulty to the creative artist in South Africa, especially the black writer, is that life itself is too fantastic to be outstripped by the creative imagination. Nkosi calls the theme of the absurd a theme of daily living in South Africa. Indeed, many writers of the absurd school would find their plots too realistic to startle anybody into serious questioning of their deeper meaning. How would the quarrel over a bench in Edward Albee's *Zoo Story* startle anybody in a country where thousands of people have been daily quarrelling over who should sit on a particular park bench, and the country's parliament has had to legislate on the matter? That's much more startling than Albee's little quarrel between two men. And Kafka himself would not have bettered the case told by Lewis Nkosi. He was arrested by a policeman who then phoned his superior to ask, 'What shall I charge him with?' Or the incident of a white man and a coloured woman who were tried for being caught kissing. The court got bogged down over the question of whether the kiss was 'platonic or passionate'. One reporter who covered the case for a local newspaper wrote: 'Lawyers and laymen are certain that the Minister of Justice will now have to consider an amendment to the law which will define the various degrees of kissing from the platonic to the passionate'.

It was not only difficult to see logic behind this sort of thing, it was impossible to detect coherent philosophical justification for it. And this is the nub of it. At its best, the achievements of apartheid society took place within the context of a moral and intellectual desert.

The extent of this moral desert has only now been confirmed. The stories of the TRC expose not only previously silenced voices, but also methods employed in silencing them. That is why the revelation of these methods has received so much attention. The silencing of voices through various forms of brutality, torture, and humiliation induced anger and bitterness. In the end, particularly for the writer, the ugly reality of oppression became impossible to articulate. This is because it itself became the only story, but one which, once enacted, had to be denied. The story of apartheid became adept at self-denial.

And so, what can no longer be denied has come out. We now learn of how people's hands were cut off and put in bottles; how a woman was forced to watch her husband being tortured. The police were later to boast to her how, in order to remove evidence of his death, they roasted his body to ashes, observing how it hissed like ordinary meat on a braai pan. It is even said that as they roasted a human body they drank beer and had meat roasting on a braai a few metres away.

We now confirm what we have suspected all along: the different methods of torture. We can confirm the details of the terrible deaths of the Mxenges. We can confirm how a man's head was reduced to blood and brains by a booby-trapped walkman, and how that instrument of death was first tested on the heads of pigs. We have heard about people being falsely accused of being informers and dying horrible deaths at the hands of fellow members of the oppressed. We could go on and on and on. But there is no need to do this. What it all represents is the acknowledgement of such pain and suffering that only now is it meaningful to ask: why? It also enables us to wait for that moment when the perpetrators acknowledge their deeds. We see pictures of alleged perpetrators in which they are dressed in business suits which make them so ordinary, like the person next door, and we begin to wonder about colleagues next to whom we may sit in a lecture hall, in a meeting; about business colleagues across the negotiation table; about fellow passengers on a plane. Could any of these have been a compulsive killer on duty? At this point we begin the search for meaning.

What kind of explanation are we going to find? I have argued before that the creative aspects of apartheid society, from the point of view of its proponents, ended when that society became inordinately preoccupied with methods of domination, which became the basis on which privilege could be maintained. Any transcendent values that may have initially informed apartheid's value system gave way to the psychology of maintenance. This was the psychology of habit which made prejudice a standard mode of perception. This mode of perception flourished in its crude aspects among members of the white, mainly Afrikaner, working class, for whom jobs were reserved in the police force, the army, railways and harbours, the civil service, and small-scale farming. The ruling elites, in both the political and industrial sectors, satisfied that they had bought the compliance of the white electorate, gave a blank cheque to the military and law-enforcement establishments. Where, in these establishments, the enforcement of apartheid degenerated into a science of torture and death, in the general society it informed social habit. It occurs to me that in this situation, black people were not hated as such; in time they simply became objects at the receiving end of elaborate institutionalized processes of maintaining domination. For those dispensing oppression, their jobs became an official vehicle for their received prejudices. Social conditioning and the work process became two sides of the same coin.

That is why the National Party is unable to apologize for the moral desert they took time to create. Their project did not succeed in being anything beyond an elaborate political programme. The political programme became everything. The resulting depravity in the polity became generalized. It is not only to be found among personnel in the security services. It is also the measure of the general moral condition among the ruling elites who are now no longer in power. Power and wealth became the dominant determinants of behaviour: two key ingredients in the recipe of socially embedded corruption.

That is why many intelligent Afrikaners still clamour for a *volkstaat* or for language rights which they already have, as if nothing significant has happened in our country in the last few years. They are unable to link the failures of the past with the need for a new moral vision which includes others. They have yet to define such a vision as a basis on which to reassess the past more fundamentally. Their demands, however valid they may be, represent the tragic failure of social conscience. In this connection, the future of Afrikaner culture may lie in its rediscovery of social morality.

Fortunately, this process has begun. In fact, there may be an informal truth and reconciliation process under way among the Afrikaners. Its contours are taking shape in the form of such novels as Mark Behr's *The Smell of Apples*. Karel Schoeman's *Promised Land* anticipated it some years back. Jeanne Goosen's *Not All of Us* gave it further impetus. I am certain that there are more such narratives which have not yet been translated. Their distinguishing feature is their focus on ordinary social details which pile up into major, disturbing statements. The ordinary Afrikaner family, lost in the illusion of the historic heroism of the group, has to find its moral identity within a national community in which it is freed from the burden of being special. Afrikaner culture and its language will triumph from the resultant honesty of self-revelation, the resonances of which will appeal to many others whose humanity has been newly revealed by a liberated present.

Somewhere the story of the agony of the contemporary
Afrikaner family will converge with the stories of millions of
those recently emerged from oppression. That point of convergence may very well be the point at which ordinary Afrikaners
recognize, through confronting their own histories, the enormity
of the horror that was done on their behalf, and which, as willing
agents, they helped bring about.

As we negotiate the difficult task of normalizing freedom, it
will be important for us to realize that a political accommodation
such as we have achieved does not imply that all the moral, intellectual, and philosophical questions have been solved. To stop at
that point is to risk repeating the apartheid mistake of making
politics everything.

Early this year, my wife and I were flying back home from
Mauritius when the pilot announced that Bafana Bafana, the
national soccer team, was ahead of Cameroon on the first game
of the African Nations Cup. My wife and I and a few other passengers cheered merrily. A wealthy corporate South African turned
towards us to ask: 'This team that we are playing, is it a good
team?' After noting the self-consciousness around the use of 'we',
I vaguely remembered the tone behind this sort of question, from
many times before. It was all too familiar: the kind of question
that evokes my resentment in a Pavlovian sort of way. Not only
did the man know nothing about the sporting preferences of his
fellow South Africans, but the glory of the Cameroon team, the
pride of Africa, had passed him by.

The tragedy of this situation is that that man felt superior in his
ignorance. And while he ritualistically sought information which
was of no use to him (as the important thing for him was to
demonstrate lack of racism in himself by seeking information
from a black person, without realizing, in the process, that he was
being his own usual inordinately condescending, racist self), we
were being reduced by him to explaining 'our people'.

As I have observed, he was not asking for information; he was demonstrating his lack of prejudice. Little did he realize what he was actually saying to us. Here is what he was saying: 'I do not know you to be good enough to beat a good European team. This other team, whatever it is, can't be that good. So you are beating a useless team. Therefore, you can't be that good either. But am I not wonderful that I am asking you?' It is highly unlikely that he would have asked the same kind of question had we had a South African cricket or rugby team, both almost exclusively made up of white players, competing in an international tournament.

I am presenting, of course, the archetypal image of the bleeding-heart, English-speaking liberal South African, who has no understanding of why he is hated so much when he sacrificed so much for the oppressed. In this connection, our fellow passenger would, of course, easily donate jerseys to a black team, as long as he was convinced these jerseys 'were going to be properly used'.

Fellow South Africans of this kind are blissfully unaware that they should appear before the TRC. They are convinced that it is only the Afrikaner who should do so. 'It is often said', Mandela has recently been quoted as saying, 'that an invisible wound is more painful than the visible one.' These are the wounds these South Africans have generally been good at inflicting. With their condescending platitudes, they have massacred hundreds of thousands of souls. I have never been to gaol, but I have, at various times in my life, been in the prison of these platitudes.

Yes, they have a story to tell. Its setting is in the interstice between power and indifferent or supportive agency. In that interstice, the English-speaking South African has conducted the business of his life. Now he was indignant and guilty; now he was thriving. This no-man's land ensured a fundamental lack of character. With a foreign passport in the back pocket of the trousers, now they belong – now they don't. When will they tell this story?

In factoring in the bleeding-heart English-speaking liberal, I am proposing one of the greatest dangers to the TRC hearings. From the point of view of one very large sector of the South African population, the TRC hearings may confirm the image of blacks as helpless victims, suffering complainants before whites who claim to understand their plight and declare themselves to be willing to help. In this way blacks will always be the numerical majority weighed down by the psychology of suffering minorities. They will be the eagle that grew among the chickens and is no longer able to fly. English-speaking South Africans have yet to acknowledge their willing compliance, by developing their own particular version of oppression, in the oppression of black people.

At the risk of setting up simplistic binary oppositions, one should state that, on balance, the guilt of English-speaking South Africans is as extensive as that of the Afrikaners. The latter were the primary agents. They had the power. They accumulated new wealth. They ruled with a firm hand. Their resulting self-confidence rendered them collectively insensitive. On the other hand, the guilt of the English-speaking South African was prone to greater moral agony, to more wrenching agonies of conscience. Those who had no power remained with their consciences, while those who had it died from within.

We cannot afford to condone any aspect of racism at a time when racism should be permanently buried. Let all the stories be told. The gift of our freedom partly lies in our ability to ensure that where oppression is no longer a major defining characteristic of the social environment, the different features of our society will now emerge as aspects of a more complex definition of that environment.

And so it is that the stories of the TRC seem poised to result in one major spin-off, among others: the restoration of narrative. In few countries in the contemporary world do we have a living example of people reinventing themselves through narrative. Only now has South Africa succeeded in becoming metaphor, in becoming a true subject of philosophy. That is why the real challenge is not in maintaining competitive levels of capability in science and technology. That is a relatively easy task. The real challenge is in grounding science and technology in lived life, in the capacity for our society to stimulate the imaginations of its peoples through voices that can go beyond the giving of testimony, towards creating new thoughts and new worlds. Only now does our experience resonate with moral import.

2

ANDRÉ BRINK

Stories of history: reimagining the past in post-apartheid narrative

> ... Falsehoods all, but he gave his
> falsehoods all the ring of truth
> *The Odyssey* (Book XIX)

EVEN IF IT WOULD BE FOOLISH to be too categorical about the nature of the link between any given historical situation and the literature produced within it, it cannot come as a surprise to anyone that, ever since the first signs of the drastic socio-political shift in South Africa, there should have been expectations of new aesthetic responses to the changing circumstances. All of us who have been involved in the transition from apartheid to what may become democracy have in one way or another been marked by our early experience. At the very least, whether it happened consciously or not, if apartheid did not altogether curtail the imagination (as some foreign critics would glibly have it), it imposed certain priorities on a writer's choice of themes – and this holds true as much for writers generally regarded as 'political', such as Gordimer or Ndebele or Serote, as for others, such as Karel Schoeman in Afrikaans or J. M. Coetzee in English, who at first sight appeared to eschew the overtly political.

One result was that, in innumerable ways, the personal was the political. And if Fugard once said, impishly, that 'the only safe place is inside a story', his own work demonstrates most

eloquently how impossible it was – in those circumstances – to
disentangle the personal from the public, or story from history (in
the terminology of William Ray, to which I shall return). In my
own work, *States of Emergency* (1988) was explicitly conceived,
inter alia, as a response to Fugard's proposal.

.   Another consequence, specifically relevant to what I propose to
discuss in this chapter, was that certain territories of experience
(gender relations, for one) and certain regions of the past (notably
those less obviously connected to the realities of apartheid)
remained unvisited, or were visited only rarely, in much of South
African literature, specifically in fiction. In the spectrum of possibilities now opening up to the writer in post-apartheid South
Africa, these silent places invite exploration, almost as a condition
for future flowering. One might even say that unless the enquiries
of the Truth and Reconciliation Commission (TRC) are extended,
complicated, and intensified in the imaginings of literature,
society cannot sufficiently come to terms with its past to face the
future.

But there is also a significant difference between the two enter-
prises: the TRC is intent on effecting reconciliation through estab-
lishing, as fully as possible, the truth, the whole truth and nothing
but the truth, about human rights infringements during the
apartheid years – 'truth', in this context, being equated with 'facts'.
The enterprise of fiction, on the other hand, reaches well beyond
facts: inasmuch as it is concerned with the real (whatever may be
regarded as 'real' in any given context) it presumes a process
through which the real is not merely represented but imagined.
What is aimed at is not a reproduction but an imagining.

Even so, it is a sobering thought that all the sets of relations
invoked so far – public/personal, history/story, facts/fiction – are
ultimately predicated on memory. The individual constitutes and
invents her/himself through the constant editing and re-editing
of memory; the confluence of innumerable records and record-
ings of memories determines the publicly sanctioned account,

which debouches into history; facts, as a Kantian *Ding an sich*, remain forever inaccessible except through our versions of them – and these versions are dependent on memory (as the testimonies in front of the TRC demonstrate with great dramatic impact). And the workings of the imagination are at the very least inspired by memory.

According to the OED, 'image', etymologically linked to the activity of 'imitating', may designate such a variety of notions as copy, likeness, statue, phantom, conception, thought, idea, similitude, semblance, appearance, or shadow – a range so wide as to be practically meaningless. We may move closer to a manageable concept if the 'image' we are concerned with is regarded as the outcome of the intervention of the imagination, that is, the shaping of an image, not by the senses but in the mind. This involves, I propose as a starting point towards a working definition, a transgression of the boundaries of an originary sensual perception, a recognition of Baudelairean 'correspondances' between otherwise disparate objects or events, while simultaneously 'making them strange' in the Russian–Formalist meaning of the phrase, infusing the ordinary with a sense of the extraordinary, the everyday with a sense of the fantastic, producing a result in which the whole is decidedly more than the sum of its parts.

In this frame of thinking, 'imaginings' would then denote the processes through which such mental images are produced. At any rate a form of interiorization is implied, through which the individual mind, itself and its workings deeply implicated in the process, may also be said to produce shapes in its own image. In other words – quite literally 'in other words' – impressions from outside and impulses from inside converge in the mental machinations that produce a quite densely textured result. In the process both sets of 'data' – that is, external impressions and internal impulses – may undergo some measure of distortion which would render them unreliable (in the sense in which some evidence in a court of law would be regarded as unreliable).

But in the light of many recent developments in historiography, as Hayden White (1978) among others has amply demonstrated, we know that this kind of distortion, linked above with the processes of fiction, has come to be seen as a *sine qua non* of history itself. We now accept that history 'as such' is simply (or, in the fashionable phrase, 'always already') inaccessible: our only grasp of Waterloo is attained through what has been written about it. 'Waterloo' is an act of language. And in the process of textualizing the event it is also narrativized: that is, the representations of history repeat, in almost every detail, the processes of fiction. In this activity, in other words, history, memory, and language intersect so precisely as to be almost indistinguishable: the 'origins' of history, as recovered through memory, are encoded in language, and each of these three moments becomes a condition for the others.

In the most literal sense of the word 'history', in this view, coincides with 'story': it is shaped around notions of a beginning, middle, and end, and whether this shape is determined by a sense of poetic symmetry as in Herodotus, or by the concept of causality that Taine brought to historiography in the nineteenth century, or even by mere chronology, narrative lies at the heart of the very process we call history. And South African historiographers – Van Onselen, Peires, Penn, and many others – during the twilight years of apartheid have done much to highlight this feature of their enterprise: in decentring the conventional point of view and breaking down the master narratives of apartheid, they have been offering not merely 'alternative' accounts of our past to redress unjust emphases and perspectives, but a radical new view of the very concept of 'history'.

If this, in very generalized terms, is where historiography finds itself in South Africa at the end of apartheid, fiction writers who wish to return to the silent or silenced landscapes of the past have to tune in to the new perceptions of what constitutes history.

Their activity, as Foucault and Derrida have demonstrated in different ways, is archaeological, inasmuch as they, too, turn to memory as a means of excavating silence. And so they, too, cannot simply pretend to write alternatives to the accepted texts by subverting, for example, the white and male-dominated constructions of the past through accounts written from the erstwhile margins of black, or female, or any other minority, experience. Simply to replace a patriarchic discourse with a matriarchic approach still respects the patterns and the model that informed the original narrative. In other words, today's writer has to take note of the fact that the possibilities of writing itself have shifted. The past cannot be corrected by bringing to it the procedures and mechanics and mind-sets that originally produced our very perception of that past. After all, it is not the past as such that has produced the present or poses the conditions for the future (this was the fatal delusion of Naturalism), but the way we think about it. Or, even more pertinently, the way in which we deal with it in language.

The kind of process I have in mind is particularly well illustrated by Margaret Atwood's most recent novel, *Alias Grace* (1996), in which the textualization of history not only determines the structuring of the plot but actually constitutes its substance. Returning to a well-known and much-commented-upon murder in Canadian history, Atwood's interest goes beyond an attempt to 'get behind' the facts of the case or 'inside the skin' of the historical character Grace Marks (accused, with James McDermott, of murdering their employer and his housekeeper/mistress in 1843). Rather than offering a new version of the history which may be accepted as emotionally or even poetically 'true', she explicitly concedes in her Author's Afterword that 'the true character of the historical Grace Marks remains an enigma' (ibid., 465). Her novelistic aim is not solving a mystery but demonstrating how historical mysteries are constructed in the first place.

As her point of departure Atwood takes the three different versions of the murder Grace Marks herself offered at the time, and the two of her accomplice: these multiple locations of memory within individuals converge to constitute public memory. And this is amplified and further complicated by incorporating into the text various other contemporary accounts, testimonies and commentaries – even a poem that circulated at the time, and drawings of the accused in court. All of these, representing various degrees of fictification, constitute, and constantly modify, shift, or even remake, the public memory (to which *Alias Grace* itself makes yet another contribution). All these components are packaged, as a frame for the narrative, with epigraphs taken from sources as far apart as Basho and Longfellow, Emily Brontë, Emily Dickinson, Edgar Allan Poe, and others. The one thing the reader is hyperconscious of at the moment of entry into the novel is that s/he is entering a textualized and storified world. Within this world, the processes of its constitution are constantly foregrounded by the manner in which Grace explicitly manipulates her narrative to suit the requirements of her interlocutors. She even changes the words of the old nursery song 'Tom, Tom, the piper's son', because 'I didn't see why I shouldn't make it come out in a better way' (ibid., 238). To express her gratitude for Dr Simon Jordan's kindness to her, she sets to work 'willingly to tell my story, and to make it as interesting as I can, and rich in incident, a sort of return gift to him' (ibid., 247). And she is aided and abetted by her lawyer who encourages her to 'say what must have happened, according to plausibility, rather than what I myself could actually recall' (ibid., 357). No wonder she becomes entangled in a patchwork (the key image of the novel) of versions: 'I can remember what I said when arrested, and what Mr. MacKenzie the lawyer said I should say, and what I did not say even to him; and what I said at the trial, and what I said afterwards, which was different as well. And what McDermott said I said, and what the others said I must have said ...' (ibid., 295). This testimony becomes especially revealing if it is read against the background of the activation of public memory in the workings of the TRC in South Africa.

The key to the whole tangle presented by Atwood is memory: but memory, as Dr Simon Jordan acknowledges, is itself notoriously unreliable: 'The mind ... is like a house – thoughts which the owner no longer wishes to display, or those which arouse painful memories, are thrust out of sight, and consigned to attic or cellar; and in forgetting, as in the storage of broken furniture, there is surely an element of will at work' (ibid., 362). And so, inevitably, when the charlatan pedlar Jeremiah, posing as a doctor, insists that 'we are what we remember', Simon points out, with equal justification, that the opposite is just as true: 'we are also ... what we forget' (ibid., 406).

Grace can remember all the different versions of her story: what she cannot – or will not – recall is 'what really happened'. History, in the conventional sense of the term, is denied or repressed in favour of story. And story is located beyond the reach of that kind of morality that normally distinguishes truth from lie: 'Did Sheherazade lie? Not in her own eyes; indeed, the stories she told ought never to be subjected to the harsh categories of Truth and Falsehood. They belong in another realm altogether' (ibid., 377).

This is of course not an answer to the problem posed in the present essay: but it is a very eloquent formulation of it. Even without the social urgencies and energies that drive the South African enquiry into the past, this Canadian text establishes the parameters and conditions attendant upon our expectations of such an enterprise.

In the end it is up to the reader to make an informed choice, and in the narrative text 'Nothing has been proved. But nothing has been disproved, either' (ibid., 388). At the same time – and this is the salient point at the moment – Atwood's text illuminates dimensions of a moment from Canadian history (the Kinnear/

Montgomery murders, the personalities involved in them, and
the social and moral context within which they were possible)
which no 'straight' history of the event could possibly have
posited.

In the light of the brief excursion into Atwood territory, we can
now return to the situation in South Africa.

Reinventing the past through the imagination involves primarily, as we have seen, a peculiar machination of memory. And
memory, which is always and even per definition selective,
comprises not only acts of recovery but also processes of suppression. 'My memory', a child in a recent psychological enquiry into
repressed memory is reported to have said, 'is what I use to forget
with' (Loftus and Ketcham 1994, 38). This accords precisely with
some of the quotes taken from *Alias Grace* in the section above.
The apartheid memory, reshaping history around the largely
imagined national consciousness of the Afrikaner, was
constrained to forget large tracts of the South African past (the
shaping of the Afrikaans language in the mouths of slaves; slave
revolts; the enslavement of indigenous people; the role of
Coloured and black labourers in the service of Boers in the Great
Trek; collaboration between black nations and Afrikaners on the
Eastern Frontier during the nineteenth century; the part played
by women in conserving certain standards of education and
morality in the deep interior, or in the Great Trek ...) and to
suppress the key roles played by 'outsiders' to what came to be
construed as the master narrative (Krotoä, Andries Stockenström,
Coenraad Buys, Estienne Barbier, Susanna Smit, Nongqawuse,
Christiaan De Wet's 'traitor' brother Piet ...). By the same token it
would be possible for the newly emerging post-apartheid
memory conveniently to forget or underplay other events and
characters in the overall narrative, ranging from collaboration
with the oppressor to atrocities in training camps in Angola and
elsewhere.

At first sight the solution may appear to lie in compiling as many diverse narratives as possible so that the resulting jigsaw puzzle – or patchwork quilt, in Atwood's terminology – would be as comprehensive as humanly attainable. But even more so than in the case of the TRC, there is the double bind that the kind of whole the exercise is aimed at can never be complete and that ultimately, like all narratives, this one must eventually be constructed around its own blind spots and silences (as, in different contexts, Macherey (1978), Derrida (1976), and Jameson (1981) have argued).

So memory alone cannot be the answer. Hence my argument in favour of an imagined rewriting of history or, more precisely, of the role of the imagination in the dialectic between past and present, individual and society.

In *Story and History*, one of the most stimulating readings of eighteenth-century fiction in English and French, William Ray (1990, vi) proposes a distinction between the two key terms of his title on the basis of representing, respectively, 'personal story and public account'. More pertinently, 'History is a story produced by reality, fable a story productive of reality, and both are presumed to stand outside of reality' (ibid., 8).

'The historicist delusion', says Ray, 'is that there can be an account of human reality that is not mediated by an act situated in human reality and vitiated by the biases of that situation ... The converse delusion is that there could be a narrative having no origins in reality, but capable of modifying – or, as is generally the charge, corrupting – reality' (ibid.).

That the confusions and complications go well beyond this I have already intimated above. But Ray's distinction between the private act of the imagination encapsulated in story and the publicly sanctioned act of history (even if that sanction is always only temporary) is useful for our present enquiry into the possibilities open to the new South African fiction to explore the

silences of the past in order to discover or invent the voices
subsumed in them.

At least three characteristics of story are relevant here, all of
which have been demonstrated by Atwood's handling of the
Grace character (who is herself a mere 'alias'): story as the
outcome of a process of internalization and personalization;
story as the construction of a version of the world; and story as
the embodiment of an imagining or a complex of imaginings.

First: in opposition to the usually more public narratives of
history ('public', as hinted above, in the sense of enjoying – or at
least appealing to – societal sanction), story explores a situation
from the inside, or internalizes what passes for facts in the public
domain. In this respect it may share many of the characteristics of
biography, as demonstrated in a remarkable text such as Charles
van Onselen's recent *The Seed Is Mine: The Life of Kas Maine, a
South African Sharecropper 1894–1985* (1996). But biography is still
produced, as is history in Ray's definition, by what is perceived as
real, whereas story constitutes a reality not necessarily commensurate with what is consensually approved as real. Even more
importantly, story involves an awareness and an implicit or explicit acknowledgement of its own processes of narrativation: every
narrative text, I should venture to say, is per definition also a meta-
narrative. Story may encompass history, in the way that sixty
years of Polish history is drawn into Andrzej Szczypiorski's
wonderful novel *Self-portrait with Woman*, but the focus is personal
(Szczypiorski 1995). In Szczypiorski's narrative, an 'ordinary' Pole,
the sociologist Kamil, is invited by a Swiss radio station to offer in
a series of interviews a personal account of his involvement in the
recent momentous changes that have swept away communism
and established democracy, a situation with quite obvious parallels to the transition in South Africa. But instead of commenting
on the political dimension of the events, Kamil elects, to the
consternation of his interlocutors, to narrate from his private life
a series of amorous encounters with women. As it turns out,

public events obtrude into the most private events, and there is no great general 'lesson' to be learned from it all: all that suffering has taught Kamil is the uselessness of suffering. What he seeks is in fact not memory but redemption from memory.

In the second place, story does not presume to bring to light 'the' truth, but at most a version of it. And its value resides in allowing the reader to compare a variety of available versions in order either to choose among them or to construct a composite image from all of them – without the kind of teleology that used to inform the older traditions of historiography.

And thirdly, even when a story tacitly narrates an event 'based on reality' it is infused with, and transformed by, the notoriously unreliable complex of private motivations, hidden agendas, prejudices, suspicions, biographical quirks, chips on the shoulder, and conditionings that constitute the idiosyncratic, individual mind.

But where does this leave the reader in search of a 'new vision of history'? If everything in a narrative text is 'pure invention' (that is, as distinct from a historical text in which the 'general reader', if there is such a creature, perceives, rightly or wrongly, at least an intention to be 'true to the facts') what weight, moral or otherwise, is to be attached to it? This was a risk I was particularly conscious of in the writing of *Imaginings of Sand* (1996) in which a centenarian woman explicitly invents the (matriarchically slanted) narrative of her tribe. After warning the reader at the outset that she disposes of a memory so amazing that 'I can remember things that never happened', she ostensibly does just that, recounting the stories of a woman transformed into a tree, another disappearing in search of her lost shadow, a third running off with a Jewish lover to Baghdad where at sunset camels perch in the palm trees to sing hymns in Latin, etc. If this is supposed to be a 'response', not only to male genealogies in my own earlier work but to the patriarchic codifications of traditional South African history, what value can Ouma Kristina's narratives possibly have apart from mere 'entertainment'? These stories are so demonstrably 'untrue', 'unhistorical' that, surely, they cannot make any dent on the granite surface of recorded history (even of 'revised' and 'revisited' history).

I should make it clear that I did not construct any grand theoretical foundation on which Ouma Kristina's stories were then based; nor did I deliberately try to create specific metaphoric variations on existing South African narratives (although a few of the narratives do indeed, as acknowledged in the book, proceed from more or less familiar versions of the histories of Krotoä, Susanna Smit, the idiots of Oudtshoorn, etc). The inventions 'happened' as the book took shape. So what I am trying to do now, after the event, is to explain, to myself as much as to others, what might have prompted the choice of such often far-fetched inventions.

It seems to me that in situations such as this what matters are not the specifics of the inventions (a woman changed into a tree, etc.) but the fact that they are resorted to at a given moment in an individual's life, or at a specific historical juncture: in this case, an old woman weaving her web of tales on the eve of the 1994 elections, speaking from the inside of a tribe in which women have always been forced by men into specific roles, against which only certain kinds of rebellion were possible at certain historical moments. In other words, the question is not primarily what 'sense', metaphorical, political or otherwise, the stories may have, taken individually or in a series, but what sense, if any, the telling of these stories by this person at this juncture could possibly make. Because this represents one (fictitious) person's response to the past, in the present, facing the future. Whether Ouma Kristina's stories contain any grain of 'historical truth' or not is immaterial in this regard. The fact that her response to a historical (or political, or social, or personal) challenge is couched in stories (and: these stories rather than others) poses, it seems to me, a much more complex problem to the reader, as it did to the writer in the first place.

Reading *Alias Grace*, we discover that what is important is not at all 'what really happened' in the life or mind of Grace Marks as she became drawn into murder, but the fact that she was driven to stories and inventions as a result of it – and that her society as a whole was likewise driven to (lurid) invention. History may remain an enigma, as Atwood suggested: but it is only through story that the nature and context of each specific enigma can be approached.

In the last instance the challenge of any fabulation (in the face of 'history') is the one implicit in Stephen Dedalus' musing in *Ulysses*: 'Fabled by the daughters of memory. And yet it was in some way if not as memory fabled it' (Joyce 1955, 21). This is the real agenbite of inwit.

What the reader is left with, in the reading of any narrative text, but most pertinently in the reading of any attempt in the 'new' South African fiction to reclaim some of the historical land from the sea of oblivion or of accepted versions, is the irreducible fact of textuality. But textuality does not obviate historicity or morality, as critics of the postmodern so readily tend to assume: because, as Derrida has so amply demonstrated over the years, the fact that there is no outside-text, that is, the fact that 'textuality' cannot be offset in any way against 'experience' or anything else deemed non-textual (and, by that token, 'real') means that our moral choices, now reinterpreted within the horizons of textuality, remain as imperative as before. If life itself is story-shaped, then the choices presented by story cannot be denied or avoided, as they coincide with the choices of life. If stories offer several versions of history, that is, of 'given' events (even though, of course, ultimately nothing is ever 'given'), the imperative of choice is even more urgent, and certainly more richly textured and more rewarding.

There is one initial act of choosing incumbent upon the reader: one may assume, with Derrida, that not just the versions of history but history itself, not just our perceptions of the world but the world itself, is text; or one may guess that, whatever the variety and the extent of 'versions' available to one in any situation, and however mutually exclusive many of these may appear to be, this does not mean that nothing happened. There is a profound philosophical, historical, and ontological difference between these two positions: but neither excludes the weight, or the need, of (moral) decisions.

In some of my early work (*Looking on Darkness* (1974), for example) there appears to be a clear assumption that 'something happened', whether on the level of history or biography, and that this is followed by attempts at reconstruction. Later, as in *The First Life of Adamastor* (1993a), the shaping of history appears to be presented as a matter of interlocking versions determined by different (eurocentric or afrocentric) perspectives. In *On the Contrary* (1993b) it would seem to me, with the illusions of hindsight, that 'pure textuality' appears to displace the earlier positionings *vis à vis* history. But I get the impression that with *Imaginings of Sand* another shift may be occurring, towards an intimation that something may in fact have happened, but that we can never be sure of it or gain access to it, and that the best we can do is to fabricate metaphors – that is, tell stories – in which, not history, but imaginings of history are invented. Myth may have preceded history, but in the long run it may well be the only guarantee for the survival of history.

3

ANTHONY HOLIDAY

Forgiving and forgetting: the Truth and Reconciliation Commission

THE PHILOSOPHER'S WORK, Wittgenstein held, 'consists in assembling reminders for a particular purpose' (Wittgenstein 1958, 127).[1] In thinking this, he keeps company with Plato's Socrates,[2] who believed that all genuine knowledge was achieved through recollection and who deployed, as a mnemonic device, a dialectical method, by means of which dedicated friends of wisdom might achieve epistemic and erotic union with the patterns of an ideal objective reality. But Plato thought and taught during the zenith of one of philosophy's rare heroic ages, in which the place of his discipline as a natural part of the cultural life of Athenian society seemed assured. Wittgenstein, by contrast, strove to articulate his reflections in the subsiding wake of another such age, and had, thus, to cope with a post-Enlightenment legacy which had turned philosophy into a rarified set of specialisms wherein only trained theoreticians and technicians could feel at home. He was, therefore, compelled – as Plato was not – to include among his reminders the caveat that the labour of assembling them was not some higher-order pastime, but an activity like any other, and that the reminders themselves did not constitute a species of occult theoretical esperanto, but belonged to the roughly textured give-and-take of conversation in a natural modality.

Now the languages in which we naturally converse not only afford us many ways of saying (more or less) the same thing, they also have scope for single expressions to range over a variety of meanings. In the latter case, we may face the clarificatory task of specifying areas of overlap and of difference arising from our use of such expressions.

To take up the case in point: there are various sorts of memory and ways of remembering, just as there are various kinds of forgetfulness and degrees of amnesia. Each of these has its own special connection to other concepts in the semantic field. When, for example, a penitent remembers a wrong done to another, that memory is bound up with remorse. For to be remorseful is an indispensable part of what it means to be a penitent and remorse is itself a form of memory, which consists in our being haunted by the distinctive presence of whomever it is we have wronged. Remorse, moreover, because it is a necessary condition for peni-tence, is a precondition for forgiveness inasmuch as a penitent is one who seeks to be forgiven. And forgiveness, in its turn, is a way of forgetting. It is not, of course, a forgetting of the fact of a harm done and suffered. For if someone has injured me by, say, cutting off my right arm, I would be another sort of being entirely if I did not remember every day of my life the injury and who had caused it. Rather, forgiving is a species of forgetting which severs the remorseful tie fettering authors of evil to those they have harmed, so that the latter no longer haunt the former. When we say to someone who expresses remorse for a wrong they have done us, 'Let's forget it,' it is a release of this order we afford them. We are offering an absolution – which may or may not be conditional on retribution or restitution – such that past evils no longer exert a claim on us or those who have visited evil on us.

It follows, moreover, that forgiveness, by reason of its concep-tual dependence on remorse, must be an intensely personal, even a private matter. This flows from the circumstance that, in remorse, one is haunted by the specific person or persons one has wronged and not by some general category under which persons are supposed to fall, such as 'humanity', 'the masses', or 'the oppressed'. When we make use of such general categories, we do so precisely in order to ignore, for special purposes, the individuality and uniqueness of those subsumed under them, in a way that makes the expression of remorse not merely inappropriate, but logically impossible.

The formulae of forgiveness, therefore, are (in a sense which I hope to clarify) outward signs of alterations to situations which are essentially inward, so that the mere public utterance of them does not of itself guarantee that the alteration has occurred. In this they are quite unlike contractual formulae, such as ship christenings or signatures on promissory notes, which constitute reasons to expect that people will henceforth call the duly christened vessel the good ship so-and-so, and that the signatory to the note will pay the bearer such-and-such a sum. Moreover, our expectations in such cases are entirely bound up with publicly acknowledged standards, which are constitutive criteria of what it is to name a ship or draw up a promissory note, since their fulfilment constitutes all the evidence we could have on which to base our expectations. In the instance of forgiveness, public performances do not exhaust our expectations in the same way. For here we demand that the penitent be sincerely remorseful and that the formulae of forgiveness are more than lip-service. Since public utterances provide no cast-iron warrant that the sincerity-conditions have been met, forgiveness is not something we can expect to happen as if it were an entitlement flowing from a contract, but only something for which we may hope.

These conceptual truths are hard to live with and are, correspondingly, easy to forget. But the concrete historical results of forgetting them can be instructive *vis-à-vis* the philosophical project of clarifying the relations between relevant notions. The Truth and Reconciliation Commission (TRC) which, at the time of writing, is conducting its public hearings, strikes me as being instructive in just this way. Its proceedings and the reactions they have excited are, I believe, vividly illustrative of two things. The first of these is the limits logic sets on what moral ends may be achieved through public institutions, designed for political purposes – no matter how laudable those purposes may be. Secondly, they are illustrative of how easily well-intentioned efforts to make the memory of past evils public can degenerate into presumption, once the limits of our language are lost from sight.

The TRC was the fruit of protracted negotiations between politicians, negotiations that culminated in the Promotion of National Unity and Reconciliation Act of 1995 (Government Gazette 1995). This Act established a commission which was to provide 'as complete a picture as possible of the nature, causes and extent of gross violations of human rights', committed between 1 March 1960 and 5 December 1993. The TRC was thus charged, in the first instance, with awakening the new democracy's memory of its protracted birth pangs during the apartheid era. It was to hold public hearings throughout the country in which the victims of human rights abuses and those who had wronged them should tell their stories.

But service as a kind of public confessional (at which the former Anglican archbishop and Nobel Peace Prize laureate, Desmond Tutu, was to serve as confessor-in-chief in his capacity as chairman) made up only half of the TRC's duty. The other half of its mandate was to grant indemnity from prosecution in the courts of law to the perpetrators of crimes committed both by the champions and by the enemies of apartheid, in exchange, not for their contrition, but only for their full confession of the evils they had committed or authorized.

The rationale for this arrangement was clear, if unspoken. It was that the TRC would accomplish the first part of its brief, namely the determination of a concatenation of historical facts and their causes, through fulfilling its second duty of dispensing symbols of reconciliation in the form of indemnities to those whose crimes were the substance of the historical truths it sought to expose. The indemnities were to serve as inducements to frank and full confessions. How and why this process would result in forgiveness, in the sense in which I have tried to explain the word, was never made plain.

Predictably, persons and events declined to conform to this neat schema. Families of some of the victims of apartheid's torturers and execution squads, far from evincing signs of unconditional forgiveness, were incensed at the prospect of being denied retribution through normal legal channels and challenged the constitutionality of relevant sections of the Act which had established the TRC in the first place. In July 1996, however, the Constitutional Court upheld the disputed legislation as being in accordance with those clauses in the constitution, stressing the need for the truth to emerge and for as wide as possible an amnesty to be granted.

By the time the court had given this ruling, however, additional complications were manifesting themselves. Some of those named, or who expected to be named as culprits at the TRC's hearings, far from rushing to confess their misdeeds, began seeking indemnities from the attorneys general in exchange for promises to testify at court trials. Thus the indemnifying process threatened to be snatched from the TRC's ambit and to become an affair of private deals struck in the anonymity of government offices. Resort to these expedients apparently stemmed from the circumstance that guilty parties could not feel absolutely sure of obtaining amnesty since, as an explanatory memorandum makes clear, amnesty could only be given for 'acts, omissions or offences' describable as being 'acts associated with a political objective' (Truth and Reconciliation Commission 1995). Such acts had also to comply with clause 20 of the internationally accepted Norgaard Principles, which required a degree of proportionality between a given human rights violation and the political objective it purported to serve. Thus, as one journalist put it, the TRC's dilemma was that 'the perpetrators of gross human rights violations will presumably not voluntarily confess to their sins unless they are confident of being granted amnesty. The commission

may use its power of subpoena, but the full truth may never out'
(Roger Friedman, *Cape Times*, 2 May 1996).

It will, perhaps, be said that these obstacles were to be anticipated, given the TRC's origins in political compromise. Surely its
having such a pedigree gave it scant chance of preserving to
everyone's satisfaction a distinction, the importance of which has
been stressed by Benita Parry, 'between a pragmatic rapproche-
ment and a forgiving of trespasses that articulates the impulse to
include within the human commonality even those who had
transgressed every tenet of a properly defined universalism'
(Parry 1995, 9). For are not political arrangements essentially the
public works of public persons (even if they are often made in
secret)? And have we not just agreed that forgiveness has to do
with what is, in the last resort, private and germane to the conceptual anatomy of the inner life and moral responses of ethical individuals? Yet, for philosophers at least, these sensible-sounding
considerations do not altogether dispel the enigmatic ambience
that surrounds the TRC's project. For it remains an intriguing
question as to what conceptions or misconceptions of publicity
and privacy informed the notion of personhood that made that
project seem cogent, let alone viable. In order to tease out some
implications of this question, I propose now to consider some of
the reasons Wittgenstein famously advanced against the possibility of devising a language which would be (in some sense of the
word 'private', which I shall try to identify) a private language.
The benefit of this exercise will be to show that concerns of an
epistemological and logico-philosophical kind are illuminatingly
isomorphic with the moral issues that trouble us when we reflect
on what the TRC was established to achieve.

The 72 sections (243–315) of the *Investigations* Wittgenstein devotes
to what might be called the problematic of meaning and subjectivity is usually miscalled 'the private language argument'.
However, as Hacker points out, these sections incorporate not

one but many connected arguments, the overall purpose of which is to expose the incoherence of a post-Cartesian vision of human nature, of the mind and of the relation between behaviour and the mental, of self-knowledge and of the knowledge of the experiences of others and of language and its foundations (Hacker 1990, 15).

This appreciation of the wide scope of Wittgenstein's concerns in these passages is indispensable to a proper grasp of the way in which his remarks speak to this chapter's purposes. All too often the private language arguments are treated as if their only foci were the areas of overlap between epistemology and semantics. That this reading is far too restrictive can be seen from the context in which the arguments about privacy occur. For they are immediately preceded by the pivotal paragraphs which introduce the crucial notion of 'agreement in judgements' (240–2), and these clearly refer to what is beyond the semantico-epistemic to fundamental issues in moral and political philosophy of precisely the kind raised by the TRC's proceedings, inasmuch as the agreement in question has to do, not directly with language as such, but with 'the framework on which the working of our language is based' (240) and with a kind of agreement which concerns, not our opinions, but our habitat within 'a form of life' (241). There is thus an implicit challenge here to social contract theory, in that a special conception of communality is being proposed as more fundamental than the usual contractarian hypotheses about civil society and social consensus – hypotheses that underpin the democratic political arrangements on which the TRC must rely to legitimize its activities.

The target of Wittgenstein's treatment of privacy is a special paradigm of human selfhood and speech which, were it not chimerical, would make it possible for an individual to devise a language which could not, as a matter of logical principle, be understood by anyone but its inventor. We are told that 'the individual words of this language are to refer to what can only be

known to the person speaking; to his immediate private sensa-
tions. So another person cannot understand the language' (243).

The metaphysical picture that seems to render this operation
credible originates in Lockean empiricism which holds the mind
to be a kind of private space, inhabited by 'ideas' derived from
sense-experience. This model at once problematizes communica-
tive interactions. In book III of the *Essay* (1959, 3), Locke tells us
that the necessity for such interaction arises out of our social
nature, humanity having been furnished by God with language
'which was to be the great instrument and common tie of
society', a bond consisting of sounds which an individual will use
'as signs of internal conceptions', making them 'stand as marks
for ideas within his own mind, whereby they might be made
known to others...'

With this move the contractarian-cum-empiricist trap is set and
the possibility of a logically private language is made to appear
cogent, so that we are not surprised when Locke concludes: 'That
then which words are the marks of are the ideas of the speaker:
nor can anyone apply them as marks, immediately, to anything
else but the ideas he himself hath...'

It is on this Lockean account that the 'private diarist' – target of
some of the most effective of Wittgenstein's arguments – must
rely. The diarist holds that he can keep a private record of the
recurrences of a certain sensation by associating it with a given
sign and using this sign to mark each occurrence of the sensation.
Wittgenstein objects that the diarist lacks a criterion for the
correct application of sign to sensation: 'One would like to say:
whatever is going to seem right to me is right. And that only
means that here we can't talk about "right"' (258).

The exchange shifts to the issue of what will constitute satisfactory criteria for determining when a name has been given a
genuine application. Wittgenstein rejects as bogus criteria supposedly set up by the imagination or established in memory. The
grounds of his rejection are that such subjective images are

publicly inaccessible and cannot, therefore, serve as objective standards of the correctness of any definition. This, he says, would be 'as if someone were to buy several copies of the morning paper to assure himself that what it said was true' (265). His point is that what the diarist appeals to is not memory, but an idle figment masquerading as memory.

But these suasions tell against one and only one version of what it is to live and speak within the confines of a private mental realm. More accurately, they nullify by exposing as incoherent a particular philosophical picture of subjectivity so as to make conceptual space for genuine portrayals of human inwardness. Wittgenstein is trying to show that a fully human natural language is essentially shareable. He is not trying to show, as communitarian theorists seem to believe, that it is essentially something shared. Indeed, he commences the private-language arguments by saying that a human being can encourage himself, give himself orders, obey, blame, and punish himself, and that we could 'even imagine human beings who spoke only in monologue, who accompanied their activities by talking to themselves' (243).

He says this because he recognizes, as those historicists who have elevated social being to the level of a metaphysical category seem unable to do, that there is nothing incoherent in imagining language use and language invention taking place in asocial contexts. That we learn to speak by following the examples provided and instruction given by other speakers is an important but, nonetheless, contingent circumstance, having to do with the route by which, as a matter of fact, we enter into the medium of language. But, just because it is a factual matter which might have turned out otherwise, it does not enter into the logical characterization of what it is to mean or to understand what we say and what is said to us. The logical character of any capacity, after all, is given, not by how that capacity was acquired, but by what it is a capacity to do.

Now the capacity to speak a language is the ability to perform a rich variety of speech acts. These typically include promises, prescriptions, descriptions, pronouncements of punishment, and – to return to the heart of our topic – confessions and expressions of remorse and of forgiveness. Some of these acts carry sincerity-requirements as conditions for their completion, while others do not. I can, for instance, with perfect propriety give a false description of some state of affairs for purposes, perhaps, of testing a hypothesis by means of counter-factuals. But, even if my description is a piece of deliberate deception, it does not on that account cease to be a description. For a counter-factual or an inaccurate description will always be a description, although not, of course, a description of what is actually the case. It is otherwise with promising: an insincere or 'false' promise is not really a promise, even where its author can be held contractually liable to fulfil it. It is the same with remorse and with forgiveness. Insincere expressions of either are counterfeits, not instances of the speech acts in question. Nor is the genuineness of either testable by the same sorts of public procedures as are applied when we need to tell true from false descriptions. In the latter case, we have only to examine the evidence and to compare it with what was said in the description. And this evidence must, if it is to count as evidence, be publicly inspectable.

In the cases provided, however, by those locutions that, like expressions of remorse and forgiveness, have a sincerity constraint attached to them, we cannot apply the same type of test as that used for descriptions. That sort of test is inapplicable, not because the condition of sincerity is in principle inaccessible to verification by others as the private diarist's sensation language was supposed to be, but because degrees of intimacy enter into the expression and scrutiny of remorse and forgiveness as they do not in the case of reports of such neutral sets of circumstances as brute-natural events or value-free narrations of historical occurrences.

In order to assure myself that someone is genuinely remorseful,

I must be able to interpret what they say with that clairvoyant sensitivity to the nuances of their speech and the behaviour that accompanies it such as is characteristic of those intimate interactions that typically hold between close friends, but also between psychiatrists and their patients, priests and penitents in face-to-face confidential encounters. By definition such encounters are not public examinations of evidence in the way that truth-tests for descriptions are, since the meaning of intimacy implies the exclusion of that anonymous majority we call 'The Public'. This is why such public bodies as courts of law pronounce on guilt or innocence but do not dispense forgiveness. It is also, perhaps, why the TRC was empowered to dispense amnesty without requiring a show of remorse from those it indemnified.

This excursion into Wittgenstein's treatment of epistemic privacy has taken us some way towards discovering the metaphysical picture on which the TRC's dilemma rests. It is the empiricist picture of the mind as a passive receptacle of experientially sourced evidence that it is the function of language to make public. That picture, as we have seen, privileges notions of value-neutral public access to the extent of excluding those conceptions of inwardness or privacy that, by their very nature, are value laden. Paradoxically, this publicist or communitarian perspective is the legatee of the selfsame Lockean theory which, as we saw, was generative of the private diarist's fantasy. Unreflective adherence to the empiricist outlook will make it seem natural to reduce language expressive of those moral realities human inwardness enfolds to evincements of emotional states. This, perhaps, accounts for the importance that those who believed in the TRC's reconciliatory capacities attached to the cathartic effect that telling the stories of the atrocities they had endured predictably had on many of the victims. It rapidly became clear that these public displays of emotion were an essential part of what Tutu and his commissioners meant by 'reconciliation'. They meant a

kind of psychotherapeutic 'healing', the efficacy of which largely
depended on its taking place, not within the cloistered privacy of
a confidential confessional, but in a public arena and under the
scrutiny of the mass media.

Clearly there is an implicit logic at work here which further
explains how the TRC's architects thought to reconcile its forensic
and reconciliatory functions. They saw the TRC as dealing with
two sets of morally antiseptic facts. On the one hand, there were
the forensic facts of politico-legal history, concerning what had
been done, by whom and to whom and the political purposes (if
any) for which these crimes had been committed. There were, on
the other hand, the psychological facts, pertaining to how people
now felt about what had been done to them. The former set of
facts served the interests of the TRC's truth-gathering task, while
the latter set, once bared in public, would be grist to the mill of
national reconciliation.

Insofar as this version of what comprises reconciliation seeks to
bind itself to some conception of forgiveness, it is obvious that
the latter notion is not, in the TRC's understanding of it, tied (as I
have argued that, logically speaking, it must be tied) to the
concept of remorse, nor is it associated with the release from
remorse made possible by that form of forgetting in which
forgiveness consists. For the emotivist, non-cognitivist ethical
doctrine – which is all the robust empiricist picture allows for –
leaves no room for that accusatory haunting of one ethical individual by another in which the reality of remorse consists. It
leaves no room for it because it confuses remorse with emotional
responses to guilt and so treats the haunting of victimizers by
their victims as psychological figments which must be banished
through the catharsis of the public confessional.

It is unsurprising that, having elected to operate with an amor-
alized and psychologistic understanding of forgiveness, the TRC
should have felt free to offer indemnities with the blithe disregard
for the requirements of natural justice, evidenced in the legislation

that brought it into being. For this legislation made it theoretically possible for a professional torturer, say, to describe in gleeful detail all he had done to his victims and earn immunity from prosecution, provided only the evidence he gave was a complete and accurate description of his misdeeds.

It is noteworthy that the TRC's chairman was, at the time of his appointment, the country's most senior Anglican clergyman and that his deputy, Alex Boraine, had been a Methodist minister and sometime head of the South African Council of Churches. Nonetheless, the conception of justice that informed the TRC's proceedings could scarcely be called 'Christian'. Indeed, if the preceding analysis is even tolerably close to the mark, those proceedings were wholly uninformed by any religious conception of justice whatsoever. How did this anomaly arise?

No body of theological doctrine can entirely obscure the truth that Christian belief (as distinct from theologically inspired Christian opinion) requires human persons to have a distinctive attitude towards one another in respect of each other's inwardness which philosophical naturalism, even in its non-reductive variants, does not require. This attitude is one born of the recognition that human individuals set limits on one another's wills, limits which are determined in the last resort by normative, and not by natural, necessities. These boundaries are what compel respect for the inner moral life of another and, in so doing, constrain our presumptions in deciding what can be done to or for or expected of other persons. Such constraints amount to a religious conception of privacy which is tied, in its turn, to a religious conception of justice, inasmuch as nothing that violates that privacy can be anything other than an injustice. Needless to say, such violations must occur when public bodies presume to usurp what belongs to the private ethical space of individuality by extending blanket absolutions to wrongdoers on behalf of those they have wronged.

The Christians who led and served on the TRC faced the

anomalies they did because they had either forgotten or, for public and political purposes, found it convenient to gloss over, the claims of a religious ideal of privacy and ethical individuality. That they did so is not altogether strange. The TRC was founded after South Africa, as a reward for having abandoned apartheid, was allowed to rejoin the world community, a community which, of course, included various communities of ideas, some dominant, some banished to the peripheries of intellectual exchange. This was and is a milieu in which religious notions of the sanctity and uniqueness of the individual person have been marginalized in favour of secular theories in which individuals are thought of, not as ensouled beings, but as 'rational choosers', whose rights are determined by social contracts. In such an environment, Wittgenstein's insights into the relation in which language stands to the forms that shape the lives of speaking beings, and into the kinds of privacy and publicity that relation permits and excludes, are almost certain to be misunderstood. The results of such misunderstandings are bound to manifest themselves in theory and in practice in the areas of jurisprudence and political morality. It has been my intention here to show that the TRC's project is, in its own special way, a salutary example of this climate of scientistic thought and this failure to understand.

4

INGRID DE KOK

Cracked heirlooms: memory on exhibition

THE POLITICAL TRANSFORMATION of South Africa, represented so powerfully on 10 May 1994 by the inauguration of Nelson Mandela as president, was interpreted by most of its citizens as triumph premised on compromise. For support of the new government and goodwill in general to be sustained, that compromise would have to be experienced as worth it: worth the pain and suffering, worth the capitulation. Since the past had to meet the present through settlement, not revolution, it needed an accompanying rhetoric about how to process the future: and that process was divined as the act of nation building. Even at the installation itself, a cultural event, 'One Nation, Many Cultures', attempted to forge out of fragmented 'ethnic' cultural expression a notional celebratory narrative called 'one nation'. Archbishop Tutu's still-much-repeated phrase 'the rainbow nation' encapsulated the euphoria, and the fiction, of the moment. Memory and representation were thus of necessity put to work early for reconstruction purposes.

Of all the institutional containers designed to sustain this reconstruction, the most controversial is the Truth and Reconciliation Commission (TRC), which began hearings in 1996. For some, it represents the cornerstone of the new dispensation, for others, it is the fatal compromise. The result of years of negotiation, 300 hours of committee hearings, and a marathon five-hour debate in the National Assembly, it stands as the country's attempt to effect national reconciliation on the basis of respect for the historical record, for human rights, for individual and collective trauma. Two types of hearing – either public or private – are being staged: for victims and for amnesty applicants. A third committee makes reparation recommendations. The TRC as a whole seeks to deal with the meaning of individual stories within the larger narrative of apartheid crime. While the stories of perpetrators are often, in Hannah Arendt's sense, banal, those of victims are always inestimably tragic – a litany of removal, terror, torture, rape, abandonment, mutilation, murder. These are the stories that the South African 'miracle' was in danger of occluding, and the TRC's attempt is to bring the disappeared stories back into symbolic currency, but within the framework of the settlement.

Criticism of the process abounds – at its most telling in Mahmood Mamdani's view that it silences the institutional effects of apartheid and narrows the notion of victim, and in his assessment that it follows a 'trajectory that has de-emphasized justice in the interest of reconciliation and realism, both local and international' (1996, 5). The TRC's brief may be both too narrow and too wide for the job it is intended to do; its design may be compromised in various respects, and its practice frequently contradictory; but it is also a potent representation of the burdens of rage and grief experienced by ordinary people, and it is this power of representation that cannot be overestimated.

An early central anxiety was the question of whether the revelations would advance or retard the fragile peace. For some, political indemnity for murderers and their bosses remains too high a price for securing the transition, and will further erode respect for the rule of law. Others argue that the bill has released a Pandora's box of difficulties – political, legal, juridical, psychic – and that it is proving impossible to manage. But by choosing to depart from models from Latin America and Eastern Europe, and with hostility to the Nuremberg Trial model, compromise was the bargain; the choice made by contesting parties whose agreement was required to confirm the compromise of negotiated political settlement.

Can structures such as the TRC contain the psychic and cultural processes involved when far-reaching social change is under way? Might they not unwittingly encourage cultural and social amnesia? Or, in Mamdani's distinction, might they not continue the process of privileging beneficiaries of the past social system by fore-grounding the acts of a limited group of perpetrators only? In the intensity of the debate, three grammars have become apparent.

The first is represented by the amnesiac rhetoric of Danie Schutte, at the time the bill was passed the leader of the National Party's justice committee. Schutte eventually supported the bill in the hopes of 'getting the past out of the way'. This is the bureau-cratic vocabulary unconscious of its resonance, forgetting what else was put 'out of the way'. The language of the 'clean break' turns into the apparently ethical consideration of 'forgive and forget' and 'life must go on'. It expresses a terror that, if we take one glimpse backwards, we may be dragged back into the apartheid underworld.

But this grammar is not restricted to the right: it emerges sometimes in the TRC's imperative to have the story – often called by commissioners 'this chapter of our history' – closed.

A second language is the rhetoric of 'national catharsis', promoting confession, or some version of 'reliving' that will purge the perpetrators and restore the dignity of the victims. Promoters include religious leaders, among others. In her account of the healing of children by spirit mediums in Zimbabwe after that country's civil war, South African anthropol-ogist Pamela Reynolds records that men, women, and children who had fought or seen bloodshed visited healers to be cleansed. The healers impressed upon their patients that unless they revealed the truth, cleansing would be ineffective, and unless compensation was paid, forgiveness would not follow. In Reynolds' view the role played by healers in assuaging trauma

was 'profound' in its contribution to the reordering of
Zimbabwean post-war society (Reynolds 1996, 67). Though some
might consider it psychologized conservatism, purposive ritual
interventions may be essential for healing and for the development of normalized social exchange in South Africa too, and such
a need for symbolic enactments saturates the TRC, with its semi-
religious staging, its confessional syntax, and its many clerical
commissioners.

The third, more suppressed, vocabulary involves a demand for
'reckoning' to resolve the relation between grief and anger. It
usually insists that cases be heard within the existing legal system,
to block amnesty applicants' attempts to evade the legal consequences of criminal acts by applying for amnesty. It asks for
'justice' to be added to the requirement for 'truth' and that 'reconciliation' be exposed as an easy sham. It asks for punishments that
fit the crime and it sometimes requires a detailed logging of
specific crimes, as if they could be added up into a total sum of
meanings. This language, which sometimes masks desire for
revenge, has the greatest valency where belief in legal justice or
divine retribution, or in the capacity of the state to act appropriately, is weak. The individual will not cede the act of revenge or
accept the mediations of the TRC.

Most people wish to avoid an obsessional attachment to the
grievances of the past which might lead to vengeance or self-
destruction. But there is also an argument that denial of the
details of the past might bind the nation to that history of grievance, and the reproducing of that history, even more powerfully
than revenge might. My view is that in most South Africans all
three languages of feeling coexist in turbulent interaction, underpinned by different degrees of guilt, pain, anger, and confusion.
The addressing of public grievance and pain, through legal
remedy and transformational social policies, is a proper job for
government bureaucracy. But the reparative capacity of government is limited, and no work of mourning, at individual or

national level, can take place without recourse to other forms of mediation. Appropriate resources need to be found in civil society itself. Healers, ministers, psychologists, and educators, among others, can mediate between the discourses of the past self and the present self in formalized ways.

Cultural institutions and artists face an especially challenging task, of permitting contradictory voices to be heard as testimony or in interpretation, not in order to 'resolve' the turbulence, but to recompose it. This involves resistance to increasing pressure on art and the public institutions to contribute directly to the psychic requirements of 'settlement' and nation building. If yoked to those imperatives, art too will become victim to the pressure to 'forgive and forget'. There is a strong impulse in the country, supported and sustained by the media, for a grand concluding narrative, which will accompany entry into a globalized economy and international interaction with the world. The press is full of praise for social engagements and cultural practices that reflect a 'break' with past politicized patterns. This impulse has the potential to produce newly energetic registers, but equally it has the potential for amnesia. Nobody believes that the TRC will or can produce the full 'truth', in all its detail, for all time. It is in the multiplicity of partial versions and experiences, composed and recomposed within sight of each other, that truth 'as a thing of this world', in Foucault's phrase, will emerge. In this mobile current individuals and communities will make and remake their meanings. This constant reconstitution is difficult labour, equivalent perhaps in individual narratives to the personal experience of mourning, recovery, and remembrance, and in aesthetic terms to the elegiac imperative.

The ability of artistic transactions to perform an elegiac function is, I wish to argue, especially valuable at a time of rapid social change. I use the notion of elegy here fairly loosely as a perspective, rather than as a literary form, and am indebted to Peter Sacks' searching study of the elegy as a practice with 'its roots in a dense matrix of rites and ceremonies, in the light of which many elegiac conventions should be recognized as being not only aesthetically interesting forms but also the literary versions of specific social and psychological practices' (Sacks 1985, 2). In his view, the imagination operates most powerfully within the spaces of absence, loss, and figuration, providing a dialectic between language and the grieving mind. In effect it brings back into our presence the disappeared, in a newly refigured form.

The central drama in elegiac construction is thus the disjunctive process of memory, its traces and asymmetrical rhythms. Loss, suffering, and shame are revisited, and their meanings revised. In this process, what Sacks calls necessary 'fictions of consolation' are constructed, and identity is recomposed (ibid.). In Derek Walcott's lyrical Nobel Prize speech, speaking of the colonial fracture of Antillean society, he says (1993, 9):

> Break a vase, and the love that reassembles the fragments is stronger than that love which took its symmetry for granted when it was whole. The glue that fits the pieces is the sealing of the original shape. It is such a love that reassembles our African and Asiatic fragments, the cracked heirlooms whose restoration shows its white scars.

This gluing together may be the key function of art and cultural education in a time of social change, but it involves seeing and feeling the fragmented, mutilating shards, before the white scar can be celebrated.

Large-scale restoration of 'the cracked heirloom' is now an established aim of the arts and arts education community in South Africa. New institutional initiatives are under way and of the existing major national institutions many are hurriedly demonstrating their adaptation to new conditions. The South African National Gallery, based in Cape Town, has in the last few years for instance made significant shifts in its policies, placing itself more firmly within African artistic traditions, as well as making educational outreach a more significant element in its commitments and staffing. Muted criticism of the pace of such change, or of the opportunistic rewriting of collection policies or other practices, has been outmanoeuvred by successful public reprofiling of the gallery. Other institutions have put their facilities to use for literacy training, language lessons, and local government initiatives. As competition for national and provincial funding intensifies one can expect various exhibitions and engagements that will speak more or less crudely to the requirements for 'nation building', the concept now guiding many publicly funded cultural institutions. The 'restoration' may prove so professional that it entirely obscures the fractures beneath, the 'white scars' that Walcott marks as the essential features of reconstitution. More compelling therefore, for my argument, are the smaller artistic initiatives burgeoning in various places in the country, often resulting from unexpected links between institutions, individuals, and communities. All involve a responsibility for public education or re-education. The two I choose to consider here are particularly successful elegiac performances: one the opening exhibition of the District Six Museum, a new community museum in Cape Town; the other a temporary installation of archival material entitled 'Setting Apart' (17 April–16 June 1995).

The District Six Museum was established by former residents to reconstruct the social history of the community and to commemorate community life before displacement. Its site is a Methodist mission building famous for serving the community in the 1940s and 1950s, and for providing a meeting place for dissidents in the 1980s. It is overtly a museum of a diaspora community intent on reassembling, and asserting, its public memory.

The context for the remembering is crucial. As is well known, District Six is a large piece of land at the foot of Table Mountain, and was inhabited for a century by working people of all races in a vibrant urban community. Its razing to the ground by apartheid planners, and the scattering of its dispossessed people around Cape Town's bleak 'townships' on the sandy Cape Flats, began in the 1960s. It has occupied a unique place in the nation's consciousness and conscience, particularly that of Cape Town. The name 'District Six' signified for years apartheid's savage attack on family life and its ruthless destruction of the fabric of functioning communities.

An apparently modest exhibition opened the museum at the end of 1994, and still underpins the various activities of the museum. Entitled 'Streets', it is constructed around the actual street signs of District Six, which were hidden for decades by a white council worker despite instructions to throw them into the sea. These hang above a map of the district which covers the hall floor and is itself covered by a clear plastic sheet. Attached to the columns in the church are notebooks for people to record memories of the streets they lived in, there is calico sheeting on the walls for people to record their names, and visitors who remember special sites, such as shops, cinemas, houses, etc. mark them on the plastic sheet cover on the floor, on which visitors walk. These are both literal acts of recording and symbolic acts of recovery, intended to generate a fuller record. Above the balcony hang banners of famous inhabitants of District Six; along the sides of the hall below are family and archival photographs of the area and reconstructions of individual houses and businesses, filled with donated family mementoes. Ordinary folk and the famous gather, as it were, on the balconies and in the streets again.

The official street registers are also in evidence, demonstrating the various periods of removals which affected the community. Named in 1867, District Six became mainly 'Coloured' when Africans were removed after 1901. In 1966 the 'whites only' declaration resulted in an agonizing and piecemeal system of removals, in which streets and neighbourhoods slowly crumbled. In 1981 the last removals took place. What happens in the register is chillingly logical: first the occupations of residents are deleted, so that there is no sense of economic activity at all. Then the names of residents become fewer and fewer and then, as the houses are demolished, even street names are no longer recorded. By the end it is as if nobody had ever lived in District Six. The strategy of the exhibition is to reverse this fascist pattern of controlled disappearance, simultaneously re-establishing the street names and places, reconstructing the names of the inhabitants, and restoring a sense of the work and community roles people occupied. The official script is thus thrown off, and replaced with a denser, fuller account.

The success of this exhibition depends upon this finely focused regenerative impulse. The exhibition pamphlet honours the oral, physical, and visual material contributed by ex-residents, their descendants, and others, called here 'the private keepers of history'. These objects are testimonials, the bridge between the past and the present that Merewether (1993, 44) speaks of as 'at once mundane and everyday, and yet also an *aide-mémoire* provoking the desire to remember'. Each individual who here reclaims personal history also participates in the versions of the past that other individuals contribute. This work of encounter is an act of mutual respect and commemoration. Reunions after twenty or thirty years of separation are common; discussions, called 'conversations', are held for one-time residents. Capetonians who never knew District Six witness, some for the first time, a history in which they were either complicit, or which has been suppressed and denied them. Families use the site as a place to pass on family history. Older people's memories are particularly revered. The exhibition, appropriately situated in the desanctified but still sacred space of a church, can be seen as a ritualistic text, with its iconography the iconography of memory. The symbolic space brings back into presence the actual, but now destroyed, place and community, and in the currents between the objects collected, the people dead and present, and the regulatory edicts, repossession takes place. Personal narratives are valorized by public expression, and memory symbolically walks the 'streets', mapping the past.

Here the 'fictions of consolation' or 'consoling substitutions' are yoked to restitution, to inheritance, which Sacks (1985, 4, 37) describes as historically and psychologically linked to the burden of mourning. There are of course dangers in the enterprise, chiefly a tendency to romanticize the organic nature of the original community before apartheid ravaged it, as well as the potential elevation of District Six to the most important of the groups of removed communities. The projections involved may mask significant divisions within the displaced community, and as they begin to focus on the *realpolitik* of reclaiming the actual land, not the symbolic inheritance, ex-residents have demonstrated sharply divergent views about how District Six should be developed now. The competition for representativeness, and the responsibilities of policy making, are certain to sharpen the divisions that naturally exist in any existing or reinvented community. But the point is surely that this community will be engaged in working through elements of its past, reconstituting them imaginatively and then applying the perspectives gained to the world again. The exhibition and its associated activities succeeds because it performs its elegiac function within such a concretely detailed set of staging devices, permitting catharsis, remembering, and the 'motives of mastery and revenge' to be contained in gestures of mourning and repossession (ibid., 18).

The second installation, though complementary, was different in style, giving bleaker witness, with a less benign trust in renewal and mediation. But it too investigated the relationship between spatial and social topographies, by interrogating the language of apartheid itself. Its attempt was to understand the relation of language to space, space to power, power to language, and thus to memory. A young architect, Hilton Judin, was the animator of the installation. Entitled 'Setting Apart', it consisted of a selection of archival documents, maps, and plans, tracing the imprint of power in the segregation of Cape Town. Judin's multi-pronged argument was mounted against the collaborationist content of architectural criticism and practice in South Africa, against the language of planning and officialdom, and especially against the introjective power of that language.

Selecting from the mechanisms of totalitarian control across the periods 1891–1909 (the last years of British colonial administration in the Cape), 1930–2 (the Ndabeni removals), and 1941–59 (the period of the transition to apartheid under the National Party government), the installation used as witnesses the mass of paper that changed hands as apartheid orders and removals took place: all in the language of a bureaucracy that had total power to talk over the heads of its ciphers. The main 'talking back' in the installation came from video sound where elderly black people spoke of the consequences of removal on individual and community life, on social trust, on consequent activism. The narrative of destruction, in voice and in document, was a mutually soliloquized text.

In the Cape Town Castle, where the installation was housed, the large-beamed official space became inhabited by words. They hung in the form of minutes, memos, letters, legal orders, maps, suspended in eleven glass display panels which themselves appeared suspended. At first sight the apparatus seemed to disembody meaning. One could enter the text and leave it at any point and interpretative signs – either from Judin himself, or in photographs, newspaper texts, slogans, overviews – were few. Viewing became a private process of discovery and interpretation.

The Castle is of course South Africa's pre-eminent architectural symbol of colonial settlement. Because of its association with military power, apartheid control, and secrecy, most people who visited the exhibition or attended the discussion forums held about it had either never been to the Castle before, or had only been as part of compulsory school outings for instruction in 'official' history. Seeing it house the evidence of repression that it now did produced poignant or shocked responses and testimonies. In the visitors' book one person reflected that 'it was important to see that our grandfathers suffered even more than we did' and others demanded that the exhibition become permanent, or be recorded in a book. This was not a bonded 'museum community', as it is in the District Six Museum example, where a community creates and is created by the exhibition, but in the room there was the palpable silence of witness.

Judin's device was to select, apparently randomly, from the archival material, resulting in fragmentary information, sequenced only by dates and haunting subheadings such as 'Tightening of wire fences', 'Permission to reside within a municipal area', 'Special trains', 'My pass is taken away'. Documents were interrupted at unspecified points in their narratives. This did not work to shroud, or mystify, official process. Rather it reminded one that these were not especially singular examples, simply representative among many. So too, the conclusion to an individual story was shown to be of no consequence to the official mind. The spatial ordering of the city, the manipulation of living environments, the public outcomes in the fulfilment of policy, all were represented by data alone: the actual written communications that determined lives and deaths. The documents testified to the way the segregation of space determined not only the unequal distribution of land and resources, but the development of a hermetic set of narratives and a rigidly closed civic language in South Africa.

Judin's installation was pre-eminently a meditation on the way language 'marks' and determines social meanings. The aim was to display and dissect the syntaxes of official apartheid discourse, the way its language conferred power by naming, ranking, and classifying by race, gender, and class. In particular it laid bare the repetitive exclusionary grammar that justified spatial zoning on racial lines, demonstrating the controlling practice of regulatory syntax itself. Formal modes of address, official designations, cross-referencing to other regulations, insignias – a whole arsenal of linguistic controls determined and reinforced the impenetrable hierarchical exchanges between the public and what were meant to be the servants of the public. Complicitous formalities such as 'It is my honour to report', 'I am directed to inform you', and 'I remain sir, your obedient servant' begin and end reports and letters. When 'illegal' black inhabitants responded, it was usually in tones of supplication ('We humbly beg'), using biblical cadences and rhythms. Of necessity, it is through the semiotics of space that activists elaborated the terms of their opposition, but the letters from organizers nonetheless seem trapped in the categories officialdom had delivered to them, and the exchanges are forced into disputes about the size of rooms, the height of walls, the number of bathrooms, etc. Authorizations, refusals, exceptions: they all enact in interchangeable language the professional complicity of doctors, planners, and engineers with government officials.

What the official discourses legitimized of course was a racial 'alert' from white and Coloured individual complainants and neighbourhood associations. 'In one word: control' is what one chairperson demands from the city council. Another individual declares that a nearby ' vile blackspot' must be removed, suggesting that this be done by 'a house to house census'. And this indeed is virtually what did happen. Judin displayed colour-coded racial survey maps, used to record the racial categories of individuals in various neighbourhoods, and filled in by white and Coloured communities and city employees like electricity meter readers. 'Europeans' were blue, 'natives' were black, 'Coloureds' were yellow, and, in the words of one resident 'the traditional South African way of life provided for under the Universal Apartheid Principles in existence today' became secured from 'a foreign race and culture'. Beneficiaries, as well as politicians and officials, become the 'architects' of apartheid.

Judin's investigation of official classifications and spatial hierarchies was intended not only to remind us of deployments in the
past; more darkly, he wished to warn of their durability in the
present. Elements of the hygiene discourse, underpinned by arguments for 'stability' and 'law and order' persist in planning documents, newspaper commentaries, and local debates even now.
What he suggested is that despite powerful resistance to it, the
apartheid state's discourse may have become so deeply introject-
ed that its constructions and representations still determine the
way we define ourselves now in space and time. Removing the
physical 'marks' has proved fairly easy. But the consequences of
such physical marking are much more difficult to erase, for segregation has become the spatial imprint of our cities and the deep
structure of our imaginations and memories. The question Judin
implicitly grappled with is: 'How does one develop a new civic
language? Is it even possible?'

The District Six Museum exhibition celebrates the possibility that
new civic forms are possible. It brings back into presence
elements of value that made the community coherent and vital in
the past, thus securing for itself a symbolic inheritance in the
future. From within 'the matrix of rites and ceremonies' that
elegiac practice provides it selects quietly assertive commemoration. It mediates the loss and destruction of the past through the
presentation of objects, the accessing of testimonies, and by the
naming of streets: by local, detailed, accessible redescription.
The 'Setting Apart' installation had a more difficult mediation
task. It brought back to our consciousness the structures of the
deep conditioning that determined our identities. Its charge was
the need to change the nature of relations, not structures. It
investigated the process of suppression that has kept South
Africans inarticulate about the syntaxes and grammar of official
control. The 'Streets' exhibition concerns itself with resurrection
images, focusing on victims, and survivors. Judin's enterprise

concentrated on the way language has made of us unwitting collaborators. As a result it was expiatory only in the bleakest of senses. His mission was an activist mission, since his claim was that memory should become a site of resistance. For him, the practice of elegiac questioning is 'to set free the energy locked in grief or rage and to organize its movement in the form of a question that is not merely an expression of ignorance but a voicing of protest' (Sacks 1985, 22). That voicing of protest, and the solace it provides, is the mediating ritual of renarration, the recontextualizing of the past.

It is understandable for a country in a historic moment such as this to attempt to erase the fouler accretions of its past, the physical signs, totems, and fetishes. As the edifices of apartheid are being dismantled, papers are shredded, signs painted over, departments renamed. American collectors are buying the old 'whites only' signs that South Africans now repudiate. Those intent on promoting reconciliation at all costs see those who wish to preserve the history of the past as spoilers at best, revenge merchants at worst. But for the project of reconciliation to succeed, individuals and the nation require the physical evidence of our suffering and complicity to be displayed as part of a new pattern. Made visible again, they need to restore to us the vocabulary of the past. The country may be in danger of making the assumption that reconciliation is at hand, or in the hand. And here Mamdani's warning that 'in the aftermath of conflict, healing is not a foregone conclusion' is salutary (1996, 5). Both these exhibitions, in different but complementary ways, reincarnated the absences and divisions that have made us what we are. They provided images of loss, destruction, and resistance, for reflection and recomposition. Both are elegiac meditations, and both ask of us particular forms of individual and social vigilance.

PART II

The remembered self

5

SARAH NUTTALL

Telling 'free' stories? Memory and democracy in South African autobiography since 1994

IN THIS CHAPTER I would like to talk about what it might be to tell a 'free' story in South Africa, about memory and democracy, and about the intricate relation between individual and collective memory. I am interested in the way that autobiography, memoir, and confession have responded to the new, more inclusive political moment in South Africa, and in the kinds of revelations and silences that this new moment is instituting.

In South Africa, the past, it sometimes seems, is being 'remade' for the purposes of current reconciliation. The wounds of the past are being opened for scrutiny, perhaps most visibly in the public sphere through the Truth and Reconciliation Commission (TRC). But this is happening within the boundaries of a carefully balanced act of political reconciliation. Although we are accustomed, especially in South Africa, to viewing repression as a form of censorship, here we see that it may occur in the name not only of partisan triumph but of a drive for consensus or reconciliation. Past conflict may be repressed in the interest of present togetherness (see Schudson 1995, 353).

At the same time, the public rehearsal of memory – through the act of testifying before the TRC, or the writing of autobiography – is always a more jagged and less controlled process than this suggests. It is a palpable, messy activity, which has as much to do with a struggle with grief, to fill in the silence, or to offer something symbolically to the dead, as it does with the choreographing of a political and social script. It is a complex composite, neither entirely ineffable and individual nor entirely socially determined (Sivan and Winter forthcoming).

Public acts of remembering – individual memory in action – will consequently require a range of careful historical and psychoanalytical readings. It will also be important to see how this messy activity of memory, this intricate crossing of the individual and social, has been subject, in South Africa, to particular pressures, and distortions.

The stories of the past that South Africans are telling try in one way or another to find a place between public resistance and private healing; and between private resistance and public healing. In 'speaking memory', they try to negotiate or recast the relation between the public and the private. Questions are also implicitly raised in these texts about the extent to which a unified self is an ongoing prerequisite for political action and personal healing in the present – and whether one can find pleasure in the acknowledgement of a self disunified across history.

Memory is always as much about the present as it is about the past, and the texts I look at are about telling stories of the past but also about working out what constitutes a collective, resistance, freedom, place, and survival in the present. I begin by making some comments about Nelson Mandela's autobiography, the kind of public–private relation it sets up, and the way that the man himself operates as a kind of narrative frame against which other lives are presented. I then look at Mamphela Ramphele's autobiography, the ways in which it both opens up further areas of speaking about self, past, and the body, but also shuts down other emotional reaches and places of the self. I conclude by looking at the confession of Mark Behr, anti-apartheid activist, novelist, and police spy.

In Mandela's autobiography, *Long Walk to Freedom* (1994), the private, apparently, is public (although members of his family question whether a 'private' self still exists). Memory is the basis on which oppression can be challenged and the political appears to set a framework for personal remembering. Memory is seen as proceeding less from the inside out, structured by an internal set of needs and desires, as from the outside in. Structured in this way, the individual or private self is vulnerable to being ignored, or seen as 'unpolitical'. This is typical of much black autobiography of the 1980s (though less so in women's writing), in which the relation between narrator and reader is still envisaged, in stronger terms than is usual in autobiography, as a rhetorical one.

The imperative is still to assert black subjectivity, and so to influence and instruct the reader. The address is still an address to an audience which may doubt the selfhood of the autobiographer. As much as an address to black freedom fighters, Mandela's text is an attempt to open an intercourse with a still resistant white world. We see its rhetorical aims in the treatment of the life as representative, its unifying sense of calling and vocation, and its stylistic sensitivity to the arts of persuasion. The writing, and reading, context is not perceived to be democratic (see Andrews 1986, 17).

'Autobiography' itself in Mandela's text comes closest to being a collective form. He makes it clear that the autobiography is a 'memory' which is not exclusively his: in prison the manuscript was 'edited', as Mandela wrote it, by fellow prisoners Walter Sisulu and Ahmed Kathrada. The monologic voice becomes dialogic: the admission of other voices into the text – though in a way that remains opaque to the reader – deauthorizes any single narrative voice as exclusively Mandela's. The production of memory is like an industry: 'We created an assembly line to process the manuscript', Mandela writes (1994, 463).

Mandela himself frequently operates in other texts as a narrative frame for personal remembrance, an emblem against which to mark private experience. In Annmarie Wolpe's autobiography *The Long Way Home* (1994), the epicentre of the narrative is the day that she and her family watched on television Mandela's 'walk to freedom' after 27 years in jail. 'It is like nothing I have ever seen before,' she writes (ibid., 5), and the release is a marker in the text, after which she presents her life as permanently changed. She will now return to South Africa, a move which recalls a past, also 27 years before, when she was 'out of control' of her life. The political event precipitates a private memory of victimhood.

In Mamphela Ramphele's autobiography, *A Life* (1995), Mandela wields a narrative power in a different way. Ramphele defines herself as a 'transgressor', a black woman operating on the margins of convention and repeatedly crossing boundaries. Yet she writes that Nelson Mandela is the 'most important transgressive' (ibid., 200). Though wanting to transgress some of the boundaries Mandela has himself observed, particularly in relation to gender, it is nevertheless he who provides the enabling impetus, the template against which the sense of her own past, and even the act of autobiography, can evolve. The public, the political, the man himself, frames, in both these autobiographies, the private memories.

That Mandela is a measure against which these South Africans mark their personal memories is not necessarily any different in a structural way from any other memory in any other nation's history. But what is significant is the terms on which Mandela is remembered by these writers. Change the frame, and one will see a different person, encounter a different set of memories. In the political frame, Mandela is the freedom fighter, the leader of the struggle against apartheid, the transgressor, and redemptive first president in the new democracy. In another frame, the memory might be different: a prisoner lonely and saying to his warder, 'Please stay with me', a harsh father and uncle, and a man called a 'dirty kaffir' by other black prisoners. In the ghost-written autobiography of James Gregory (1995), Mandela's warder during most of his years in prison, an account often riven with plagiarism, fantasy, and self-justification, we nevertheless do glimpse a different Mandela, a man who admits to wearing a mask, and bearing agonies that remain invisible in the 'national epic' which is Mandela's own autobiography.

Not only does Gregory's book (*Goodbye Bafana: Nelson Mandela, My Prisoner, My Friend*) unsettle the terms on which Mandela presents himself in public memory, but new and more complex facts continually surface about the lives of the men and women involved in the liberation struggle, cracking the narrative frames that have been adopted. Govan Mbeki recently disclosed that Mac Maharaj (current minister of transport in the ANC government), presented to the public, not least in Mandela's autobiography, as the indefatigable and disciplined yet cavalier member of the ANC High Command, tried to commit suicide on Robben Island with broken egg shells. In André Malraux's classic novel of the revolutionary left, *Man's Fate* (1934), one of the characters offers his comrade half of a cyanide pill. It is a narrative quite other than the book's predominant political message and the characters' sworn allegiance to the cause of socialism.

What might the difference be between the 'freeing' of memory and the intervention of an autobiographical form that will free others – one that is still in the service of a cause, not necessarily that of the struggle, but that of bequeathing a 'model' life? In Mamphela Ramphele's autobiography, *A Life*, there is a shift from 'cause' writing to a more personal kind of writing, one that is conventional in a different way. There may be a need for 'role-model' autobiography, such as one finds in much African-American writing, both in terms of South Africa's current attempt at political reconciliation and because of its dearth of black success stories. But it is interesting to compare a work such as Ramphele's with the much more open, and more tormented, autobiography of Bloke Modisane, *Blame Me on History*, written in 1963. This, along with other writings such as the work of Arthur Nortje, is a brilliant, jagged account of what it means to be the victim of racism, how this is marked on the body, and the compensatory mechanisms that this brings into play. I shall return to this comparison later on.

Ramphele's text seems to shift from the first objective – the 'freeing' of memory – to the second – the bequeathing of a 'model' life. In fact her book is more accurately described as memoir rather than autobiography, making use as it does of the looser conventions of this form. Whereas autobiography is writing from a beginning towards a destination, memoir has often to do with a portion (usually an obsessive or troubled one) of a life – a pathological experience, or an experience of victimhood. This is frequently accompanied by a pressure on the ending to stage a recovery. It may have to do with a wider cultural disposition for uplifting endings, or with a culture's discomfort with untranscended tragedy – or both. Certainly the Nelson Mandela/ democracy/truth-and-reconciliation moment puts a lot of pressure on current South African autobiographies to be publicly uplifting and conciliatory. In memoir, there is less of an attempt to contain a life – to see it 'whole' – than to open it up. The title of Ramphele's book is interesting: 'A Life' suggests that it is non-centralized; that other versions of it could be told. But it also resonates with the notion that it is exemplary – both ordinary, yet somehow to be followed, a precursor life. Although, again, there is perhaps room for this kind of story in South Africa, it also contradicts claims that memory is necessarily being 'freed'.

Ramphele apparently takes advantage of the new political moment to write her story. The act of writing a life becomes a very public way of declaring herself free, of defining freedom and then assigning it to herself in defiance of her bonds to the past. She writes early on in the text that she has felt 'not the desire to serve but a passion for freedom to be my own mistress in a society in which being black and a woman defined the boundaries within which one could legitimately operate' (1995, 44). One imperative of the story is to write out silences, silences in her family about

politics, birth, sex, and death, silences about women who transgress the conventional boundaries of womanhood, but especially
a silence about her triangular love affair with Steve Biko. Memory,
apparently, loses its inhibitions and speaks of silences, restores a
missing past, leading to what Nadine Gordimer (1995, 13) has
termed 'the liberation of openness'.

One of the important silences she breaks is about the effects of
political activism itself. Reared as a student in the early 1970s in
Black Consciousness activism, she writes how she began to associate her own life so closely with the life of her country that it
took her two breakdowns to sever one from the other. As the
country's transition to democracy approached, her 'instability'
grew: 'I had invested too much physical and emotional energy in
this society to countenance the possibility of a negative outcome
of the liberation struggle' (1995, 190). Her earlier moment of
transformation revisits her as a 'powerful but deadly combination' which has sown the 'seeds of self-destruction' (ibid., 184).
The self which is so closely bound to the historical process is
presented as a self in distress.

Ramphele expresses the need for the individual self to cleave
away from a self that is more collectively defined. Yet at this
moment there is an effacement of self in the text. The more individual self she seems to be wanting to reach is banished from the
text, from her autobiography. Rather than turning inward at this
point, there follows an increasingly less convincing set of 'trans-
gressions'. Her need to 'split off' the self from the political fate of
the nation, though traumatic, is also used in part to justify her
'guilt' at leaving political activism in order to pursue an academic
career. And this move, too, is set up in such a way in the text so as
to avoid the really close scrutiny of self-identity that the text was
moving towards. Terms such as 'transgressor' or 'survivor' lose
their narrative power even as she is supposedly expressing
moments of the greatest freedom. Her academic writing is
presented as transgressive, and so is her recognition of her global

citizenship. Her mother and son are both described as 'survivors' and it becomes a cliché in the text. Significant also is her incantation of the guilt of the survivor, which ties her success and survival repeatedly to Biko's death; his becomes another life, like Mandela's, which supports and interprets hers.

In a text that has so much to do with the projection of agency, Ramphele frequently talks of her relationship to her body. She writes of 'the frail body' which had 'a lot to learn to incorporate the emerging activist' (ibid., 69); that 'my small frame took severe punishment' (ibid., 41); of 'frail persons like me' (ibid. 42); and of her heart pounding in her 'tiny chest' (ibid., 39). When talking of her body she seems able to express some of the feelings of vulnerability and fragility which do not for the most part otherwise surface in the text. But the glamorous and tiny body is also a strong presence. Towards the end of the narrative in particular, her body becomes a mark of her agency. A friend in New York takes her to her weekly pedicure and manicure (Ramphele describes it as an introduction to 'American decadence'), and Ramphele remarks: 'I have learnt to enjoy paying attention to my body. This, I believe, is a necessary part of the healing process I personally have to undergo' (1995, 223). Healing from a process of collective political struggle, an inverse individualism comes to the fore.

I have suggested that towards the end of Ramphele's book the self-interrogation stops, and the identity she fought hard to establish, through an ability to change and transgress, reaches a kind of stasis. But the ending requires an intricate reading, which has a great deal to do with the meaning(s) of 'healing'. The book stages, and responds to, the need to heal. Jay Winter (1995, 5), in a discussion of the search for an appropriate language of loss following a period of trauma (in this case, the period after the First World War), writes of the strength and preponderance of traditional narrative forms, because of their ability to mediate bereavement. Whereas modernist forms, with their multifaceted sense of dislocation, paradox, and the ironic, could express anger, melancholy, and despair, and did so in enduring ways, they could not heal. Continuity, not transformation, reiteration, not alteration, were features of post-war narrative, Winter argues, disputing the claims of modernists who presented a binary break between the traditional forms of the past and the modernist features of modern, post-war memory (ibid., 54).

Ramphele opts for a narrative 'wholeness': contrary to those who might favour the maintenance of 'traumatic memory', refuse the premature smoothing over of real contradictions and insist on a certain 'refusal to mourn', she favours healing through a 'narrative memory' which works through the past by telling intelligible stories about it. This corresponds with most autobiographical work in South African since 1994, in which the rudiments of hope, of the redemption of suffering, and of transcendence over evil are never far from the narrative that is being constructed. Following Winter, the language of the sacred is not so much disputed as reworked. Both in autobiography, through 'conversion narratives' and 'redemptive moments', and in the TRC, where notions of sin and forgiveness operate powerfully, such narratives may speak of the emotional distress or intense personal conflict that precede and make way for, say, the redemption at the end of the narrative. The practices of psychotherapy, one could say, address themselves to the same contradictions mediated by such narratives.

Modisane's earlier *Blame Me on History* was a response to a specific, and very repressive, period in South Africa's history. This accounts in part for the different set of responses to memory and mourning that it presents. The distortions that the trauma of racism causes are reflected in the ritual revisiting of a perversely pleasant pain. The full obscenity of apartheid, and its 'devouring' memories, can only be captured through a literature of debasement. 'I am afraid to vomit the accumulation in my stomach,' he writes, 'the violence would be too great for me to control' (1986, 70). Images of frustrated sex, or sterile sex, are the terms he chooses to talk about being black in South Africa. 'Every endeavour, every action is like an orgasm in a bed of which the sheets are soiled, but there is no release of the sexual tensions', he writes (ibid., 251).

The imperative, for a consciousness such as Modisane's, and those of a number of others of his generation, was perhaps towards death, or exile, rather than towards healing. The narratives they wrote, existing as they did within, and not beyond, apartheid, and with an intimation that the apartheid system was getting more brutal and repressive, would not, and could not, heal. Modisane died in exile in West Germany in 1986. He writes in his autobiography that he feels 'disillusioned beyond reconciliation' (ibid., 139).

Ramphele writes in a historical period in which the process of healing can more easily be staged, and responded to. But is any version of healing a kind of closure, somehow problematically holistic and harmonistic? Martin Jay (forthcoming) has recently written how Walter Benjamin steadfastly defied all attempts to heal the wounds caused by the First World War. Benjamin refused to seek some sort of new symbolic equilibrium through a process of collective mourning that would successfully 'work through' the grief. Scornfully rejecting the ways in which culture can function to cushion the blows of trauma, he wanted to compel his readers to face squarely what had happened and confront its deepest sources rather than let the wounds scar over. Rather than rebuilding the psychological 'protective shield' that Freud saw as penetrated by trauma, he laboured to keep it lowered so that the pain could not be numbed. He was profoundly at odds with the post-war, international culture of 'commemoration' that drew on all the resources of tradition and the sacred it could muster to provide meaning and consolation for the survivors.

Benjamin's attraction to the endless, repetitive 'play' of mourning or melancholy, as opposed to the allegedly 'healthy working through' of grief, was more than a response to the war experience in general, Jay finds. It was specifically linked to his reluctance to close the book on his friends' anti-war suicides. Making sense of these acts in terms of sacrifice, atonement, and reconciliation could only reinforce the evil power of mythic fatalism.

If Jay is critical of Benjamin's insistence on 'valorizing catastrophe', rather than trying to heal it, he sees, too, that Benjamin's views preserved the notion of a dissociation between past and present, 'the temporal delay of the trauma itself, that made a constellation, not a collapse, of the two possible' (forthcoming).

The integration of the past into the present may be one stage in a process of healing, or in the making of memory, but to heal, and to remember, is also to find the freedom to ask more questions, to let the unspeakable, both then and now, filter in, to disturb, to open out consciousness. Does this bring us back to a modernist – and postmodernist – alienation? Does it ask those who might have tried, and perhaps succeeded, in recovering to mourn again?

Yes and no. Of a text such as Ramphele's, which does transgress the conventional narratives of the self in black autobiography in some ways, there are other questions to be asked. What would it mean to speak too revealingly of the black self? How much are the demands of telling the 'truth' about the past, and the 'other woman' role she plays (and which black intellectuals have criticized her for) at odds with self-preservation? What remains 'unspeakable'?

To see that one has not located the truth about the past, but only an ongoing narrative of self – to see the subjectivity of the versions of the past one has offered to oneself, binaries, perhaps, which have been able to hold the weight of one's sorrow, to guard against a void of meaning and understanding which one most fears – can be newly painful, in its allowance of the disjuncture that Benjamin wanted us, perhaps too insistently, to see. But it can highlight in a newly self-conscious way the complexity of memory's meanings and motives.

If Ramphele's book centred on a set of psychologically loaded fragments in her personal and political life, leading towards some form of catharsis or 'restoration' in the present, confession is a more obsessively focused, and fraught, genre, structured around the naming of a transgression in order to win re-entry – restoration, forgiveness, healing, and return – to the boundaries of moral society. The confession of Mark Behr, author of the acclaimed novel *The Smell of Apples* (1995), that he had been a spy for the South African security police until 1991 reveals the totalitarian potential of a literary self-consciousness we might otherwise welcome in autobiography.

One commentator has remarked of Behr's confession, which was delivered to an interdisciplinary academic conference called 'Faultlines': 'There is no chink in the words for us to enter and engage with him. He has pre-empted any possible criticism by exhaustively criticising himself...We are left unable to engage with the truth' (Borain 1996, 27). The confession is framed by the notion of the limitations of memory and language to describe truth. His confession is undertaken, Behr says, to 'shatter an autobiography of denial'; undertaken, then, apparently, in order to tell the truth, or a truth, about his life. At the same time he speaks, he says, with a voice that is tainted, and perhaps cannot tell the truth: the 'voice of betrayal: a voice that cannot be trusted, is incapable of truth...in words more broken and more suspect than others'. This is the condition of language itself: given what he calls the 'limited relationship between reality, language and memory', not only is the shame that he is to speak 'too momentous to verbalise' but 'all language will always slight the trauma of the people in this country' (1996, 1).

Language is not seen as producing a reality; instead language will manifest its 'own' truth. But, as J. M. Coetzee writes in an essay on confession, where the confessor takes the approach of confessing with an 'open mind', acknowledging from the beginning that what he avows as the truth may not be the truth, 'there is something literally shameless in this posture' (1992, 274). To present memory as language bound, as Behr does, is also to disavow the possibility of truth where 'truth' matters – 'truth' in the sense of which story you tell, or who you make your apologies to. Autobiographical memory, here, may proceed from knowledge, but not self-knowledge, as Coetzee has elsewhere observed; the account may have no more authority than an account given by a biographer, or a stranger (ibid., 271).

Behr's text raises questions about the purpose of confession and who its beneficiaries are. Confession typically presupposes a constellation of notions about the private self tormented by guilt and the private conscience exposed to self-criticism. However, the fact that people confess to their crimes does not necessarily imply a compulsion to confess as an escape from a burden of guilt. For Behr, the conscience of memory may be less at stake than the fear of exposure before the TRC in the present. Confessions, as Hepworth and Turner (1982, 35) point out, are constructed and not discovered.

Memory theorists have often remarked on the consistency of the range of narratives that people, or cultures, employ to tell their stories. Such narratives, or patterns, weave webs across translations and dislocations, guiding memory, and creating a seeming unity in multiplicity. Certainly the autobiographical accounts I have discussed in this chapter, despite the intricacies they reveal, display a kind of cultural intertextuality. This is both in relation to the negotiation of the public and the private self, and the use of religious tropes to mediate the narratives of the self that are being constructed. It is a culture from which I, too, write: I have only to think of the difficulty I have in subjecting Mandela, both the man and his writing, to the kind of critical scrutiny I might want to practise in 'ordinary' circumstances, to acknowledge the pull of the latter-day saint that he seems to me to be, to read my own writing as part of the culture of which I write.

We are never, Winter has remarked, the first people to know who we are. But if collective memory is the outcome of agency, in South Africa it may often seem that we need to approach the construction of memory from the other way round: Is it less, here, that private memories shape collective remembrance than vice versa? Does the challenge then become how we can create a collective memory that is multiple, flickering with the many meanings that individual experience can collectively bring to it?

Memories, like stories, can never be 'free'. They will always be laden with meaning – less crudely ideological, always, than narratorial (which may nevertheless constitute a kind of 'freedom'). But what I have meant to show here is just how difficult the 'freeing' of memory – not a 'fullness' so much as a more fully realized vision of the social and private dimensions of experience – is proving in South Africa.

6

GARY MINKLEY and
CIRAJ RASSOOL

Orality, memory, and social history in South Africa

THE FIRST HALF OF 1996 was marked by significant events for the reworking of memory and the production of history in South Africa. Two such events, the start of the hearings of the Truth and Reconciliation Commission (TRC) into gross human rights violations, and the release of Charles van Onselen's 649-page epic, *The Seed Is Mine*, occurred almost simultaneously. These separate events, on very different scales and in settings quite removed from each other, raise the issues of the relationship between individual testimony, evidence, and historical memory.

The TRC has been hearing personal narratives – presented as testimony – of the apartheid era from both victims and perpetrators. It is concerned to document these as part of the process of remaking collective memory of the past on an inclusive and national scale. Van Onselen's life history is of Kas Maine, a sharecropper who lived on the Highveld. It is built upon the deep layering of oral testimony as biography, and is concerned with the cultural and social meanings of memory. The TRC, on the other hand, is concerned with a politics of memory in which the past is uncovered for the purposes of political reconciliation in the present.

The two processes, though seemingly unrelated, are not quite as much at odds as they might seem: *The Seed Is Mine* publicly places the social experience of black rural lives into a collective memory of cultural osmosis, interaction, and reconciliation; the

TRC deals with the telling of individual memory that defies the categories most familiar to those who wish to collect these stories. They each raise a similar set of questions about how historical and personal memory have been approached in South Africa.

Van Onselen's history is meant to be read as a monumental counter-memory to the official record of segregation and apartheid, the biography of a man who 'never was' (1996, 3). The TRC reflects an official recording, on an extraordinary scale, of counter-memories to the silence imposed by apartheid. Both the book and the official body rely primarily on personal memory to counter official and documentary 'black holes'. Between the social history of the life of Kas Maine and the TRC's quest for political mastery of collective memory lies the claim by both to being vehicles for the histories and everyday stories of ordinary South Africans.

This chapter begins by exploring the notion of submerged memory in South Africa. It looks at the claim by recent social historians that they have been facilitators of its emergence through the generation of oral testimony and remembrance. Social historians have seen their work as characterized by the attempt to 'give voice' to the experience of previously marginal groups and to recover the agency of ordinary people. The documentation of these pasts, conceived as 'hidden history', sought to democratize the historical record. They were seen to be able to create an archive for the future and an alternative form of historical documentation.

We raise questions about, firstly, the chronologies, periodizations, and narratives of social history; secondly, the 'domination versus resistance' model it has employed; and thirdly, the practices and processes of the authoring and translation of memory through oral text into 'history'. Our discussion of the translation of personal memory into collective remembering is broadened by looking at the uses of oral history in the story of Kas Maine, and in the hearings of the TRC.

The historical narratives produced by South African social historians have relied on the idea of 'lived experience', as communicated through oral testimony, as a means of overcoming the silences of written sources. This approach saw oral testimony as the voice of authenticity, and memory as being transparent. Paul La Hausse, writing in *Radical History Review* in 1990, argued that the general character of South African oral historiography reflected the tensions between 'life histories', the recovering of 'subjective popular experiences' in rural and urban settings, and the retrieval of largely unwritten and non-literate 'underclass' experiences. The focus of social history in South Africa ranged across apparently diverse fields, from portraits of black lives on the Highveld to the 'moral economies' of urban mineworkers and squatter proletarians; from the local traditions of resistance amongst rural workers to migrant organization, criminality, and working class-life under urban apartheid. Yet La Hausse (1990), as well as much of the historical work he reviewed, was markedly silent about memory as either a theoretical or historical category.[1]

Tim Keegan has been one of the few to point out that 'individual memory is usually an indispensable source of evidence at the historian's disposal' but that 'human memory is given to error, misconception, elision, distortion, elaboration and downright fabrication' (1988, 159–62). At the same time, Keegan argues that 'in the narratives of ordinary people's lives we begin to see some of the major forces of history at work, large social forces that are arguably the real key to understanding the past' (ibid., 168). Here the concept of memory represents more than individual experience and stands for collective social and economic experience, particularly as it relates to class.

In the 1980s the emergence of the ANC front organization, the United Democratic Front (UDF), saw the emergence of a perspective which collapsed national and class teleologies into one of 'the people'. 'History from below' was 'people's history' and was connected to struggles for 'people's power' and 'people's

education'. Authentic 'voices from below' became those of
nationalist leaders. More importantly though, social history came
to be mobilized in support of building a national movement on
the basis of the dominant resistance politics of the 1950s.
Individual memory, sourced through 'resistance voices', recollected 'the memory of a people' and implied an unstated collective
memory of resistance. The 'people', imagined as a visible, assembled body, were granted collective memory through the accumulation of their leaders' voices, through the integrity ascribed to
the memory and identity of individual nationalist leaders.

Social historians, such as those involved in the History
Workshop at the University of the Witwatersrand, became
involved in popularizing the South African past and making academic knowledge 'accessible'. Three popular histories, written by
Luli Callinicos, were produced.[2] In addition, a series of popular
articles for the weekly newspaper *New Nation* was published later
as a collection, *New Nation, New History*. A slide–tape production
on squatter movements in Soweto, called *Fight Where We Stand*,
and a six-part documentary entitled *Soweto: A History* have also
been produced. While *Fight Where We Stand* used actual transcripts it consisted of the motionless images and projected voices
of actors; the video series, largely inspired by the model of the
slide–tape, consisted of 'real people in motion', synchronized
with 'real voices', conveying 'real experiences'. Here, oral history
had been used as the 'voice of the people', or even the 'voice of
the worker', authenticating academic research and the 'scholarly
findings of the new school' (Bonner 1994, 6). In the place of
national leaders, the previously submerged 'ordinary' voices and
images construct the analogies of community and class identities
as ideal and representative of collective memory.

South African engagement with social history in the 1980s took
the form of two narratives. One was academic, based on culturalist notions of class and consciousness and the other popular,
located within the cultural politics of nationalism. These were

parallel and compatible resistance narratives. While social history claimed to draw its inspiration and its knowledge from the working class, its research was largely focused on the sphere of 'reproduction'. People's history produced a politics of history as weapon, tool, and vehicle for empowerment, as part of 'a broad project to develop an education for a post-apartheid South Africa'.[3] Both narratives drew on the notion of the community as a metaphor for everyday experience, as the place for locating divergent strands of political consciousness.

The compatibility of these academic and popular narratives was demonstrated in Leslie Witz's *Write Your Own History*, produced under the auspices of the History Workshop. In its presentation of the relationship between 'critical history' and 'political activism', history as 'process' was promoted. Both narratives relied on constructing identities through the mobilization of an implicit politics of memory that assumed fixed practices of oral signification. Collective memories, we argue, were analogous to the remembrances of individuals, linked by the group experiences of race and class in communities and shared by the ideal memory and identity of these individuals. Multiple individual voices equalled collective memory and represented collective identity (Schudson 1995).[4] Oral history was the connection between the past and political struggle, between historians and the voice of community, between social and political history, between the individual and the collective, between knowledge and power, and between memory and history (see Witz 1988; 1990).

This framework has continued to characterize most oral history work in South Africa. The main roads into the past remain those tramped by classes, communities, and organizations engaged in resistance in the form of a journey – a procession with an origin, a course, and a destination. In Johannesburg, resistance was 'orally' inscribed as a process of consciousness formation by classes and individuals; in Natal, it was recorded in biography as the agency and organizational careers of ordinary people, and in

Cape Town these two strands were brought together in a nostalgia of ordinary people's experience, constructed as a community splintered by state intervention.[5]

From the early 1990s, however, oral history as the 'democratic practice' of social and popular history in South Africa has come under increasing strain. Its assumption of inherent radicalism and transformatory intent, in both method and content, predicated on its apparent access to the consciousness of experience, has begun to be questioned. Alongside this, the mythology of 'history as national struggle' and the partisan 'ventriloquisms' of people's history have implicitly begun to be questioned (Rousseau 1994, 82–119); Qotole and Van Sittert 1994, 3). We wish to suggest that social history in South Africa brought together modernist appropriations of oral discourses with nationalist and culturalist teleologies of resistance to generate a grand narrative of experience, read as 'history from below'. Unwilling to engage the issues of power embedded in the conversational narratives, South African social historians imposed themselves and their 'radical' methods on 'ordinary people', inscribed them into an authenticated historical narrative, and made them 'mere representative allegories of 'correct political [and historical] practice' (Rousseau 1994, 42).

There is a growing realization that in even more complex ways than has previously been the rule in new social history, apartheid did not always produce resistance, and that resistance was not always occasioned by apartheid. Rather, alongside difference and inequality lie more subtle forms of economic, cultural, and intellectual exchange integrally tied to the layers in which past and present are negotiated through memory, tradition, and history, both written and oral. Equally important is the sense in which the periodizations of resistance have begun to alter, but also to fragment the overall nationalist narrative as one no longer containing incremental modes negotiating modernity. The 'ordinary voices' do not fit the dominant narratives and it has become increasingly difficult to read history from left to right, across the page.

In some ways, social historians continue to produce studies full of vigour and insight. Rich and complex histories have been written that do not easily romanticize and essentialize the past through a simple dichotomy between apartheid and resistance. These histories have drawn on the 'many voices' of communities and classes, highlighting the dynamics of gender, race, and ethnicity, and of age, migrancy, and urban–rural spatiality.[6] Those 'voices' within the state and its institutional 'presences' have also begun to receive attention (see e.g. Posel (1991); Lazar (1987)). The determining framework for most of these studies has, however, remained materially based. As Isabel Hofmeyr (1994, 181) succinctly puts it:

> One result of this [social history] approach is that traces of economic determinism are always present. To have a detailed concern for words and their impact in the world in this climate is often difficult since one is seen to be speaking of issues which are far removed from, and so apparently irrelevant to, the major forces that shape people's lives.

A number of recent studies have begun to explore the pathways suggested by Hofmeyr. Bozzoli with Nkotsoe (1991), Moodie with Ndatshe (1994), and Nasson (1991), among others, all draw extensively on oral histories (or testimonies) as the basis for re-examining experience and unravelling constructions of resistance at the core of South African historiography. Bozzoli with Nkotsoe, for example, point to the more complex and less coherent forms of identity and agency collected through peasant testimony among various women of Phokeng.[7] Moodie with Ndatshe argue for a similar process of reassessment, drawing on the changed content generated through migrant testimony. The surprising aspect of this recent work is the continued limited engagement with the form, structure, and social processes of memory. An important exception is the work of Bill Nasson

(1991), which begins to address issues of oral remembrance and storytelling in relation to memory and tradition, myth, and legend, in the making of rural and cultural identities.

In an article prior to the publication of *The Seed Is Mine: The Life of Kas Maine*, Charles van Onselen (1993) reflected on the methodology of reconstructing a rural life (that of Kas Maine) from oral testimony. This piece is particularly interesting in its engagement with the 'difficulties that come between the oral historian and his quarry' and for the manner in which oral testimony and personal memory begin to be reassessed. Van Onselen identifies the difficulties of the changing 'knowledge transactions' between interviewer and interviewee over time, the differences of age, colour, class, and gender, the issues of language and translation and those of subjectivity, memory, and reliability. In particular, Van Onselen points to the ways that language choice in a multicultural setting can influence the researcher's effectiveness, and that when material is 'generated' in a second or third language, 'the resulting product will in itself partly determine the voice and style in which the final historical presentation is made'. In the case of Van Onselen's work on Kas Maine, this meant the 'almost unavoidable' need to 'eschew cryptic quotation and revert to the third person'. He suggests, though, that Kas Maine's 'narrative skills' did help 'to shape and direct the resulting work', albeit in a 'remote and indirect fashion' (ibid., 506–10). The other key point Van Onselen makes, in relation to the further refinement of oral history practice, is that more critical energy and attention should be focused on the theory and method of 'data collection rather than interpretation'. He provides a fascinating example, drawn from the Kas Maine oral archive. Using an unusual, traumatic moment of recollection, spoken in a form uncharacteristic of Maine, Van Onselen argues that this moment 'not only tells us about the state of the subject's cognitive processes at the time of these events, but also reveals one of the codes that he had employed to store and retrieve the results of an important set of events'. While this is part of a wider defence of oral history as an indispensable and legitimate source for submerged histories, it also begins to probe language, memory, and history in important new ways in South African studies (ibid., 511–13).

In spite of this far more suggestive concern with issues of 'how peasants speak', these advances are not sustained in Van Onselen's book. The story of Kas Maine does offer major new insights, drawn from detailed examinations of the black family, the share-cropping economy, and the gradual erosions, by the encroaching tide of capitalism and virulent forms of racism, of complex paternalistic relations. The most dramatic elements that attend to the form of personal memory, however, are largely internal to Van Onselen's story. The ways that Kas Maine used memory as a resource, a storehouse of oral knowledge about prices, markets, contracts, and agreements, and about weather, movement, and family, is highlighted. Van Onselen appears less concerned with how this tells its own story of remembrance, forgetting, and narrativity than with a continuing conventional approach to memory.

This rests on the recovery of that 'forever lost to official memory' (hidden, submerged) and the difficulties of dredging personal and public memories through oral evidence into a 'body of historically verifiable facts'. It might involve 'rare ability, courage, dedication and vision' on the part of the informants, as well as the powerful senses in which 'history lives on in the mind', as exemplified by Kas Maine himself, who 'never once ceased to amaze with the accuracy, depth and extent of his insights into the social, political and economic structures that dominated the southwestern Transvaal', but this does not significantly alter the dominant sense of memory as remembrance within social history. The implications of this approach are that memory remains treated as transparent, prior to history, and subject to tests of verification. Memory, in this view, continues to belong to the imprecise world of the emotional, the inaccurate, whose validity depends on the reliability of remembrance.

Van Onselen argues that 'Kas Maine's odyssey was but a moment in a tiny corner of a wider world that thousands of black South African sharecropping families came to know on a journey to nowhere'. Personal memory or memories stand for collective ones, sifted, checked, ordered, referenced and cross-referenced, evaluated, and processed by the historian into a construction of consciousness, the remembrance of real collective experience (Van Onselen 1996, 8–10).

We suggest, then, that the story of Kas Maine is much more Van Onselen's story. While he proposes that Kas Maine's own narrative – his voice and style – can be found in the shape and form of the resultant work, this may be difficult to sustain, even in a remote and indirect fashion. Memory, for Van Onselen, is not Maine's medium of history. For a 'laconic man ... who was often almost monosyllabic in his replies' and who apparently relied on 'a short, clipped, economical style of communication that seldom gave clues to context, mood or emotions that he had experienced', the narrative voice that emerges is Van Onselen's (Van Onselen 1993, 510–13). It is his translation of the imagined and represented content of Maine's life history, drawn from testimony and the orality of memory, into 'totalising history', that marks this as 'a classic work' (Nasson 1996, 3).

The ironic consequence of many previous attempts to place categories of people 'hidden from history' at the centre of historical studies 'from below' was that these studies had deepened their marginalization and perpetuated their special status. The hidden and the silenced were inserted into histories largely as a 'contextual device' (Rousseau 1994, 41). Kas Maine suffers a similar fate. Hofmeyr has argued that while there has been a lot of work based on oral historical information, this scholarship has tended to mine testimony for its 'facts' without paying much attention to the forms of interpretation and intellectual traditions that inform these 'facts' (Hofmeyr 1994, 9). More importantly for our purposes here, social history continues, within finely textured accounts, to collapse oral interviews into historical realist narrative. Oral history becomes a source, not a complex of historical narratives whose form is not fixed. In this historical practice, it 'imposes as grammar the mathematics of history' in the South African context, and simultaneously 'makes things with words', and memory into a 'written layer' (Jewsiewicki and Mudimbe 1993, 4–9).

The consequence has been a particular conception of individual and collective memory in South African historiography. Collective memory is seen as the collective meanings that belong to the political field, while individual memory is also seen to be primarily part of this field as it makes sense of historical details in direct relation to political legitimacy. This field is configured by the literate racial and class worlds of the modern South African state and its equally literate and modernist oppositions. All oral testimony becomes the vehicle for 'voicing' the collective memory of consciousness and documenting the collective experience of modernity. Tradition, memory, and orality cease to be arenas negotiating society's relationships between past and present. This is left to history and the written word.

In crucial respects, this history, whether in its intellectual or political manifestations, has structured the 'seamless continuity' and performed the 'cohering task' of defining public, urban, and 'modern' collective memory in South Africa (Minkley and Rousseau 1995, 4–16). Oral transcripts, their construction, and their re-presentation in history typically reflect a process of selecting, editing, embellishing, and deleting the material of individual memory into an identity intimately bound up with the stages of modern domination and resistance. The individual is inscribed into this collective memory as resister, or a variant thereof. Oral history has been less conversational narrative and more dramatic monologue which binds, affirms, and entrenches the collective memory of this history.

7

MICHAEL GODBY

Memory and history in William Kentridge's *History of the Main Complaint*

WILLIAM KENTRIDGE was commissioned to make the animated film *History of the Main Complaint* for the 'Faultlines' exhibition that was held at the Castle in Cape Town in the winter of 1996. This context suggests that the film, like the exhibition as a whole, was intended to address the issues of memory, truth, and reconciliation that engage South Africa at this time. Until now, Kentridge has used the genre of landscape, in drawings, animated films, and installations, as the medium of memory in which the past is made present: images of civil engineering in his landscape drawings, for example, or the assimilation of massacre victims as landscape features in the film *Felix in Exile*, render geography as the product of nature and history. In *History of the Main Complaint*, the vehicle of memory is the body of the protagonist which is made to carry within itself the trauma of recent history.

Inevitably, any presentation of the film is a poor substitute for the experience of seeing the film itself:

A siren wails somewhere beyond the panorama of a deserted street. A gust of wind blows a newspaper down the street.

In a hospital ward with polished floor and bare walls, curtains screen from view a patient's bed. The soundtrack plays the haunting music of a Monteverdi madrigal.

Beyond the screen, Soho Eckstein is shown lying in bed dressed in pinstripe suit and tie: Soho is a familiar figure from Kentridge's earlier films who stands for both rapacious business interests and, because of a sense of alienation and displacement, more generally, for white South Africa as a whole. Soho is unconscious and his breathing is assisted by an oxygen mask connected to a pump on the bedside table. A scanner that is also on the table displays briefly the damaged state of Soho's intestines – before the image changes into the words of the title.

The screen then displays X-ray images of the patient's broken pelvis, the spinal column, individual vertebrae, and bruised organs. A physician, who wears a suit like Soho's, materializes from the medical equipment and places his stethoscope on Soho's body. The scanner again shows the damaged organs. A second doctor, identical to the first, appears with a stethoscope and also examines Soho. In a close-up of the first doctor leaning over Soho, it becomes apparent that he is a self-portrait of the artist.

An X-ray of a torso in profile reveals the movement of the end of a stethoscope down the spinal column to the sound of a steam engine on a railway track. The stethoscope end comes to rest with the sound of sparks flashing; and, as a third identical physician joins the group, two similar devices attach themselves to the X-rayed form like electrical connections. These forms metamorphose into a lever punch that operates to expel the first stethoscope. The other two make contact in a flash, set an alarm bell ringing, and transform into a telephone which sounds and is answered.

There are now five identical physicians examining the patient.

The damaged organ displayed on the scanner metamorphoses into a landscape with a road running straight into the distance. The scene moves along this road from a featureless rural landscape into a built-up area similar to that shown in the opening scene. The movement is accompanied by the regular bleep of the electrocardiograph. This electronic pulse is changed into the sound of an actual heartbeat, punctuating the now familiar singing, as the view is adjusted and shown through the windscreen of Soho's car. Soho is shown from behind, as if from the back seat of the car, and his eyes seem to fill the rear-view mirror. In fact, these disembodied eyes look like those of the artist, and so another autobiographical reference is made.

The car windscreen is replaced by the medical scanner and the view returns to a section of Soho's body as it is examined by the doctors. The noise of electrical contact recurs when their stethoscopes touch the body. Numbers on the screen indicate sites of bruising and trauma. The sound of the beating heart accelerates as the scanner moves rapidly through a series of images, from Soho's bruised organs, to a place-setting that is swept away and replaced by a teleprinter, a ringing telephone, and an X-ray of Soho's pelvis area. The heartbeat calms down as an old-fashioned desk blotter is superimposed on the X-ray and absorbs the little red crosses that denote trauma. Now ten physicians examine the patient. For a moment the madrigal ceases while machine noises accompany the metamorphosis of the abdomen into a typewriter. The image of the abdomen and the sound of singing return together.

Once more the tempo quickens as the sound of electrical contacts keeps pace with a rapid rotation of images. The scanner displays in succession a view of Soho's bruised intestines, a joint of meat on a platter, a foot tied with string, and other views of a body.

The scene returns to Soho, prostrate on his hospital bed.

Next, Soho is driving down the road – his car windscreen fills the view and the ambiguous eyes stare back from the mirror. He passes a body lying unnoticed on the road. Soon the viewer becomes aware of an assault taking place on the road ahead. The scene briefly cuts back to Soho comatose in hospital. Returning to the road, the assault comes closer and increasingly violent. The representation of the assault is translated from the view through the windscreen to the medical scanner; and the wounds of the victim are transposed to Soho's body. The head of the victim fades into an X-ray of itself, marked by the red crosses that indicate trauma, before rematerializing as Soho's head, seen for the first time in profile as he continues his drive. Seen from the front, the windscreen becomes covered with these same red crosses, which Soho attempts to clean off with his windscreen wipers. A quick view of the rear-view mirror shows the eyes closed.

The scene fades to the hospital bed which is again curtained.

The electrocardiograph bleeps as the scene returns to the road where, very faintly, many prostrate bodies are shown. The landscape darkens as the road enters a dense avenue of trees. A light-toned figure darts across the road. The sound of heartbeats quickens. A second figure runs across the road in front of the car. Another figure is caught in the headlights, lifted onto the car bonnet, and smashed against the windscreen. At the moment of impact, the scene reverts to the hospital bed where Soho opens his eyes. Back in the car, the mirror shows Soho watching impassively the agonized writhing of the man he has hit. As the windscreen shatters, it transforms into the scanner that displays in rapid succession the head of the victim, his arm with a wristwatch that explodes, and his annihilated lower leg.

Soho sits up in bed, apparently recovered. A detailed view of one eye shows it to be clear. The medical paraphernalia of his life-support system implodes and transforms into different pieces of office equipment, all of which have appeared before – the desk blotter, the lever punch, the telephone, etc. The sound of the electrocardiograph is drowned out by the renewed noise of office equipment as the scene returns to the curtained hospital bed. The curtains part to reveal a revived Soho Eckstein sitting up in bed as if at his desk directing his business empire.

The scene fades to the sound of an elevator bell.

Even from this rudimentary account it will be clear that the basic structural form of *History of the Main Complaint* is narrative and that this narrative has been substantially elaborated. Since the film is clearly concerned with history, it may be useful to begin by comparing its use of narrative with recent developments in the use of narrative as a means of explanation in the discipline of history.

Reviewing recent trends in the discipline, Peter Burke (1991, 233–48) notes the re-emergence of narrative after years of neglect by historians practising the structural analysis of the Annales school. But instead of the traditional narrative of nineteenth-century historians that appeared to encompass all events from a single authoritative point of view, the trend now, according to Burke, is for historians to present a narrative fragment (usually termed a 'micronarrative') and to situate it in the historical structures (or 'grand narratives') of the institutions, social or economic frameworks, modes of thought (mentalities), etc., in which it takes place.

To describe this development in the discipline, Burke coins the term 'thickened narrative' on the basis of Clifford Geertz's idea of 'thick description' for the technique of anthropologists interpreting an alien culture through the precise description of particular events. Like anthropologists, Burke suggests, historians can describe 'social dramas' that reveal underlying tensions and so illumine social structures. But Burke recognizes that many of the strategies used by historians to thicken narrative in this way derive from contemporary literature. Thus historians have begun to use the literary device of multiple narratives to render the complexity and contradiction of historical experience and so signal their conviction that history is not simply what happened, but a particular view of what happened. And they seek to insert themselves in their narrative in order to advise the reader that they are neither omniscient nor impartial. With these negations of the traditional unitary and totalizing authorial viewpoint, the actual style of writing history has changed radically. In place of the seamless narrative of conventional history, on the one hand, and the rational analysis of structures, on the other, historical writing is now purposefully heterogeneous and replete with poetic and dramatic vocabulary and syntax. But in reviewing artistic forms as models for writing history, Burke expresses particular interest in the potential of film. He cites with enthusiasm Gillo Pontecorvo's *Battle of Algiers* (1966), and suggests that the techniques of flashbacks, cross-cutting, and alternation between scene and story may be used by historians both to relativize past experience and situate it within historical structures. Indeed, Burke goes so far as to suggest that further developments of this kind would lead to a form of regeneration of history.

These developments in the discipline of history have occurred because of changes in the conception of truth. Postmodern borrowings from literature and film serve to deconstruct and disperse the notions of objectivity and truth. But history, needless to say, cannot become the fiction it appears to emulate. History is committed to the past and all the new rhetorical devices are focused on it. In an art work, on the other hand, these strategies are turned on the spectator. Thus in *History of the Main Complaint*, whose subject is the past, the project is not to understand history for its own sake but, rather, the relationship of the individual to the past. The truth and reconciliation process itself is concerned as much with the present as with the past. And, in his film, Kentridge constantly renews and extends this present by engaging the individual spectator in the process on each occasion of viewing. The spectator, therefore, effectively becomes part of the film in a way that is simply not possible with a historical text. Put another way, the idea of truth which, in history, no matter how deconstructed, inevitably remains attached to the object of study, becomes, in *History of the Main Complaint*, the medium of memory that connects the spectator to the past.

The conception of time, upon which narrative of any sort is dependent, is thoroughly problematized in *History of the Main Complaint*. Indeed, if narrative is understood as the development in time from the first scene to the last, the narrative of the film is the single event of Soho Eckstein recovering from coma. In fact, for the greater part of the film, time is actually reversed in order to explain the opening scene of Soho in hospital. And the film uses discrete experiences of time, both in cuts from scene to scene and, in a different way, when the acceleration of the sound of the heartbeat signals a heightened sense of drama. Moreover, in the incident of the wristwatch exploding, the film suggests that time might be experienced as actually stopping.

The fracturing of time in *History of the Main Complaint* is one of

the features of the film that separates it from conventional historical description. The different presentations of time relate not to a
shared sense of reality but to subjective experience and the
uneven process of memory. Similarly, Kentridge's use of anima-
tion appears to dissolve the fixity of the objective world. His
extensive use of fantasy, most conspicuously in the ceaseless
mutation and metamorphosis of objects, gives space to the
viewer's imagination. And the extraordinarily graphic style of his
drawing in charcoal, which is simultaneously powerful and
suggestive, invites completion by the spectator.

The structures that encourage the spectator's participation in
the film assist also in the conversion of the narrative from a simple
sequence of events into an allegory of recent South African
history. Because of these devices, the representation of the car
journey through a landscape of violence is readily understood as a
metaphor of the recent past; and the assault in which the trauma
of the victim is transferred to the witness can be taken as an allegory of the indivisibility of South African society. The overload-
ing of the fragmentary narrative by an extensive rhetorical vocabulary demands metaphorical interpretation for every significant
image. Thus Soho Eckstein's body becomes the sick body politic
of an unreconciled state; and this metaphor is extended in the
group of physicians who attempt to heal the patient without
being able to diagnose the cause of his sickness. The business
paraphernalia of telephones, punches, blotting pad, etc. seems to
stand for continuity in the exercise of economic power but, simultaneously, for the tendency of that power to absorb or deny the
violence on which it is based. And the climax of the film, in Soho's
recognition of his complicity in this violence, and the liberation
that flows from this epiphany, appears to relate to the function of
the truth and reconciliation process in South Africa today.

Perhaps the image that most forcefully includes the spectator
within the dramatic structure of the film is the repeated view of
eyes in Soho Eckstein's rear-view mirror. As Michel Foucault

(1986, 22–7) has demonstrated, the person reflected in a mirror is simultaneously present and absent. Kentridge's mirror, of course, seems to reflect the eyes of not only the driver of the car, but also the spectator of the film. The image thus slips through both time and reality, from the time of the fictive event represented to the time each spectator confronts his or her own participation in history. Through this device, the spectator is made to share the experience of the driver as he witnesses the assault and becomes involved in the accident: the spectator shares the experience – and the responsibility. The climax of the film in Soho's recovery at the very moment of his recall to memory of the accident suggests that liberation from the burden of responsibility comes only with each individual's acknowledgement of his or her complicity in the violent history of South Africa.

The artist does not exclude himself from this statement of the need for a general anamnesis – that is, the process of remembering and mourning that leads to healing.[1] The eyes in the rear-view mirror, as well as being Soho's and the spectator's, are, at least for the moment of making the drawing, the eyes of the artist: in fact, these eyes look very much like Kentridge's own. Moreover, the artist includes himself more substantially in the narrative in the role of Soho's physician, who appears eventually in no less than ten manifestations. Kentridge writes that initially he intended the doctors to be other representations of Soho himself – and their costume of suit and tie remains from this idea – but that, somehow, in the process of drawing, the doctors passed through the identity of Felix Teitelbaum – Soho's nemesis and Kentridge's alter ego in his earlier films – before settling into the identity of the artist himself (personal communication).

The idea that the artist is not separate from the society he seems to observe is one indication among several in the film of the indivisibility of South African society. We have seen that the injuries of the victim are transferred to Soho as witness; and the fact that Soho and the physicians who attend him wear identical suits and ties renders the idea of moral responsibility utterly circular: the physician is hardly distinguishable from his patient who, though only a witness, bears the injuries of the victim. Moreover, this collapsing of identities within the narrative is extended beyond the boundaries of the film. The artist's self-portrait connects the film with the real world; and the spectator participates by responding to the drama of the film.

The confessional mode in which the spectator is asked to relate to the film ensures a heightened psychological quality in this participation. This is consistent with the dramatic structure of the film, which clearly makes sense more in psychological than in objective terms. Similarly, the truth that is claimed to liberate those who acknowledge it is as much a psychological as historical truth. Kentridge puts the spectator in contact with this truth by utilizing the surrealist devices of fantasy and collage. Fantasy, in the form of dream imagery and chance, provides a medium through which the spectator may connect with the drama of the film; and the collage devices of flashbacks, cross-cuttings, etc. create a psychic space in which viewers may ponder their own history.

The heightened state of consciousness in which the viewer engages with *History of the Main Complaint* corresponds with the allegorical status of its narrative. Whereas the micronarrative of postmodern history remains a fragment of the past, with perhaps a symbolic relationship to it, the narrative of the film is clearly metaphorical. Thus, on one register, as we have seen, Soho's body represents the body politic and his car journey South Africa's recent past. Moreover, in terms of historical structures, Soho's role in the film may be seen as an allegory of capital. But these metaphors, and others, are presented in the form of a micronarrative, a story from the life of a single person. On this register, the narrative engages with individual experience and the relationship of individual to collective memory.

Even before South Africa's democratic revolution, and the

subsequent implementation of the peace and reconciliation process, William Kentridge had warned of 'the disease of urbanity' in South African society, that is the 'ability to absorb everything, to make contradiction and compromise the basis of daily living' (1988, 15–19). According to Kentridge, this desensitization, particularly in relation to violence, amounts to a form of disremembering. With *History of the Main Complaint*, Kentridge provides a vehicle – literally, in the image of Soho Eckstein's car – for those South Africans who would tend to identify with the political and economic power represented by Soho to revisit the past. Although the final image of the film, a restored Soho Eckstein conducting business as usual, would seem to indicate the ability of capital to survive any crisis, the film clearly calls for memory to be preserved even in the midst of forgetting what coming to terms with trauma inevitably entails.[2] The representation of memory in the commonplace form of a car journey allows, or rather demands, that each person acknowledge his or her involvement in the violence of the past, not necessarily direct political involvement, obviously, but complicity through some degree of knowledge upon which the apartheid state depended. In this sense, the mundane image of the car journey represents the collective experience of apartheid – which is interpreted individually by each person involved. And the representation of injury in the mute form of the driver's body allows each witness gradually to discover the extent of his or her own hurt.

8

CARLI COETZEE

Krotoä remembered: a mother of unity, a mother of sorrows?

THE PERIOD SINCE the democratic elections in South Africa has seen the emergence of a number of new nationalisms. Kerry Ward and Nigel Worden, in their chapter in this book, discuss the rise of Coloured nationalism, and Steven Robins refers to Griqua nationalism. Afrikaner nationalism has undergone many changes, some of these in an attempt at a sympathetic response to the changing political situation, others a perpetuation of the claims to land, such as is seen in the calls for an Afrikaner *volkstaat*. In this chapter I discuss a relatively new trend in popular expressions of Afrikaner identity, namely the attempts of Afrikaners to try and find a connection with an African identity. In an attempt to create such an identity, however, there is the risk of remembering the country's history in a way that ignores the oppositions of the past.

On the night of 8 February 1669 in Cape Town, two children were removed from the care of their mother, the Khoikhoi woman Krotoä. She had been living in a cottage (furnished by the Dutch East India Company) under the name Eva, and was the widow of Pieter van Meerhoff, a Danish surgeon who had joined the DEIC garrison in 1659. After the children were removed from her care, the house was boarded up, and the children put in the custody of a respectable member of the (white) Dutch community. These children grew up as part of Cape Dutch society, and became the founding members of many Afrikaner families.

Ann Stoler, in her work on turn-of-the-century French

Indochina (1992), has shown that 'abandonment' was a term used to refer to métis children born outside marriage who were not provided for by their European fathers. The term was used regardless of whether the child remained in the care of the mother. These children were thus considered 'abandoned' for as long as they remained with the native mother, who would be able to give them only a 'native' upbringing. Ideally, from the point of view of those who were concerned with what Stoler calls 'racial frontiers', these children were to be removed and handed over into the care of state institutions, where they would be given an education commensurate with the 'blood' and name of the father.

This chapter traces the ways in which Krotoä, who is known to us only through her appearance in official DEIC records, has been remembered in South Africa. Her banishment to Robben Island (Deacon 1996, 19), where she died, had for long been presented as the fitting end to her life, and her role as the biological ancestor of many was long denied in the all-white versions of Afrikaner history. In 1995 an Afrikaans-speaking performer wrote a one-woman show in which Krotoä is referred to as '*onse ma*' ('our mother'). How is it that this woman, whose contribution to white South African identity (especially Afrikaner identity) has been disclaimed for nearly three centuries, has come to be remembered by Afrikaners as 'our mother'? Krotoä is one of a number of women whose life stories have recently been written as part of a project to make known hitherto ignored parts of South African history. Many creative writers and artists are, in South Africa as elsewhere, using the lives of women (especially women who are members of oppressed or colonized groups) as metaphors for alienation and a perceived lost wholeness.[1] In André Brink's most recent novel, *Imaginings of Sand*, a woman hears the stories of the foremothers of her family; and learning of their strengths and resourcefulness, herself is healed.

Many will want to resist the idea of woman as healing, and will want to question metaphors that promise wholeness if the feminine principle is acknowledged and restored. But in a time of political transition, such as we are experiencing in South Africa, the desire for wholeness is sometimes impossible to resist. This chapter considers one such example of a quest for unity through memory: Krotoä, a woman renamed Eva, typecast for centuries as an example of her 'kind' and as a bad mother, and now hailed as an Afrikaner foremother. Her life story, one of destruction and breakdown, has come to function as an analogue of the state of the imagined South African nation. Her 'blood' is now claimed by those whose ancestors denied any relation with her ancestors.

South African history books used to start with the arrival of the Dutch East India Company's first commander to the Cape, Jan van Riebeeck, with his three ships; and hence Cape Town has been called – and remains – the 'mother city', the first city, where 'our' history began. Africanist versions of South African history, and histories written with the making of a wider South African nation in mind, will want to move the focus away from Cape Town, and in the press many are accusing the city of racism and intolerance to black South Africans. Even in narratives about the 'mother city' the focus is shifting. Instead of the spotlight falling on the Dutch man (whose portrait used to be represented on all South African banknotes), it falls on a Khoikhoi woman; his Europe meets her Africa, and she is the symbolic, if not the historical, champion.

The Cape, in this new version of the story, was once a good mother to those who lived in her, and at some point was forced to abandon her own indigenous children, who were taken over by a cruel white 'father'. And thus the 'mother city' was forced to become a bad mother to her own children. In current versions of Krotoä's life, she is being constructed as the mother of us all, the mother of the nation who was banished but can now be reconstituted. The political gain of this move is the acknowledgement of mixed blood and the Khoi contribution to South Africa. This is especially useful to Afrikaners, many of whom had long denied their 'non-white' ancestry publicly. By reclaiming as their fore-mother the Khoi woman Krotoä, these South Africans can gain what seems like legitimate access to the new rainbow family.

Attempts at radical rewritings of South African history which situate themselves at the early Dutch Cape run the risk of perpetuating the myth of 1652 as founding moment. The dangers are clear: Krotoä's life serves as the image of a promised sense of fullness and completeness, a return to an origin, to fulfilment and reconciliation. While all new nations need to imagine origins, and unity, this particular version has other liabilities: again one places the beginning of South African history during the first decade of Dutch settlement. Before the Dutch arrived, it is implied, there was as yet no family worth writing about or remembering. It is the mother whose children were fathered by Europe who is our significant mother. And it is in this way that her life story (about fragmentation and breakdown) begins to function as an interpreting metaphor for white identity. Because now it is South African whites who often find themselves, uncomfortably, in a world in between.

The uses to which the idea of the mother have been put by South African nationalisms are well documented (see e.g. McClintock 1991, 1993; Kruger 1991; Gaitskell and Unterhalter 1989). Many writers have pointed out that both Afrikaner and African nationalism construct the mother as central; and in the literature one finds two neatly paralleled traditions. Krotoä, it seems, is being constructed as the mother of the nation which has yet to be constituted, of Afrikaners 'returning' to their roots. This 'return' operates in very different ways from the Africanist call *Mayibuye iAfrika* – let Africa return. Instead the return to Krotoä necessitates amnesia about how and why this mother of the Afrikaner nation came to be forgotten; through remembering her now, these forgetful children hope to gain a claim to an African identity.

The earliest twentieth-century references to Krotoä come from literary works such as Adriaan Francken's play *Susanna Reyniers*

(Francken 1908). Francken read Van Riebeeck's *Dagjoernaal* in the Dutch transcription, and prepared a lecture on the journal. In his play of 1908, Krotoä appears as Eva, but there is no reference to her marriage to Meerhoff, nor of her acceptance into elite Cape Dutch society (Coetzee 1996). The play was written by someone involved in early Afrikaans language movements, and the representation of Krotoä serves a clear racist and exclusivist purpose.

In a similar vein two articles on Krotoä appeared in the popular magazine *Huisgenoot* in 1942. At the time many Afrikaner intellectuals were involved in a project to define (and create) 'Afrikaans' culture, and the contributions on the 'Hottentots' were linked to a programme of constructing a 'pure' Afrikaner racial identity. The series of articles also serves, anachronistically, to justify separatist thinking by finding reasons for it at the early Cape. The articles on Krotoä are presented as proof of a certain kind of biographical trajectory. She is mentioned as a *'Hottentottin'* (female Hottentot), and the articles focus on her 'fall' and banishment from Company circles; her behaviour is explained in terms of her inescapable 'hottentot-ness'. The author, Bosman, writes: 'As baptism offers no guarantee of Christianity, so civilization offers no proof of virtue. In Eva's case both Christianity and virtue were very superficial, simply a veneer. Repeatedly, she lapses into her original state of barbarism...'[2] His conclusion is that a life such as hers is proof of the fact that racial prejudice developed historically, and is a result of 'habits and characteristics of the Coloureds and not of the inborn prejudice of the whites'.[3]

In the second article on Krotoä, Bosman writes that he had, some time before, suggested that Herry, one of the other important Khoikhoi figures known to us from Van Riebeeck's journal, may be a suitable hero for a historical novel. Now, he writes, he wonders whether it might not be possible to see Herry as a patriot and folk hero, and 'Eva as a female Quisling'.[4] Bosman's reference is to Vidkan Quisling, the Norwegian politician and collaborator with the Nazis, who was executed three years after Bosman's articles were published. The interpretation he gives here, which presents Eva–Krotoä as a woman who betrayed her people, is a fascinating one, and in complete contradiction to Bosman's political programme. For seeing Eva–Krotoä as a traitor means acknowledging the Khoi point of view, and the DEIC as a foreign enemy to be resisted, or with whom one can collaborate to the detriment of one's own people. The opposition between the roles of victim and betrayer in the interpretation of the lives of indigenous women who act as interpreters and sexual partners is one that is familiar from the literature on Dona Marina (Malintzin/ Malinche) in Mexico and Pocahontas in New England. Recent work on Malintzin, by writers such as Cherrie Moraga and Nora Alarcon (see e.g. Moraga 1986) has attempted to evaluate her role not only as a national symbol (as Octavio Paz (1985) sees her), but as a precursor of women's position in contemporary society. Moraga reads Malintzin as a traitor, but sees her actions as predetermined by her gendered role in society. Interesting is the fact that the only version of Krotoä's life that casts her as traitor comes from a conservative, racist position. For writers such as Bosman, she served to make an argument about racial identity and inherent inferiority. To more recent writers, it is more important to acknowledge the complexity of her role as cross-over figure, and to try to place her life in the context of the fort as well as her kinship relations as a female member of Khoi society.[5]

The version of Krotoä's life and significance that I turn to is the one-woman show *Krotoä* by South African performer Antoinette Pienaar. Pienaar had been working on the piece for a number of years, and it is clearly influenced by the work of Karen Press, who has written a children's book and a poem cycle based on the story of Krotoä's life (Press 1990a, 1990b). Pienaar's work is regarded as among the most interesting being produced at the moment, and has a strong focus on women. *Krotoä* was first performed at the Klein Karoo Nasionale Kunstefees (Little Karoo National Arts Festival) in Oudsthoorn, and was awarded the festival's 'Herrie' prize. When the show moved down to Cape Town, *Sarie*, an Afrikaans women's magazine, partially sponsored the production, and gave away free tickets in a competition for its readers.

Part of the reason for this association is of course Pienaar's popularity; but the strong 'Afrikaans' flavour of the production is interesting. Pienaar does not sing in Afrikaans only; but the audiences were mainly Afrikaans speaking. Mother-tongue English speakers tend to be the most resolutely monolingual group in the country, so productions that make use of another language rarely draw them as an audience. In Pienaar's work, the main narrator is Pieternella, daughter of Eva and the surgeon Van Meerhoff. Candy Malherbe (1990, 51) writes that Pieternella and her brother Salamon, the two younger children of Krotoä's marriage, were taken to Mauritius in 1677, and that Pieternella married the free-burgher Daniel Saayman. Pieternella returned to the Cape in 1709, and had eight children. The second daughter was named Eva. As in the other interpretations, artists want to take Krotoä beyond her death, since her death does not capture the significance of the story as they see it. Using Pieternella as narrator is an interesting way of dealing with this problem. However, Pieternella as interpreting consciousness has changed the tone of the narrative: Pieternella is the daughter of Khoi and Dane, of Krotoä and van Meerhoff. Having her as the narrator makes this a story about birth rather than death; of survival rather than destruction.

Krotoä offers Afrikaans-speaking South Africans a way into a South African identity, rearticulated in an African context. Krotoä becomes the mother of all, and her daughter the one who survives, and whose survival will signal that the forgiveness of all that has gone before is finally possible. Pieternella sings of being the daughter of Eva and van Meerhoff, of the sun and the moon. There was a time, we hear in one of the stories told by 'our mother' Krotoä, when the sun and the moon were one. This time, it seems, can be regained in some way by Pieternella. If she finds a way of telling her mother's story as one of healing and reconciliation, the time when the sun and the moon were one will return.

And what better moment than the time of the rainbow nation? Pieternella, the show assures us, is 'us', daughter of 'our mother'. The final song is a plea from Krotoä that 'we' plant an aloe on her grave, so that the roots will grow into her heart and the aloe be made sweet. Here is forgiveness from the grave for all who acknowledge their mother's pain, and will remember her. On the poster advertising the show, a naked woman dances behind an aloe and a sunflower. Her face is undifferentiated: the nose is shown in profile, the single eye full frontal. She has no mouth.

This version of Krotoä's life is an attempt to embrace a different history, especially for Afrikaners. 'Our mother', long denied by white Afrikaners, has to be remembered and acknowledged. The Heeses, a father-and-son-team of historians doing genealogical work, have done remarkable archival work showing the ancestry of Afrikaner families. When, in the early 1970s, they published their findings that present-day Afrikaners had a high percentage of Khoi and slave ancestry, their work was dismissed, angrily, by many Afrikaner intellectuals and political leaders. Now, in the mid-1990s, a largely Afrikaans-speaking audience sits and hears Krotoä described as 'our mother'. And in amateur genealogical circles, white people compete to discover that they are descended from Krotoä, the *stammoeder* (founding mother) of the Afrikaner. The admission of, or the claim to, hybrid identity and Khoikhoi blood can have a conservative impulse: it risks forgetting the conflict and destruction involved in the mix. The danger of such an interpretation is the sense of completeness it brings. Claiming Krotoä as the foremother who will make everything better because all will be forgiven risks distorting the significance of her life. Better it is to remember her as Yvette Abrahams does in her recent piece in *Kronos* as the mother of conflict, at the centre of whom some of us are; a mother of sorrows rather than of unity. Better to remember that her silence is not a sign of forgiveness.

9

STEVEN ROBINS

Silence in my father's house: memory, nationalism, and narratives of the body

DURING 1996 AND 1997 South Africa was in the throes of a traumatic revisiting of the political terror and state violence of the apartheid era. Night after night television news broadcasts began with harrowing Truth and Reconciliation Commission (TRC) testimonies of murder and torture by apartheid's death-squad killers. Former policemen confessed to 'necklacings' and blowing up tortured bodies of dead interrogation victims with limpet mines. In March 1997, five former policemen collectively admitted to their involvement in the murder of 65 people during their reign of terror in the mid-1980s (*Mail & Guardian*, 14 March 1997), and in the same month the exhumed remains of ANC activists were discovered at police 'death farms' in KwaZulu-Natal. Yet, to a numbed nation, the TRC hearings of March 1997 did not appear dramatically different from the hearings of previous months.

These testimonies capture the horror of the apartheid years. They also raise questions as to exactly how such accounts of murder and torture will be written and reconfigured into official histories of the new nation, and how they will be remembered and recollected by ordinary South Africans. Although official accounts of the apartheid past emerging during the mid-1990s seemed to comprise coherent nationalist narratives of heroism, sacrifice, and resistance, the television sound-bites and journalists' reports of the 'rivers of tears' of TRC witnesses recollecting these traumatic memories at times appeared fragmented and dispersed.

How will these personal, fragmented recollections and televisual images of traumatic experiences be represented, remembered, and memorialized in the years to come? Will the new nation state be the sole author of the official script of public memory, or will collective memory continue to lie elsewhere, in embodied memories, in the privacy of homes and within remembered spaces of violence? What about the millions of ordinary black South Africans who suffered the more mundane, everyday aspects of apartheid and who, unlike the activists, were not singled out for 'special treatment' by the state? How will these ordinary people relate to official accounts of apartheid that focus on the experiences of ANC activists and privilege specific sites of memory such as Robben Island? These questions take us to the heart of issues of memory, identity, and historical representation.

Saul Friedlander (1993, x) writes that for scholars such as the French philosopher Jean François Lyotard, Auschwitz has become 'the paradigm of historical catastrophes which cannot be represented directly by way of our usual "modern" discourse'. Similarly, for Harold Kaplan the Holocaust 'is where discourse stops as before the unspeakable'. It is an event in terms of which attempts to seek human motives, explanation, justifications, descend to idiocy (Kaplan 1994, x). Similarly, Claude Lanzmann, the director of the documentary film *Shoah*, suggests that attempts to interpret or explain the reasons for the Holocaust tend to descend into 'obscenity'. Reflecting upon these positions Saul Friedlander (1993, x) observes that 'we are confronted with an insoluble choice between the inadequacy of traditional historiographical representation and the need to establish as reliable a narration as possible'.

While recognizing the nature of these problems of representation, it seems that to challenge the persistence of Holocaust denial, as well as the Holocaust revisionism of neo-nationalist historians of the mid-1980s *Historikerstreit* (German historians' debate), requires the production of as reliable a narration of this apocalyptic event as possible. However, the problem of historio-graphical representation is further compounded by the tendency of both official and popular accounts of collective suffering to serve (ethnic) nationalist agendas. Instances of this would include ideologies of Afrikaner nationalism, India's sectarian Hindu nationalism,[1] and Israeli Zionism, all of which seek to legitimize exclusivist and discriminatory ethnic nationalisms.

Jonathan Boyarin (1994, 24) makes the more general observa-tion that ethnic-nationalist discourses tend to draw on metaphors of the body. These links between the body and the nation operate at both the level of the organic metaphors of nationalist ideology, and the fact that 'nationalist ideologies really do recruit bodies' (ibid). Mary Douglas also recognized the salience of narratives of the body when she wrote that 'the human body is always treated as an image of society and ... there can be no natural way of considering the body that does not involve at the same time a social dimension' (Douglas 1970, 10). Following this anthropologi-cal line of inquiry, Allen Feldman analyses narratives of the body in ways that illuminate the staging and commodification of the body as an embodied transcript through political violence. Feldman (1991, 8–9) shows how bodies become violently staged political texts as part of a process of ideological production in Northern Ireland's violent conflict between 'Loyalists' and 'Republicans'. Drawing on similar theoretical threads, David Bunn (forthcoming) provides a fascinating study of burial and exhumation practices on the nineteenth-century Eastern Cape Frontier in which mutilated Xhosa and European bodies were staged as embodied transcripts and political texts in gruesome exchanges of violence. This chapter draws on these insightful writings to explore how narratives of the body are produced in the construction of national identity and the body politic.

The shattering of bodies through violent encounters with colo-nialism, Nazism, and apartheid is often recast as totalizing nation-alist rhetoric that does symbolic violence to the personal and embodied memories of these traumatic experiences. Through the reworking and rescripting of individual testimonies of violence, embodied personal memories of trauma are often erased and rewritten in the name of nationalism. The recasting of personal memory as nationalist narrative reconfigures and erases the fragmented character and silences of embodied experiences of violence.[2] This chapter examines these processes of erasure and disembodiment, processes which nonetheless tend to draw on metaphors of the body to narrate the nation and the body politic. It will trace the presence and absence of bodies in the production of ethnic/nationalist narratives within specific sites of public memory: the 'Miscast' exhibition that focused on KhoiSan material culture and history; and the TRC. The chapter also discusses in some depth instances in which the fragments and silences of embodied memories of trauma and violence are not spliced onto ethnic-nationalist narratives. These cases will be discussed in relation to two spaces of memory: firstly, the place of Holocaust memory in my family home in Port Elizabeth; and secondly, the 'Coloured' Reserves of Namaqualand, where during the 1980s there was a dramatic recuperation of fragments and the submerged and silent traces of Nama (Khoi) social memory.

   In the opening section of the chapter I discuss my own encounters with Holocaust memory which led me to choose to live with fragments and silences rather than embracing totalizing narratives of collective suffering, national redemption, and destiny (i.e. Zionism). The fragments of memory and my father's silences around Holocaust memory may be deemed to constitute more 'authentic' and embodied traces of shattering encounters with Nazism than the nationalist narratives of Zionism. However, it seems that the problem of representing the Holocaust does not necessarily mean that there is no need for historiographical representation of the Holocaust or apartheid. Such historical narratives may indeed be necessary to recollect and make sense of these traumatic pasts, especially in the context of attempts at denial or revision. This chapter explores the implications of this apparently insoluble solution through a reflection upon a politics and ethics of living with the fragments of memory. This may manifest as a tactic of resistance to totalizing narratives, as in the case of my opposition to splicing accounts of my family's fate in Auschwitz and Riga onto Zionist discourses of nationhood.

Silence in my father's house: living with the fragments of memory

Holocaust memory has been shaped by museums and monuments in very different ways in the United States, Israel, the former Soviet Union, and Europe (see Young 1988; Huyssen 1995). These different appropriations of Holocaust memory point to the multiplicity of ways in which national identity shapes, and is produced by, processes of memorialization (Young 1988; Huyssen 1995). In responding to the (mis)appropriations of the Holocaust for various nation-building projects, Andreas Huyssen draws attention to the instability of both personal and collective memory. He concludes that all memory is to some degree 'abused' or compromised by the passage of time. 'The ways we remember', Huyssen writes,

> [d]efine us in the present. As readers of Freud and Nietzsche, however, we know how slippery and unreliable personal memory can be, always affected by forgetting and denial, repression and trauma, and more often than not, serving the need to rationalize and maintain power. But a society's collective memory is no less contingent, no less unstable, its shape by no means permanent and always subject to subtle and not so subtle reconstruction. (1995, 9)

Both personal and collective memories are unstable, suffer the degradations of time, the pressures of the present and are often subject to self-serving revision and manipulation as well as the forgetting, silences, denials, and repression that traumas produce (Richards 1996; Huyssen 1995; Samuel and Thompson 1990). Writing about these deceptions of memory, South African artist Colin Richards (1996, 6) concludes that 'mostly I trust the voice of memory less than silence'. Given the variety of ways in which events such as the Holocaust have been appropriated to legitimize nationalist political projects, I am sympathetic to Richards' distrust of the voice of memory. My early childhood exposure to knowledge about the Shoah was the official Zionist version in which Holocaust memory is appropriated to legitimize Israeli nationhood. It was only in my thirties that I was able to begin to experience the Shoah at a personal level. This happened after years of submerging my Jewish identity and understanding the Shoah as an event that happened to other people, at another time on another planet. Like my father's silence about the Holocaust, it seems likely that millions of black parents are unable to express what they feel about the humiliations and pain of their everyday experiences of racism under apartheid. Perhaps the rage about systemic racism will only be expressed in future generations. Like my father, millions of black South Africans may be too concerned with survival, and perhaps only their sons and daughters will be in a position to revisit their parents' and their own traumas.

The immediacy and pervasiveness of white racism and state repression during the apartheid years also contributed to a silencing and deferment of any real engagement on my part with the Holocaust. The plight of black South Africans living under apartheid closed off any space for me to deal with Holocaust memory. Throughout my student years, apartheid figured as the space of terror and oppression. Moreover, my Jewishness was experienced as inextricably bound up within apartheid's categories and constructions of whiteness. Under such circumstances, it was impossible to either engage with my Jewishness or confront Holocaust memory. After all, the 'authentic' victims were black South Africans, while Jews were beneficiaries of apartheid. With the collapse of apartheid in 1990, it finally became possible to begin to confront these submerged and repressed identities and memories.

It was only a few years before my father passed away in 1990 that I began to want to know more about how the Shoah had impacted upon his and my own life. In 1988 I had interviewed him on tape about his life story. Apart from two photographs, my father's thick German accent, and his account of his dramatic flight from Nazi Germany in 1936, there was virtually no trace of his family's fate – my grandparents' deaths in Auschwitz and Riga – in our Port Elizabeth home. There were only two photographs of the Robinski family: one is of my grandfather, David Robinski, standing outside his shoe shop in Erfort with his wife, Cecile, and his children Siegfried, Herbert, Arthur, Edith, and Hildegard.[3] Only my father, Herbert, and his younger brother Arthur managed to escape. The other photograph is a portrait of my paternal grandmother and her daughters.

Writing about memory, history, and the Holocaust, Saul Friedlander (1993, 48) elaborates on the process whereby memory eventually becomes 'mere history':

> For a whole age group, still active on the public scene, this past remains part of personal memory. With the passage of two or three decades at most, the memory of the Shoah will be essentially ritualized for some and historicized for the great majority, like any other event saved from oblivion. The destruction of the Jews of Europe will become an empty formula and, in any case, 'mere history'.

My personal memory of the Shoah resides precisely in the silences and fragments of my father's past, rather than in the selective, ordered, and simplified logic of the coherent narratives of collective suffering and national redemption – namely Zionism – that I was exposed to as a child attending Theodor Herzl Primary School in Port Elizabeth.

My grandfather (right) and his family

My grandmother and her daughters

Fragments, fictions, and 'ethnic' truths

Drawing on Eric Hobsbawm and T. O. Ranger's notion of invented tradition, South African anthropologists Emille Boonzaier and
John Sharp (1994) describe the 'rediscovery' and public performance of Nama (Khoi) identity in the 'Coloured' reserves of
Namaqualand in the Northern Cape in the late 1980s and 1990s as
a case of 'staged ethnicity'. Observing that these performances
seemed to vanish following the 1988 Supreme Court case victory
which reinstated communal tenure, Boonzaier and Sharp
conclude that Namaness was enacted in self-consciously instrumental ways by Coloured Namaqualanders in order to strengthen
their claims to Nama traditional lands. Once the court case was
won, they argue, these performances lost an appropriate context,
audience, and rationale, and expressions of Namaness once again
disappeared from the more thoroughly missionized
Namaqualand reserves such as Leliefontein.

During a visit to Leliefontein reserve in 1996, the earliest
accounts of the past I was able to elicit from residents referred to
Reverend Barnabas Shaw, the first missionary to arrive at South
Africa's first Methodist mission established in 1816. It almost
seemed as if there was no local history prior to Shaw's arrival.
The pre-colonial Nama past seemed to have vanished from the
public historical imagination. Boonzaier and Sharp explain these
silences and the submergence of Namaness by observing that in
the past missionized Nama responded to the racist and derogato-
ry connotations that Europeans assigned to the category
'Hottentot' ('Khoi') by distancing themselves from their Nama
language and cultural identity and by adopting Afrikaans,
Christianity, and the identity of Baster or Coloured. In my own
work on Namaqualand (Robins 1997) I suggested that the silences
and submergence of Namaness amongst Leliefontein's residents
were not as complete as Boonzaier and Sharp suggest.

I also critiqued Boonzaier and Sharp's concept of 'staged ethnicities' by suggesting that, rather than seeing these public performances as fictional and instrumentalist, one ought to view them as acts aimed at the recuperation of Nama social memory. I argued that it was precisely the devastating encounters with colonialism and apartheid, and the cultural hybridity, fragmentation, silences, and inconsistences that these encounters produced, that made contemporary attempts to reclaim and re-present Nama identity appear to be merely fictive invention. It is the legacy of these colonial encounters that has rendered today's Coloured descendants of the Nama incapable of producing convincing and coherent narratives of cultural and historical continuity. Yet, fragments of Nama collective memory can indeed be traced in the 'off-stage' acts of collective memory, in the silent shadows of everyday life. It is in the material culture of traditional *matjieshuise* (mat huts), oral histories, place names, and the fragments of Nama language that we may find traces of these plundered and shattered subaltern identities. Contrary to Boonzaier and Sharp's analysis, I conclude that public displays of Nama identity are not purely instrumental staged ethnicities, 'made up' by thoroughly assimilated and missionized Coloureds in order to buttress claims to land. Instead these are collective efforts aimed at the retrieval of the fragments and silences of Nama social memory.

The 1990s have however witnessed a number of attempts to appropriate KhoiSan memory to serve the political project of KhoiSan and Coloured ethnic nationalism. KhoiSan and Coloured nationalists have challenged what they claim is the marginalization of the KhoiSan past and the privileging of black (African) historical experience of the recent apartheid past. Some of the more vocal of the KhoiSan organizations such as the Griqua National Conference of South Africa have demanded that the new ANC government recognize pre-colonial aboriginal land claims and political and cultural rights. They accuse the ANC of ignoring the plight of the descendants of the KhoiSan and favouring their African constituency. An essentialist ethnic-nationalist politics of temporal priority seems to be emerging in which some KhoiSan ethnic nationalists are claiming autochthonous status, thereby transforming both Europeans and Africans into outsider settlers. These KhoiSan activists have also challenged official accounts of South Africa's past for marginalizing and silencing the KhoiSan history, memory, and identity.

The TRC has indeed privileged a modern temporal frame, with the past half century of apartheid as the starting point for a process of publicly accounting for human rights violations.[4] This temporal bias of the new nation state has been challenged by activists claiming to be the direct descendants of the KhoiSan. 'Miscast', a controversial exhibition that opened in Cape Town's National Gallery on 12 April 1996, provided the public space for a volatile KhoiSan politics that challenged official representations of South Africa's past.

Public responses to 'Miscast' reveal that many visitors did in fact view the exhibition as a type of Truth Commission. 'Guilty whites' experienced 'Miscast' as confessional space that forced them to confront European colonial violence and genocide in ways similar to the TRC's interrogation of apartheid's past. For nation building to take place, some visitors wrote in the 'Miscast' comments book, there needed to be a process of national catharsis through the revelation of truth. These statements revealed visitors' perceptions of the link between 'Miscast' and the TRC. Sue, a white woman in her twenties whom I interviewed at the exhibition had the following to say about 'Miscast':

> It gives you the idea of the Holocaust, you know, just masses and masses [of bodies]. No use for them anymore, we've done with that now. Just a nameless, nameless burial... I think it's our story here in South Africa, along with things like the Truth Commission. It all seems to come together.

Once you know what happened you have a responsibility,
you suddenly become part of what politicians did before you
were aware...

This revisiting of the trauma of colonial violence has been a
process that the new nation state has thus far been reluctant fully
to take on board. By restricting itself to the last three decades of
apartheid rule, the TRC has been silent about KhoiSan experiences
of colonialism, and this has angered some KhoiSan activists.
Rather than living with the fragments and silences of colonial
violence and domination, KhoiSan activists have sought to
construct totalizing ethnic-nationalist narratives that draw upon
collective memories of suffering.

Despite the complex ancestry of these KhoiSan nationalists,
many have claimed biological and cultural continuity to pre-
colonial KhoiSan ancestors such as Saartje Baartman and Krotoä
(Eva). The ways in which these KhoiSan female bodies were
appropriated and reclaimed reveal the symbolic potency of links
between the corporeal body and the body politic. The following
section investigates the complex ways in which the 'Bushman'
body featured in the KhoiSan identity politics that surrounded the
'Miscast' exhibition.

The medicalized body, the museum, and the body politic

During a recent visit to the Holocaust Museum in Washington,
DC I was struck by the ways in which the exhibition drew
attention to how the Jewish body was measured, photographed,
and categorized in order to develop Nazi racial theories of Aryan
collective identity and supremacy. The exhibition displayed
photographs, charts, and measuring instruments used by the
Nazis to buttress the official Nazi view that human races were as

different as species. Hair- and eye-colour charts and nose-measuring instruments, used to determine whether individuals were racially 'Aryan' or 'alien', were also on display. The Holocaust Museum also showed how bodies were measured and classified for the Nazi population census. Walking through the exhibition it became clear to me that the metaphor of the nation as a 'body' was at the heart of the Nazi rationale for human classification and population census. For example, Nazi census technology was seen as an instrument through which 'the physician of the nation' (the Nazi Party) would be able to diagnose illness and prescribe remedies.[5] Similar charts and instruments for measuring and classifying KhoiSan bodies were displayed at 'Miscast' in order to challenge the romanticized and ahistorical portrayals of pristine and primordial 'Bushmen' displayed at the dioramas of the South African Museum. The display of charts, measuring instruments, and resin casts of KhoiSan bodies revealed the role of western science, particularly anthropology, museology, and anatomy, in the construction of the 'Bushman' and 'Hottentot' body (see Gilman 1985). The display of the resin casts of naked 'Bushman' bodies that were commissioned by the South African Museum in the 1920s also drew attention to the measurement, classification, and construction of KhoiSan bodies by means of technologies similar to those deployed in Nazi racial studies of Jews and Roma (Gypsies).[6]

Through a process of critical engagement by the public with the exhibition, 'Miscast' became a catalyst for the production of collective memories and the articulation of KhoiSan and Coloured ethnic nationalism. The exhibition's guest curator, the Cape Town artist Pippa Skotnes, had created a public space within which it was possible for a variety of KhoiSan groupings to put forward their claims to custodianship of KhoiSan bodies and suppressed and submerged memories, histories, and identities. The exhibition generated a multiplicity of competing readings and interpretations of KhoiSan historical memory and what it means to be KhoiSan.

A number of KhoiSan intellectuals challenged the right of the curator, a white woman, to represent 'their' past. They also claimed that she was appropriating KhoiSan historical experience for her own intellectual and personal agendas. Upon entering the main exhibition hall one encountered a large photograph of a nineteenth-century European woman, Lucy Lloyd, the sister-in-law of German immigrant and philologist Dr Wilhelm Bleek. The name of Lucy Lloyd also appeared in the dedication of the *Miscast* book edited by Skotnes. From their Mowbray home, Lloyd and Bleek recorded thousands of pages of /Xam San folklore and learnt the San language from members of an extended family of /Xam San that had served a sentence at the Breakwater prison in Cape Town for stock theft (see J. Deacon 1996). Living with these /Xam San in their Mowbray home from the 1870s, Lloyd and Bleek developed complex and intimate relationships. Skotnes sought to redeem and rehabilitate the tenacious and dedicated ethnographer who worked ceaselessly under the shadow of the illustrious philologist Bleek. Skotnes' project of engendering memory and reclaiming Lloyd as a humane and sensitive ethnographer of KhoiSan culture and history was criticized by some KhoiSan activists as an improper appropriation.[7] Gauging their responses, it would seem that James E. Young's concluding comment, 'better abused memory than no memory at all', would have little relevance or bearing.[8]

Claims to propriety over KhoiSan bodies and the 'emotional reserves' of the San genocide were made by representatives of a variety of KhoiSan groups including the Griqua, the Brown Movement, and the militant Coloured Nationalist Kleurling Weerstandsbeweging (KWB). The biological essentialism of some of these groups elided the historical fact that many of the people referring to themselves as Brown, Coloured, and Griqua are in fact of slave–European–African–Khoi–San ancestry. However, rather than recognizing this mixed ancestry and cultural hybridity, many KhoiSan activists claimed a 'pure' KhoiSan identity based on notions of biological and cultural continuity. Others did not deny their mixed ancestry but asserted biologically based claims to KhoiSan identity to gain custodianship over the KhoiSan body and collective memory. For example, even though he had been classified white under apartheid, Mansel Upham, the Griqua National Conference's legal representative, insisted upon making public his claims of genealogical links to a founding Khoi ancestor, Krotoä (Eva). The following section discusses the ways in which the naked and clothed 'Bushman' body featured in discourses on KhoiSan identity emanating from debates surrounding 'Miscast'.

A representative of 'the Brown Movement' vehemently attacked the curator for inviting the semi-clad Kagga Kamma 'Bushman' delegation to the public forum at the exhibition opening, and thereby contributing to the objectification of the bodies of 'the Brown people'. For these KhoiSan critics the visual imagery of the 'half-naked clan' from Kagga Kamma resembled a living Bushman museum diorama and conformed to popular representations of 'Bushmen' in film and fiction:

> We are sick and tired of naked Brown people being exposed to the curious glances of rich whites in search of dinner table conversation. Our shocked eyes were greeted by the spectacle of a half-naked clan sitting on the steps of the Gallery... The exhibition [is] yet another attempt to treat Brown people as objects... Where is the Khoisan view... Where are our representations of the people who came here to steal our land, make us slaves and deprive us of our culture and our history? When do we get to mount an exhibition?...

The Brown Movement was also extremely vocal in its criticism of Skotnes' display of resin casts of naked 'Bushman' bodies. These casts were originally made for the South African Museum in the

1920s from live 'Bushmen', purportedly for scientific study and because the 'Bushmen' were deemed to be becoming 'extinct'. By displaying the casts of naked 'Bushman' torsos, Skotnes sought to highlight the dichotomy between what is stored in museums out of public view and what is displayed. KhoiSan representatives, however, were angered by this display of nakedness and claimed custodianship over KhoiSan bodies, including those of Saartje Baartman, a nineteenth-century Khoi woman who was taken from the Cape to Europe where she was publicly displayed as a sexual freak, the 'Hottentot Venus', and where, until recently, her brains and genitals were on display in the Musée de l'Homme in Paris.

While the semi-naked Kagga Kamma Bushmen have become an international tourist attraction, as well as a televisual icon of public imaginings of authentic hunter-gatherers, a public statement from the !Hurikamma Cultural Movement expressed shock and outrage at the presence at the 'Miscast' opening of 'the semi-naked clan' of Kagga Kamma Bushmen. The statement indicted this display of nakedness and the fact that the Kagga Kamma people's livelihood 'depends on acting out the sick dramas played out by archaeologists, anthropologists and art historians'.

Another vociferous objector to this display of nakedness was Mario Mahongo, the spokesperson of the !Xu San of Schmidtsdrift in the Northern Cape. Mahongo, a Dutch Reformed Church minister, officer in the SANDF, and a veteran of the Angolan and Namibian wars, insisted that the Kagga Kamma delegation ought to have dressed in western clothing. Mahongo seemed to desire to cover their bodies, for reasons similar to those of missionaries in Africa who sought to transform the naked heathen body through the civilizing cover of clothing (Comaroff 1993). From this perspective, it seems plausible that Mario Mahongo, the Dutch Reformed Church minister and San leader from Schmidtsdrift, may have been more concerned with Christian signs of clothing and civility than with indigenous cultural injunctions. In other words, these calls to cover the naked bodies of the Kagga Kamma

Bushmen possibly embodied a Christian belief that 'clothedness was next to godliness' (ibid., 3).[9]

The 'Bushman body' became the key site of contestation and commentary on memory and identity at the public forum. The link between the body and the (ethnic) nation was vividly illustrated in the dramatic ways in which the story of Saartje Baartman was recently reinserted into public consciousness, for example, through media coverage of Griqua demands for the French government to return her bodily remains for reburial in South Africa.[10] Mansel Upham, the Griqua legal representative, made the following demands at the 'Miscast' public forum:

> [The Griqua demand] the immediate surrender by the French Government and the return of the remains of the late Miss Saartje Baartman to the Griqua for burial in her native land; the immediate release by the Anatomy Department of the University of Witwatersrand and reburial of the remains of the Griqua chief Cornelis Kok II; and the ending of all dehumanized portrayal of the Khoisan ancestors of the Griqua.

Cape Town historian Yvette Abrahams asserted a 'Brown' identity that gave a personal resonance to her claims on the body of the seventeenth-century Khoi woman Krotoä (Eva). Abrahams claimed that Eva was raped by a Dutch settler, a view that has been challenged by scholars who argue that her marriage to one of Jan van Riebeeck's doctors was of her own volition and who represent her as an ambitious 'career woman' with agency, rather than seeing her as simply a victim (Wells 1997). Carli Coetzee's fascinating account of the complex identity politics and negotiations around Krotoä's body in the new South Africa includes reference to white Afrikaner attempts to claim ancestry from this recently redeemed seventeenth-century woman. The 'Miscast' public forum illustrated how live and deceased KhoiSan bodies were appropriated and recruited to produce such collective memories, ethnic-nationalist identities and ideologies, and essentialist narratives of biological and cultural continuity.

Like Zionist appropriations of Holocaust public memory, Coloured nationalists such as Mervyn Ross of the KWB appropriated the San genocide and suffering to produce narratives of national redemption and destiny. This Coloured nationalist rhetoric stressed the autochthonous status of present-day 'Coloureds' as the direct descendants of the aboriginal KhoiSan in ways not that different to Afrikaner nationalist appropriations of the suffering of Afrikaner women and children in British concentration camps during the South African War of 1899–1902. Given this legacy of the splicing of collective accounts of suffering onto dangerous ethnic nationalisms, how can we remember traumatic events such as the Holocaust, the British concentration camps, and apartheid, and yet resist the totalizing tendencies of nationalist rhetoric?

Black South Africans and Palestinians know at first hand how collective memories of suffering can be deployed to create more suffering for those whom Edward Said refers to as 'the victims of the victims'. This raises important questions as to how future generations of Coloured and black South Africans will make meaning of apartheid without resorting to new ethnic absolutisms. How will the public histories and collective memories of apartheid deal with this past without silencing those deemed not to have the necessary biological, historical, and cultural background to legitimately speak about 'black experience' under apartheid? For example, will new public histories marginalize experiences of Coloureds on the grounds that they did not suffer under apartheid as much as black South Africans?

Miscasts, (mis)appropriations, and the making of national identity

The TRC testimony of the sister of Maki Skosana, a woman brutally 'necklaced' by an angry crowd in the 1980s for allegedly being an informer, reveals how the TRC hearings have complicated the production of seamless heroic resistance narratives.[11] It also shows how personal memory and pain can be reconfigured through multiple mediations. This was graphically demonstrated in an SABC news broadcast of Skosana's sister recounting to the Commission how, after her sister was burnt alive, she went to the mortuary where she saw that her grotesquely mutilated corpse had a broken bottle inserted into the vagina. This gruesome recollection of the horror of Skosana's terrible death was interrupted by the commissioner's call for a minute of silence to salute Maki's heroism and martyrdom. This silencing of the witness sought to transform the woman who had been necklaced as an *impimpi* (informer) into a hero of the struggle, a martyr whose body had been sacrificed in the name of the new nation. Through this reworking and reappropriation of the traumatic memory of the mutilation of Skosana's tortured body, a heroic narrative of the new South African nation was manufactured for consumption by millions of television viewers.

Despite the TRC hearings' role in complicating sanitized heroic resistance narratives, the televised testimony of Maki Skosana's sister illustrates how the TRC and the media are manufacturing a new nationalism from painful personal memories and shattered and mutilated bodies. This seems to be part of a broader process in which the incarcerated bodies of Robben Island political prisoners assumed almost mythical status in a heroic narrative of sacrifice and defiance. This focus on Robben Island could, however, ultimately elide the more banal and mundane everyday aspects of apartheid such as influx control, Group Areas Acts, and the Separate Amenities Acts.[12] Meanwhile, the Skosana hearing suggests that even the dismembered bodies of innocent victims and bystanders are readily appropriated for this collective project of sacrifice and nation building.

Conclusion

Recently, during my visit to the Holocaust Museum in Washington, I was able to find information about the transportation of my family to Auschwitz and Riga. This knowledge is now permanently etched in my memory. Visiting the building in which my father's brother Siegfried Robinski and his wife Edith lived in Berlin's Kreuzberg District, now a Turkish working-class neighbourhood, embodied and materialized my knowledge about my family's terrible fate. Standing in front of the building on a bitterly cold winter night produced a profound materiality to what had once been a vague and repressed knowledge about my family's past. In the past this knowledge had been disembodied, submerged, and repressed – mere history, part of a nationalist narrative about the making of the Israeli nation. Now I have reclaimed a Jewish identity that is tightly enmeshed within the memory of this apocalyptic event, yet outside religious or Zionist appropriations of this past.

Sifting through the fragments and silences of Berlin's sites of Holocaust memory, after more than thirty years of being emotionally distant and dissociated from this apocalyptic event, has rendered the Shoah no longer mere history or nationalist rhetoric. As I reflect upon living with these fragments of memory, my thoughts keep returning to questions as to how the thousands of TRC testimonies are likely to be recollected and represented once the TRC's hearings come to a close. It remains to be seen whether South Africa's contested past will be remembered in a form that does not privilege particular historical experiences, collective memories, and nationalisms, and elide others. It is also unclear whether shattered bodies mutilated by colonialism and apartheid, as well as the gasping and choking voices of TRC witnesses such as Maki Skosana's sister, will be edited and erased in order to serve the needs of totalizing narratives of resistance, heroism, and nationalism. I remain undecided as to whether 'abused memory' is better than no memory at all.

PART III

Museums, memorials, and public memory

10

PATRICIA DAVISON

Museums and the reshaping of memory

> We must reckon with the artifice no
> less than the truth of our heritage.
>
> Lowenthal, *The Past Is a Foreign Country*

IN POPULAR MEMORY the South African Museum (SAM) in Cape
Town, the oldest museum in the subcontinent, is associated with
the natural history of 'Bushman, Whale and Dinosaur'.[1] Since the
early decades of this century a series of plaster casts of the indigenous inhabitants of southern Africa has been a consistent visitor
attraction. Indeed, surveys suggest they are the most memorable
of all the museum's exhibits. Complete in every physical detail
and revealing a mastery of technical skill, these casts are quintes-
sential museum specimens, dehumanized objects of scientific
inquiry, exhibited for the public gaze. If the casts seem at home in
the contrived realism of a diorama, this is not surprising since
both are constructs of museum practice, re-presentations that
mediate the memory of people classified as Bushmen.

Millions of museum visitors have viewed the plaster figures of
thirteen /Xam women and men who were living near Prieska in
1912 when they were cast to preserve an exact physical record of a
'nearly extinguished' race. Although by the time they were cast,
this group of /Xam no longer wore traditional clothing made
from animal skins and had long since been dispossessed of their
hunting grounds, their history of resistance and subordination

was not presented in the museum. Instead they were reduced to physical types and exhibited unclothed, except for small aprons and loin-coverings, as examples of a primitive race. The compellingly lifelike casts gave tangible form to stereotypes of KhoiSan physical difference that had been well established during the preceding century in photographs and drawings. They echoed the public display of living 'Bush people' at the shows of London and Europe in the mid-nineteenth century, and recalled the sensation surrounding the earlier exhibition in London and Paris of Saartje Baartman, the 'Hottentot Venus'. For decades casts of the /Xam and other KhoiSan people were prominently displayed in glass cases inviting contemplation of anatomical features, such as stature, skin colour, and steatopygia. In the 1950s the thirteen /Xam figures were removed from the display that explicitly emphasized physical attributes and repositioned in an idealized diorama, depicting a nineteenth-century hunter-gatherer encampment in the Karoo. Intended to evoke memories of a past way of life, of bush craft and survival skills, the diorama shows the casts, surrounded by artefacts of everyday use, in a carefully constructed 'natural' environment. But, despite their new setting, the figures inevitably retained the connotations of stereotyped otherness that gave rise to their production in the first place (Davison 1993). In 1989 a display was mounted adjacent to the diorama to draw attention to the history of the people who were cast, and the ideas that gave rise to the casting project.

The visual rhetoric of the diorama medium evokes associations with the realm of nature – in other galleries fossils, fish, and birds are found similarly displayed. The inclusion of anthropology, but not cultural history, in a museum devoted mainly to natural history affirms this association. The problem is not that human beings are grouped with natural history but that only ethnographic 'others' are categorized in this way. Such spatially encoded classifications embody theoretical concepts that shape both knowledge and memory. The investigation of classificatory

constructs therefore becomes of critical importance in illuminat-
ing how museums institutionalize certain forms of knowledge,
and perpetuate stereotypes in the name of scientific inquiry.

Pippa Skotnes, artist and curator of the recent exhibition
'Miscast: negotiating KhoiSan history and material culture',[2] set
out to interrogate in visual form the historical relationships that
gave rise to misconceptions surrounding the people that outsiders
had collectively labelled 'Bushmen'. Listening to public responses
to the diorama at the s AM had confirmed her view that the
Bushmen were indeed 'miscast', fixed in a timeless depiction of
an imagined past that occluded the public memory of their
dispossession and decimation. Her project was to illuminate the
power relations of this history through imagery, artefacts, and
ethnographic narrative. The 'Miscast' installation stimulated
unprecedented controversy and will remain a landmark in exhibition practice. Later I return to 'Miscast' and consider the conflicting reactions it evoked, but first I reflect briefly on museums as
places of memory and outline the changing contours of local
museum practice over the last decade.

Museums as mirrors of power

Museums, like memory, mediate the past, present, and future.
But unlike personal memory, which is animated by an individual's
lived experience, museums give material form to authorized
versions of the past, which in time become institutionalized as
public memory. In this way, museums anchor official memory.
Ironically, the process involves both remembering and forgetting,
inclusion and exclusion. In making decisions about collecting
policy, museum curators determine criteria of significance, define
cultural hierarchies, and shape historical consciousness. The institutionalized neglect, until the late 1980s, of African art by national
art galleries in South Africa is a case in point, as are the more

recent moves to redress this exclusion.

Every preserved artefact is a tangible trace, a crystallized memory, of its manufacture and use, but at the same time attests to conceptual and spatial displacements resulting from acts of acquisition, classification, and conservation. Once assembled, collections are complex and revealing artefacts of museum practice, as well as fragments of former social milieux. Objects held by museums constitute a material archive not only of preserved pasts but also the concerns that motivated museum practice over time. These concerns can seldom be separated from relations of power and cultural dominance. Museums have often been described as places of collective memory, but selective memory may be a more accurate description.

Although museum presentations are always subjectively shaped, they are widely associated with authenticity and objectivity. Consequently, museums have become privileged institutions that validate certain forms of cultural expression and affirm particular interpretations of the past. In many countries state-funded national museums have tended to pursue projects that further the national interest, even if this is not openly acknowledged. 'The ordering and reordering of objects and representations in national museums can serve to legitimate or "naturalize" any given configuration of political authority' (Steiner 1995, 4). Museums are thus used by nation states to represent themselves to themselves, as well as to others. But, as Steiner notes, defining 'themselves' and what constitutes national identity is not uncontested or unchanging – the concept of nationhood, like a sense of community, is a construct of the mind, an imagined reality. In practice the situation on the ground is more complex – there are always tensions between differing interest groups, overlapping constituencies, and opposing interpretations of events. For political reasons new versions of the past may become the official version and claim authenticity, but former structures and mechanisms remain unchanged.

In practice, despite changing power relations, collections designated as 'national' are assembled by museums and held in trust
for future generations. The history of these holdings and their use
in exhibitions provide insight into the shaping of national identity
and public memory. Moreqver, internal museum processes also
have specific histories, often taken for granted because they seem
self-evident. The conceptual frameworks that order collections
and underpin exhibitions also mirror dominant forms of knowledge. Change may occur imperceptibly but at certain moments,
as in contemporary South Africa, it becomes programmatic.
Taking its cue from political transformation, the revision of
heritage practices has become overt – the reshaping of public
memory is an explicit project.

'In keeping with the spirit of the new South Africa, the South
African Cultural History Museum at the top of Adderley Street is
rethinking the history of the country it wants to reflect.' This
quotation from a press report (*Weekend Argus*, 6–7 January 1996)
underlines both the expediency of rethinking the past in the
context of a new present, and the selectivity inherent in the
process. The version of the past represented in this museum is
being reworked to accord with an emerging new orthodoxy.
Historical narratives, such as those relating to slavery at the Cape,
that were previously excluded have become politically acceptable,
even marketable as part of heritage tourism. The museum is
housed in a building that, in much altered form, was the slave
lodge of the Dutch East India Company at the Cape from the late
seventeenth to early nineteenth centuries. Despite an ever-present
spatial echo of slavery, this chapter of Cape history was not, until
recently, interpreted at the museum for the visiting public –
selective amnesia prevailed. Within the current political climate,
however, memory has returned and the museum's slave connection is regarded as an important heritage resource and visitor
attraction. A new tourism initiative is seeking to develop a local
slave route that would create awareness of the legacy of slavery in

the Western Cape, and eventually link up with slave routes elsewhere in the world.[3]

This is but one example of a museum responding to South Africa's new national agenda. State-funded museums have been called upon by the Ministry of Arts, Culture, Science and Technology to redress past inequities as part of the national reconstruction and development programme. Funding is a powerful agent of change, and it has been made clear that financial support will be awarded to those heritage projects that contribute to transforming national consciousness. However, this policy of project-based funding has yet to be implemented. The National Heritage Council that will become the statutory body in control of funding is expected to be constituted during 1997. It is anticipated that appointments to the council will be made following a process of public nomination.

A number of recent exhibition projects have been directly concerned with reshaping memory. Among the most remarkable are a series of exhibitions undertaken at the Castle of Good Hope, the oldest surviving colonial building in South Africa. The Castle, resonant with complex histories of colonial power, slavery, and resistance, has become a venue and symbolic space for challenging the ideologies that supported apartheid, and for reclaiming histories that had been marginalized. The history and culture of the Muslim community was celebrated at the Castle in 1994 as part of the Sheikh Yusuf Tricentenary Commemoration. This was followed by a poignant exhibition of official documents and recorded testimony relating to the racial segregation of the city of Cape Town. Freedom to express views within the confines of the Castle that might formerly have been suppressed in that setting gave the exhibition heightened significance. Also operating within an evocative cultural space, the District Six Museum, founded in 1992, reclaims the social histories of people who were forcibly removed from the area under Group Areas legislation – it is also a memory bank of human resilience in the face of adversity.

My focus is on much older institutions that must confront the burden of their own history in shaping a new future. My central concern is with the SAM and other large state-funded museums. In different ways these institutions are all striving to embrace transformation and develop strategies for creating new constituencies.[4] However, the process is complex and uneven – the need for structural change may be accepted in principle but resisted in practice. In considering how museums are responding to political imperatives, I do so as an anthropologist whose personal memories of museum practice go back to the 1970s.

During most of the apartheid years the SAM and many other state-funded museums tended to assert that they occupied a neutral zone where knowledge was generated and communicated to the public. Museums that emphasized their research role were reluctant to recognize the relationship between knowledge, power, and privilege. Predominantly white museum professionals regarded their work as objective and apolitical. The 1975 entry in the international *Directory of Museums* suggested otherwise:

> The museums of South Africa are the museums of white South Africa. The non-white majority is represented, not in the planning and the organization of museums, but in ethnographical collections and exhibits – the European section of the population is, for some reason, not considered suitable material for ethnography ... History is invariably presented from the point of view of the white man.
> (Hudson and Nicholls 1975, 385)

Until the 1980s little criticism of museums emerged from local sources. The Culture and Resistance Symposium held in 1982 in Gaborone, Botswana, although not directly concerned with museums, signalled an increased engagement in cultural practice by the democratic movement. From 1983 when the racially segregated tricameral Parliament divided museums into Own Affairs and General Affairs on the basis of presumed 'group' interests, the argument that museums were neutral became untenable. The South African Cultural History Museum (SACHM) was classified as white Own Affairs, despite having large collections that did not fit into this category,[5] while the SAM and the South African National Gallery (SAMG) became General Affairs museums. Criticism was voiced by the Southern African Museums Association (SAMA) but many of its own members accepted the status quo, and did little to counter the prejudices and misconceptions that many museums perpetuated (Webb 1994).

This complacency was challenged increasingly within the profession.[6] Critical questions were raised regarding whose heritage was preserved in museums and commemorated in monuments, and who had the right to decide what should be preserved. An undeniably eurocentric bias was shown by the fact that less than 1 per cent of about 4 000 declared national monuments in South Africa related to pre-colonial African heritage (Deacon 1993). The development since 1990 of a number of new projects reflects a post-apartheid shift in priorities. Notable among these are the site museum at Tswaing, north of Pretoria, designed as an eco-museum that integrates cultural and natural history and serves 'the total South African society, especially hitherto marginalized communities' (Kusel 1994), the restoration of the stone-walled capital at Thulamela,[7] occupied between about AD 1400 and 1700, and the planning of the Robben Island Museum to commemorate the struggle for human rights in South Africa. Significantly, these projects are striving to set up negotiated decision-making processes that involve local communities in long-term site management. The co-operation between academic archaeologists and Venda chiefs in resolving sensitive issues relating to the excavation and reburial of skeletal remains at Thulamela has been hailed as a model of successful negotiation. Venda people have taken immense pride in the excavations and the restoration project. At the official opening of the site the importance of Thulamela as a place of public memory was stressed – it affirms the complexity of African culture in southern Africa centuries before the arrival of white settlers and reclaims a significant chapter in Venda history. In this context ethnic identity has become a positive community resource.

Ironically, because apartheid policy used ethnicity to classify African people and deny them South African citizenship, the mobilization of ethnic consciousness by Africans themselves was, until recently, compromised. Cultural traits had been used too often to perpetuate racial stereotypes, and ethnicity had been used to justify separate 'homelands' for different 'tribes' or 'nations'. In post-apartheid South Africa this has changed and cultural diversity has been embraced within the symbolic construct of nation building. In practice, however, accommodating ethnic difference without resorting to essentialist notions of race and culture remains a challenge.

From the late 1980s, academics who had previously distanced themselves from museum debates became involved in the politics and poetics of museum practice under the banner of public history.[8] At the same time many museums started rethinking classificatory boundaries within collections and between institutions. In 1990 the formerly separate history and anthropology sections of the SAMA merged to form the humanities group. This symbolic realignment signalled a growing momentum to tell 'hidden histories' that had been suppressed or distorted under apartheid, a new respect for oral histories, and a call to democratize museum practice at all levels. A number of museums targeted new audiences among previously disadvantaged communities and employed black education officers in their outreach programmes. Acquisition policies came under review. Apartheid 'memorabilia', such as 'Whites Only' signs, became sought after by museums. Art galleries were quick to expand their collections to include material of African origin. However, authority to decide what to collect and exhibit did not extend to African people – existing power relations remained unchanged.

New exhibition projects challenged conventional oppositions, such as art/artefact, with varying degrees of success. 'Art and Ambiguity' shown at the Johannesburg Art Gallery in 1991 emphasized the sculptural and aesthetic attributes of works in a collection that could equally well have been presented in ethnographic or historical context. The Brenthurst Collection of Southern African Art proclaimed itself as 'Art' by definition, location, and visual rhetoric. Although the ambiguities of the collection were largely eclipsed by the mode of presentation, the exhibition succeeded in focusing attention on memories waiting to be recovered. The arresting forms of headrests, staffs, snuff-boxes, and domestic objects, simultaneously aesthetic and functional, also embodied non-verbal histories that had yet to be fully explored. Coinciding with the return of many political exiles, the exhibition seemed to celebrate a heritage regained.

While temporary exhibitions adopted new conceptual approaches, these were less easy to implement in large museums with semi-permanent exhibitions that inhibited rapid change. In theory the division between cultural history and ethnography had been dissolved but in practice relatively little changed at the SAM. In 1993, as an interim measure, a series of 'dilemma labels' were installed in the anthropology gallery under the heading 'Out of Touch'. The intention was to highlight problems of interpretation and omission in the ethnographic displays, which had been mounted in the early 1970s. The introduction to 'Out of Touch' read as follows:

> From looking at these exhibits you might think that all black South Africans lived in rural villages, wore traditional dress and used only hand-made utensils. The objects shown in this hall date from the late nineteenth century through to the mid-twentieth century. During this period, African people were profoundly affected by economic changes, following

the discovery of diamonds and gold. Men migrated from rural areas to work in the emerging mining and manufacturing industries. Despite laws preventing black people from living in cities, many settled illegally in areas surrounding major urban centres. This process, however, is not shown in the displays of traditional African life. Instead, African culture is portrayed as trapped in an unchanging past.

A series of contrasting images was superimposed on the existing showcases to create a visual counterpoint to the ahistorical depiction of traditional life. Images of San men in the South African Defence Force were placed over exhibits of hunter-gatherer material culture, the dress of African female executives was contrasted with traditional clothing, western religious ceremonial attire was juxtaposed with the African equivalent. The counter-images deliberately destabilized the narrative of the gallery. Predictably, many visitors found this confusing, while for others it successfully focused attention on critical issues surrounding the interpretation of cultural difference. If public memory is to be more than a dominant mythology, new ways of evoking multiple memories will have to be found.[9] Museums are well placed to take long-term perspectives on complex issues surrounding the shaping of cultural identities. Instead of assuming in advance that identities are fixed, museums can demonstrate how people shape their identities through cultural strategies (Hamilton 1994). Culture is a resource that people draw on in relation to ever-changing circumstances and shifting identities. A single individual may embody a range of identities, communicated in dress, language, or any other form of cultural expression. For example, the public attire of Chief Buthelezi, leader of the Inkatha Freedom Party, reflects a masterly mobilization of cultural symbols – ceremonial Zulu regalia on occasions of tribal significance, European suits for business meetings, and African printed shirts for stressing solidarity with the rest of the continent. By posing questions, such as 'What does it mean

to be Zulu?', museums could explore complex issues. At a macro
level the same could be done in relation to national identities. In
effect national museums need not simply reflect a constructed
national identity but could show the processes involved, and how
national identity shifts over time. A similar approach could be
applied to issues of cultural ownership. Who owns Robben Island?
Although it is state property and has been declared a national
monument, there are competing claims to the heritage of the
island. The dominant claim at present is that of political prisoners
who were gaoled there under apartheid legislation, but the recently revived Robben Island Historical Society voices other claims to
the island's past, as does the Muslim community for whom the
island is a site of pilgrimage. The right to interpret the history of
the island for the visiting public is not uncontested. '*Esiqithini*: The
Robben Island Exhibition', which opened in 1993 at the SAM, set
out to raise discussion about the island's future, informed by a
presentation of its remote and recent past.

Robben Island at the entrance to Table Bay has been described as
the most symbolically charged site in South Africa – historically, a
place of exile for political dissidents, and confinement for lepers
and the insane; from the 1960s to 1991, a high-security prison and
metaphor for the inhumanity of apartheid. Since the release of
Nelson Mandela and other political leaders, the island has become
a symbol of transcendence over oppression, an icon of hope.

   Until 1990, the views of banned ANC leaders were relentlessly
censored from the media. For decades it was illegal to publish or
display photographs of Nelson Mandela in South Africa. The
history of the struggle for human rights was excluded from state-
funded museums. State propaganda and school textbooks
presented distorted versions of South African history, and ignored
the perspectives and interests of the black majority. In museums
African history was usually reduced to static ethnographic
descriptions of timeless traditions.

'*Esiqithini*: The Robben Island Exhibition' arose from an unlikely partnership between a long-established national museum and
the newly established Mayibuye Centre, committed to recovering
the history of the liberation movement. The two institutions had
different perspectives on the past, different skills and resources,
different constituencies, and different missions. The impact of the
exhibition depended in part on these creative tensions. The timing
was significant – in 1992 when the exhibition was initiated the A N C
was not yet in power, and the A N C-aligned Mayibuye Centre saw
itself as engaging critically with the establishment (Odendaal
1994). From the museum's perspective, this was an opportunity to
provide a public forum for debate on the future of Robben Island,
informed by its remote and more recent past. It was also an
opportunity for the museum to attract new audiences, and to
show its willingness to participate actively in an emerging
discourse on museum practice in post-apartheid South Africa.

The exhibition evoked memories of prison life on the island
mainly through the personal possessions of former political prisoners. Objects and documents were used as mnemonic devices,
visual prompts to personal and shared recollection. Former political prisoners were part of the exhibition team, and their memories informed the script and shape of the exhibition. The hardship
of prison life was juxtaposed with the commitment of comrades
to continuing the struggle behind bars. Recollections also evoked
personal memories of wives, mothers, and friends on the outside.
Although female political activists were never imprisoned on
Robben Island, the exhibition also recalled their roles in the liberation struggle. The official perspective of the Department of
Correctional Services was not excluded. In short, no attempt was
made to present a seamless version of the Robben Island story.

Although the post-1960 period was the main focus of the exhibition, an illustrated time-line traced the island's long history
from its geological past to the present. At the time of the exhibition, no decision had been taken on the future of Robben Island

and viewers were invited to comment on the issue. Responses covered many other issues as well. Some viewers felt that the exhibition was overtly political and biased in favour of the ANC; many applauded the opportunity to learn more about Robben Island. Both positive and negative comments underlined the fact that locating 'Esiqithini' in the SAM was a significant affirmation of the importance of Robben Island in the social history of South Africa. It was also a symbolic shift to the mainland – the island was no longer 'a place apart'. Four years later, the island has been declared a national monument and, in due course, it will be proposed as a World Heritage Site.

Since the exhibition at the SAM closed, the Robben Island collection has been publicly displayed at the Mayibuye Centre and at an exhibition centre at the Waterfront. Can the artefacts of prison life retain their poignancy after multiple displacements, or will their capacity to move the viewer diminish? The Robben Island Exhibition, which was situated in a Caltex service station complex, showed many of the same objects and documents that were part of 'Esiqithini' at the SAM but they conveyed different meanings because of the commercial setting. Context is a crucial cue to meaning, and there is no doubt that the validating context of the SAM evoked respect for the objects – the setting and manner of display added value to the material. This was not the case when the collection was exhibited at the Waterfront. Although regarded by the Mayibuye Centre as a temporary measure, a stepping-stone to a purpose-built museum, it represented a commodification of heritage as visitor attraction.

As a site of memory, Robben Island presents a set of problems for those concerned with its development and management. The physical situation of the island and its history are invaluable heritage resources. Since the early 1990s the high-security section of the prison has become a place of homage, visited by dignitaries from all parts of the globe. But how will the island's past be packaged for large-scale tourist consumption without irrevocably changing it? This is the implicit paradox of preservation – in the words of Lowenthal (1985, 410) – ' ... preservation itself reveals that permanence is an illusion. The more we save, the more aware we become that such remains are continually altered and reinterpreted ... What is preserved, like what is remembered, is neither a true or stable likeness of past reality.' In the early 1990s, when journalists were first allowed into the prison, the cells had been given a new coat of cream paint, a practical cover-up prior to press scrutiny; more recently picturesque murals appeared in some places, seeming to parallel a growing nostalgia among prison officials as their stay on the island drew to a close.[10] The eventual departure of warders and their families at the end of 1996 was marked by tearful reminiscences and sadness at leaving their island home. Signs of tourism development to follow were already present in the local shop: Robben Island T-shirts, souvenir teaspoons, and bottles of wine, successfully marketed as Robben Island Red.

In January 1997 Robben Island was designated a museum and regular tours to the island were started by the interim management body responsible for administering the island museum until a formal council had been appointed. The number of tourists wanting to visit the island soon exceeded the official limit of 265 people per day. Inevitably market forces and private-sector interests put pressure on the authorities to allow greater freedom of access to the island. This was strongly resisted by those in charge, underlining the critical issues of control and moral authority in planning the future development of the island. The unauthorized use of the name Robben Island in commercial products has also been strenuously opposed. A private venture to market Robben Island memorabilia under the label 'The Original Robben Island Trading Store' provoked an outcry from former prisoners and those involved in the preservation of the island. The swift moves to close this venture reflected the significance of the island in popular memory as a shrine to the liberation struggle (see *Cape*

Times editorial, 9 June 1997). The salient issue, however, remains one of control.

Recasting memory

If museums are agents of official memory, individuals and groups continually intervene to contest and reshape orthodox views. Indeed, public memory emerges from an intersection of official and vernacular versions of the past (Bodnar 1992). Curatorship, which can be regarded as a process of institutional memory making, is in itself complex and seldom has predictable or stable outcomes. This was demonstrated by reactions to the exhibition 'Miscast: Negotiating Khoisan History and Material Culture' which opened at the SANG in April 1996.

The SANG has energetically embraced the challenges of transformation. At the recent Faultlines Conference the director declared: 'The process of redress started in 1990, and since then, every function of the national art museum has been reassessed and tested against the needs and requirements of a changing South Africa' (Martin 1996). The concept of 'Miscast' was in keeping with the overall mission of the gallery to redress past inequalities. The aim of Skotnes' project was to illuminate the colonial practices that had mediated perceptions of people classified as Bushmen and Hottentots, and cast them as objects of scientific study. Using aesthetic and textual tools the exhibition starkly exposed the unequal relationship between observer and observed. Harrowing images and artefacts of human suffering, humiliation, and objectification formed the visual burden of the installation, while transcribed texts from San oral literature, finely crafted objects, and rock art evoked the sense of a heritage lost. No redemption from shame was offered; no affirmation of survival. On the contrary, one gallery was designed so that viewers could not avoid walking on images of KhoiSan people, signifying inescapable complicity with past oppression. But who was Skotnes implicating? What reactions did she anticipate from people of KhoiSan descent? And what of her own position as curator? If unequal power relationships characterized the colonial past, surely this continued to be so in the present. Far from applauding the exhibition, angry KhoiSan descendants contested the authority of the curator to represent their history, and accused the SANG of perpetuating the colonizing practices of the past. Their reactions were summed up in the comment 'To show these things here is just as bad as the people who did these things long ago. It is continuing the bad thing.' Ironically, this was diametrically opposed to the stated mission of the gallery.[11]

As Paul Lane (1996) has noted, KhoiSan responses to 'Miscast' suggest that the ironic intent behind the use of many images was misunderstood. Severed heads, fragmented body parts, and naked torsos were not read metaphorically but literally as another form of violence. People claiming KhoiSan descent asserted that the exhibition was aimed at white people; they themselves did not need to be reminded of the humiliations suffered in the past. Controversy surrounding 'Miscast' did not, however, extend to the South African Museum diorama. Skotnes' own response to the diorama had originally motivated the 'miscast' concept but her indignation was not shared by KhoiSan viewers. On the contrary, the diorama tended to be favourably regarded (Davison 1991, 187–93). Perhaps a reason for this contradiction lies in the fact that, although problematic in other respects, the diorama does not represent San hunter-gatherers as victims. Klopper (1996) stresses this point in a perceptive assessment of KhoiSan responses to 'Miscast'. She also notes that despite criticism of the installation, the occasion was used strategically by KhoiSan descendants to advance their current claims to land. Survival in the present is the most pressing concern for marginalized people, and it is a remarkable indication of resourcefulness that the exhibition could be used to serve current interests.

A public forum held on the day after the opening, and another before the closing of the exhibition, affirmed that power relations remain at the centre of critical debates on museum practice, but that museums themselves are public spaces that can be used for contesting and negotiating these relations. There is no single authentic voice – exhibitions, like other artefacts, are open to imagination and interpretation. A character from *In the Fog of the Season's End* (1972), by the late African writer Alex La Guma,[12] recalls waiting for a fellow political activist at the South African Museum. In the zoological gallery, he 'had been alone, a stranger in a lost dead world…' but in the anthropology section he had mused: 'These Bushmen had hunted with bows and tiny arrows behind glass; red-yellow dwarfs with peppercorn hair and beady eyes. Beukes had thought sentimentally that they were the first to fight' (cited in Voss 1990, 66).

The tangibility of objects is particularly salient in relation to memory. Museum collections, like monuments and sites, bridge the past and the present and provide cues to recollection. They embody memories of the past and evoke memory in the present. The /Xam casts made in 1912 are material reminders of ideas that were current at the time but, having been exhibited for over eighty years, they have accrued other meanings over time. Similarly, over a far longer period, Robben Island has accumulated many layers of memory. The significance attached to particular events in the past changes in relation to the politics of the present. But there remains a surplus of meaning waiting to be made and remade. Museums hold and shape memories but they cannot contain them.

II

HARRIET DEACON

Remembering tragedy, constructing modernity: Robben Island as a national monument

Introduction

THIS CHAPTER EXPLORES the role of Robben Island in the process of reformulating public (indeed, national) memory during a time of social and political transition in the 1990s. Seldom has one small piece of land been so heavily imbued with a symbolism which remains, like understandings of its past and hopes for its future, so deeply contested. It is impossible to embrace the complete range of meanings surrounding the island and its history in one chapter, using a small range of sources. We can nevertheless identify the outlines of a public memory of the island by examining a few eddies of interest and debate in public discourse which have emerged and re-emerged within the vast silent pool of possibilities. These eddies of debate are now part of a broader contest over the structure and meaning of the new South Africa and how to interpret its past. Always in the process of formation, the debates draw their strength from exchanges between various personal and public memories of the island, memories which are often unequal in scope and power, expressed in different media and through different channels of authority.[1]

For the last three-and-a-half-centuries Robben Island has been the 'hell-hole' of Table Bay, South Africa's Alcatraz, an impregnable place of banishment for those who have opposed the status quo. During the last few decades, debates about the future of the island, as nature reserve, holiday resort, and museum, have represented competing attempts by various political groupings to reformulate the meaning of the island and its role as a national symbol. The now dominant representation of the island as a place symbolizing triumph over apartheid is linked to a reformulation of national identity based on a particular view of modernity represented by the discourse of 'human rights'. This will be compared to a similar (although ultimately unsuccessful) reformulation of the island's role during the mid-nineteenth century, when the 'humanitarian' reform of the island's mental asylum was linked to claims for modernity made by a new settler government which had just been granted some legislative power by Britain.

Robben Island has been used for many different purposes and held various contrasting meanings for South Africans during the course of its history. During the early years of European sea travel to the East (from 1488) and settlement at the Cape (from 1652), sailors used it as a stopping place, the island's seals and penguins kept the early settlers alive, and Dutch East India Company stock were fattened there. For them, the island was thus associated with safety and security. The indigenous inhabitants of the Cape Peninsula did not try and reach it by sea until they were offered a passage by Europeans in the 1640s and they left the island soon afterwards, when its meagre resources had been exhausted. During the eighteenth century the island became a place of detention for those defined as the worst criminals and most dangerous political opponents of the Dutch East India Company. In the latter half of the nineteenth century it was primarily used as a hospital for the insane, lepers, and the sick poor. The image of the island as a healthy place, suitable for curing the sick and the mad, struggled against the weight of its image as a place to which the incurable and dangerous (both patients and prisoners) could be banished. When the last medical patients were removed in 1931 there was much discussion about the potential recreational uses of the island, but by 1939 it was commandeered (as *SAS Robbeneiland*) to protect the country against foreign invasion during the Second World War. In 1961 it became a maximum-security prison.

Although the island's Alcatraz image became something of an international embarrassment to the National Party government in the 1970s the island prison continued to be touted as a symbol of its authority and strength. For the political prisoners and their families, the island was a place of sorrow, suffering, and, in some cases, also a 'university' for the struggle. The Robben Island prisoners were unusual in that they were able, despite internal differences, to create a subversive culture within the prison, developing a common identity (as Robben Islanders), and pressurizing the prison authorities (by appealing to human rights conventions) to give them greater privileges after about 1976. Some of the Robben Islanders have been important cultural brokers in the process of redefining public images of the island through the publication of prisoner memoirs and interviews in the press.

Throughout South African history Robben Island has thus performed a vital symbolic role. Oliver Tambo commented in 1980: 'The tragedy of Africa, in racial and political terms [has been] concentrated in the southern tip of the continent – in South Africa, Namibia, and, in a special sense, Robben Island'.[2] Yet within the public memory of the new South Africa, it has now also become an important symbol of the triumph of human rights over the horrors of the atavistic system of apartheid, a symbol of national transformation. For many South Africans, Robben Island symbolizes 'the indestructibility of the spirit of resistance against colonialism, injustice and oppression' (Lubbe 1987, 49; see also Jacobs 1992, 74). At the outermost edge of the country and yet so deeply part of its history, the island's position, which formerly made it a perfect place for exiling opponents, now makes it a suitable place to situate a critique of the past within a 'new' country, remade under the 'rainbow' of cultural harmony. Partly because of its long historical association with political imprisonment, although the only prison buildings that now remain are those built after 1960, the island was proclaimed a national monument in January 1996. A project is under way to construct a museum on the island which will symbolize the 'triumph of freedom and human dignity over repression and humiliation' (*Argus*, 7 June 1993). Like the death camps of the Holocaust (Young 1994, 23), the island prison, a site of repression built by its inmates, is to be the first monument to the death of apartheid. Yet it is not constructed primarily as a place to commemorate martyrs, those who sacrificed their life and liberty for the struggle against apartheid; instead it is to be a place to celebrate victory, where South Africans mark the attainment of mass democratic rule and the demise of apartheid. It has become a symbol of the future of the new South Africa rather than its past. South Africans' understanding of the island as symbol is thus of vital importance in mediating an understanding of South Africa's past and hopes for its future. The significance of the island today lies not so much in what actually happened there as in how its history has been interpreted and represented. The island figures in the national memory partly through its more distant past as prison and hospital (specifically for lepers), but largely through its history as a prison for anti-apartheid leaders (especially Nelson Mandela) who have played such an important national role subsequent to their release. There were other prisons housing anti-apartheid activists, some with even harsher regimes than that of Robben Island. Many other activists contin-ued to fight against apartheid within the country and in exile. But the Robben Island prison and its inmates stood out as particularly significant. The National Party government chose Robben Island for a prison precisely because of its historical use as a place of banishment – it was the most horrific site imaginable. Only those anti-apartheid activists who were considered the most threatening and dispensable (thus, no women and no white prisoners) were sent there. Although the Robben Island prisoners were, by some accounts, treated better than some other political prisoners during the apartheid era, their imprisonment has come to represent the crimes of apartheid, their release the victory over apartheid. Their personal experiences of imprisonment on the island have helped to reconstruct its political significance. In giving meaning to their imprisonment through autobiography some political prisoners have intertwined historical and personal memories, and explicitly identified themselves with black leaders from the Eastern Cape who were imprisoned there in the nineteenth century. These accounts, supplemented by a rash of histories of the island, have been particularly significant in reconstructing public memory because most South Africans have never been able to visit the island, and many have no knowledge of its broader past.

Contesting the future of the island

During the 1970s, as political tension rose surrounding the use of the island as a prison for anti-apartheid activists, a public debate about an alternative role for it was generated. There was a political contest between broadly right-wing proposals to make Robben Island into a leisure resort or nature reserve and broadly anti-apartheid suggestions to build an educative museum or a peace centre there within an ecologically and historically sensitive development. This debate was part of a contest over the public memory of the island which because of its symbolic importance had important consequences for national identity. For the resort planners, seeking to deflect criticism of the National Party government, publicly remembering the island's 'natural' environment allowed a public forgetting of its political role. For the museum planners, seeking a site on which to concentrate criticism of apartheid, publicly remembering the horrors of the prison was part of a project of reconstruction and celebration more than a simple commemoration of heroic activists.

During the 1970s and 1980s plans to turn the island into a holiday resort and nature reserve were invoked to naturalize (and neutralize) the violence of its history and, by extension, the violence of apartheid. By this time tourism had become an important source of income for South Africa, which was struggling with a poor international image. Robben Island, where most of the anti-apartheid leaders were incarcerated, represented the harshness of apartheid rule; scandals about the treatment of prisoners there sparked debate in Parliament about its closure. The conversion of Robben Island into a resort would scupper its image as 'apartheid's Alcatraz' and allow it to signify the 'true' side of the country: 'braaivleis [barbecue], rugby, sunny skies, and Chevrolet' as an advertisement of the time put it. The *Argus* (10 April 1975) explained that Robben Island would be 'far pleasanter to point out to guests of the Cape' if it were a nature reserve or holiday resort rather than a prison. In 1981 it reiterated (21 August):

> If (or when) all this [i.e. the resort plan] comes about, Robben Island would be free at last of the stigma that has hung over it for hundreds of years – that of a penal settlement, leper colony and outpost for the insane.

Where once it had been the antithesis of what was socially acceptable, the island was now represented as 'a God-given opportunity to create something special right in the maw of Table Bay' (*Argus*, 12 May 1973), an 'integral part of the Cape' (*Argus*, 18 July 1985). It had become a potential symbol of the 'natural' Africa – without any pesky 'natives' – embodying the 'silence and the smell of unspoilt land' (*Cape Times* , 6 June 1985).

Proposals to make the island 'a great place to escape to'

(*Weekend Argus*, 10 November 1990) for leisure and pleasure have a long history: the island was associated with health even before the establishment of a hospital there in 1846. As early as 1820 Thomas Suter, a cabinet maker from Pepper Street in Cape Town, asked to stay with Mr Murray on Robben Island for his health and a change of air after a long illness (Memorials, CO 3918, 6 May 1820). The fresh sea breezes and the open atmosphere on the island were considered very healthy at a time when miasma theories of disease saw foul air as a major causal factor. Climate was so important in medical considerations that records of rainfall, wind, and temperature were religiously kept on the island between 1888 and 1891 (Superintendent's diary, Robben Island 1888, RI 139). In 1886, the *Robben Island Times*, a news-sheet for staff at the island hospitals, noted 'what a splendid health resort could be made on the Island if an Hotel were allowed to be started at Murray's Bay' (*Robben Island Times*, 1886, 4). But besides unofficial hunting trips to the island (for rabbit and quail) little was made of its leisure potential until the closure of the lunatic asylum in 1921 and the leper hospital in 1931.

The Cape Geographical Society suggested in 1934 that a health resort, with hotel, golf course, and tennis courts, and possibly also a sanatorium, could be built on the island (*Cape Times*, 7 November 1934). The resort idea was floated again in 1945 (*Argus*, 29 November) and in 1959 (23 May), when the *Cape Times* noted with regret that the island's 'tragic history' would reach full circle with the establishment of a maximum-security prison, again missing the opportunity to turn it into a holiday resort, nature reserve, or tourist attraction. But as in all the proposals before the 1970s, official control and the isolation or stigma of the island deterred investors from making any serious offers to exploit its leisure potential. On the cessation of war, a newspaper reporter commented (*Argus*, 6 September 1945):

> Once again Robben Island has become a problem. A fine
> settlement has been built but who would wish to live there?
> ... I should like to think of Robben Island as a treasure island
> but really it seems to have no value at all between the wars.

Proposals to put a fishmeal factory there and to maintain the
rights of fishermen and yachtsmen to land on the island seem to
have had more commercial viability than tourism in the late 1950s
(*Argus*, 23 June 1959, 27 July 1960). On the eve of the island being
turned into a maximum-security prison the mayor of Cape Town
commented: 'I do not think Cape Town cares very much about
Robben Island. After all, it was a leper colony for nearly a hundred
years until 1931. Since then very few people have visited the island'
(*Argus*, 23 May 1959).

Proposals were put before Parliament in 1973 with the support
of several MPs including Piet 'Weskus' Marais, who had an
anthropology degree from the University of Stellenbosch and a
yen to make the west coast into a tourist haven. The prison buildings would serve as unusual accommodation for tourists enjoying
the 'beautiful nature reserve', casino, five-star hotel, airport, and
yachting marina on the island (*Argus*, 12 May 1973). Influential
commercial interests backed the resort proposals while others,
such as the minister of prisons, suggested withdrawing it from the
public eye completely by turning it into a wildlife sanctuary (*Cape
Times* 25 April 1975; *Argus*, 14 February 1976). Debate intensified in
1978 when it was announced that the prison would be closed in
five years' time (*Cape Times*, 14 March 1978). Financial considerations supposedly caused a delay in the transfer of prisoners to
mainland prisons, but to reduce the political value of the island to
the anti-apartheid movement many of the anti-apartheid leaders
were relocated in 1982 (*Cape Times*, 23 June). The public debate
about the future of the island resumed three years later with the
appointment of a government committee on the subject and the
resumption of commercial offers to turn it into a tourist resort. A

decision was made to retain the island as a prison, but to defuse any political capital being made out of this the Prisons Service declared its intention to permit more public visits (*Cape Times*, 6 July 1986). Although the remaining political prisoners were removed in 1991 it was another two years before the government finally announced its intention to close the prison in 1996 (*Weekend Argus*, 6–7 March 1993).

As part of its plan to change the image of Robben Island the Prisons Department had already begun in the early 1980s to stock the island (rather inappropriately) with eland, ostriches, and springbok, and to re-establish the penguin colony there. A coastal reserve was established, although the prison staff still enjoyed the fish and crayfish from it (*Argus*, 7 June 1993). The nature reserve idea meant that although the island was dry and largely devoid of its original plant and animal life (*Die Burger*, 8 June 1985) it could now be hailed as a 'forgotten paradise of teeming bird and marine life' (*Weekend Argus*, 14 May 1983), its ecological importance used as a barrier by the department against any unwelcome development plans. When the department opened the island up to visitors in 1986 the focus was not to be the prison, which was still operative, but the nineteenth-century buildings, the Second World War installations and the natural environment (*Cape Times*, 6 July 1986). Private entrepreneurs were poised to take over once the prison was closed: then the prison history could add gothic appeal, like the leper graveyard, rather than making a political point. The island's real historical asset was its quaint Victorian village (or what remained of it after the Prisons Department 'renovations'). As Nick Malherbe of the Future of Robben Island Committee put it, Robben Island would become 'a tasteful tourist destination in tune with the Victoria and Alfred dock development' (*Argus*, 27 October 1990): a 'larger Matjiesfontein [a small Victorian-style tourist resort in the Cape]' (*Weekend Argus*, 11 May 1991).

There was some opposition both to the initial hotel resort proposals and to later plans for a Victorian-style holiday spot. The commercial resort proposals – particularly the hotel and casino plans, first floated in the 1970s and backed by Sol Kerzner in 1985 (*Cape Times*, 8 June 1985) – were rapidly scaled down to a 'low key recreational facility for all' during the 1980s (*Cape Times*, 29 June 1985). By 1991 a survey in the *Argus* newspaper (which has a largely white and Coloured middle-class readership) demonstrated more support (65 per cent) for the 'nature reserve and restored Victorian resort' than for a casino (25 per cent) – about a third approved of turning the prison into a hotel. Most respondents decried any developments that would create a 'rich man's paradise' (*Weekend Argus*, 18 May 1991).[3] The National Monuments Council and the Cape Town city council and tourist board also supported the more low-key proposals. If the island was to be a leisure venue for the 'man in the street', however, there was still great unease, particularly in ANC circles, about the way in which the recent history of the island was being downplayed. It was soon apparent that the island was too politically sensitive a site for an easy and wholesale reconstruction of its symbolism in the public memory, an erasure of its past.

The contest over the island's future thus became a contest about what elements of its past were important and how they should be commemorated. Fuelling the debate was the issue of who had the political power and the moral right to determine what happened to the island. The reassurance from Nick Malherbe that Mandela's cell would be retained as a museum within the Victorian resort drew a furious response from the ANC (*Cape Times*, 17 November 1990). Nelson Mandela protested that the island would be turned into a 'circus' (*Cape Times*, 2 December 1991). Ahmed Kathrada, a former prisoner on the island and now a government minister, later argued against the 'vulgar commercialism' of plans to put casinos and nightclubs on the island and proposals that exploited the popularity of Mandela (*Argus*, 7 June 1993). Dr André Odendaal, in charge of the 'applebox archive' of Robben Islanders' possessions at the University of the Western Cape, said: 'It is not for white businesspeople or the Minister of Justice of the regime responsible for creating this monstrous prison ... to decide on the future of Robben Island' (*Cape Times*, 16 May 1991).

How, then, was the future of the island – and its meaning as a national symbol – to be decided? Odendaal envisioned a museum like the Holocaust Museum in Israel for the island, teaching visitors about apartheid, as part of a broad educative experience including the ecological and earlier history of the island and South Africa as a whole. In 1993, an exhibition about Robben Island, entitled '*Esiqithini*', emphasized the continuities between the past and the more recent history of the island, and the ways in which imprisoned political leaders were able to transcend their oppression. As the 'green scene' reporter John Yeld said after the exhibition: 'The real environmental significance of the island lies [not in its flora and fauna, but] in its incredibly rich cultural history and in the lessons which this history holds for all South Africans' (*Argus*, 7 June 1993).

Ex-Robben Island prisoners have been crucial players in defining an educative role for the island. It has long been dubbed the 'university of the struggle' because many of the anti-apartheid leaders educated themselves and others in practical politics and academic matters while on the island.[4] The more prominent prisoners have told us what they learned from the island. These lessons are not just their memories, but a model of what South Africa should learn from its past and a sign towards the path to true liberation. Many of them, for example, have stressed the way in which they have put their bitterness at imprisonment aside (*Argus*, 25 July 1994). At the opening of the '*Esiqithini*' exhibition Ahmed Kathrada said the island should 'not ... be a monument to [former prisoners'] ... hardship and suffering [but] ... a monument reflecting the triumph of the human spirit against the forces of evil, a triumph of freedom and human dignity over repression and humiliation' (*Argus*, 7 June 1993).

The idea of Robben Island as a university has spawned many

new proposals among which are a peace centre and a new home for the Centre for Intergroup Studies of the University of Cape Town. These ideas have been taken up by those who wish to see Cape Town 'retain its status as the country's legislative and diplomatic capital' at a time when it is threatened by proposals to move Parliament to Pretoria. Cape Town would supposedly become the 'Geneva of sub-Saharan Africa' (*Argus*, 30 January 1993). A number of non-governmental organizations (including the Centre for Intergroup Studies, Idasa, and church groups) have formed a pressure group called Peace Visions, which wants to establish a training centre for conflict resolution on the island. This seems to be partly inspired by the institution on Goree Island off the coast of Senegal, promoting democracy and understanding in Africa, which the Dakar conference delegates visited in 1987 and which has close ties with Idasa (*Argus*, 14 May 1994).

In January 1996 the island became a national monument and came under the jurisdiction of the Department of Arts, Culture, Science, and Technology. The departure of the prison staff families from the island in 1996 and 1997 was an emotional moment, not just for those who had lived there for so many years or for those destined to take their places, but for the country as a whole. Because of a much slower and less marked change in mainland-based civil service staff over the period of transition, the island changeover was one of the most concrete and public signs of a movement away from the old regime in staffing patterns. The Robben Island Museum, established under the temporary leadership of Professor Odendaal in January 1997, is now a reality, entrusted with the task of presenting both positive and negative memories of the island to a still divided and uncertain South African public which has been part of the creation of those memories and continues to be deeply invested in their representation. One of the challenges facing the museum is to present a positive side of the island's history without effacing its role in the tragedies of South African history and the difficulties facing the country's future.

The island as a symbol of moral maturity

There have only been two major moments in the history of the island in which it has been able to symbolize what is positive rather than negative about South Africa. These moments of redefinition both occurred at a time when a new government sought to emphasize its moral modernity, specifically to an international audience, and to construct a new source of national pride. The first moment was during the mid-nineteenth century when a rising Cape Town middle class wished to earn self-rule from Britain. The second was during the recent transition to democracy. The story of the first reform of the island's image, usually subsumed within the dominant memory of its dark past, can provide an interesting commentary on current attempts at national reconstruction, and a deeper understanding of the ambiguous and recalcitrant nature of public memory.

In the 1850s an emergent white middle class in Cape Town wanted to transform the Robben Island lunatic asylum from a backward-looking place of punishment into a modern curative institution, as a symbol of the humanitarianism, modernity, and maturity of the colony which had earned the responsibility of self-rule from Britain. The attempt to transform the island's image only succeeded briefly – after the granting of responsible government in 1872 and the death of the reformist doctor in charge of the asylum in the same year, the white middle class gradually stopped supporting the institution with paying patients and a good press. Over a century later South Africa has undergone a new political transition to a wider local democracy, again under the critical eye of the western world. In opposition to attempts to naturalize the island's past, a group of ex-Robben Island prisoners have brokered a reinterpretation of the island's meaning, as the university of the struggle and the crucible of change in South Africa. Through the recorded memories of Mandela and others, the prisoners' liberation within the prison and from the island has become a symbol of national liberation, moral modernity, and ethical maturity. This interpretation has also been important in underlining for an international western audience the fitness of the new power brokers – the urban black middle class – to take the reins of the 'rainbow nation' in the context of the failure of other African states to maintain democracy after independence.

The positive reformulation of the island's symbolic meaning in the public memory during the 1990s can be compared with a similar reformulation in the mid-nineteenth century. In 1846 the colonial secretary, John Montagu, had established a general infirmary on Robben Island for lepers, 'lunatics', and the chronically ill. The infirmary was designed as a place where the incurable and offensive among the sick poor could be kept away from society in a cheaper and more centralized institution; it was not envisaged initially as a place of cure. A series of public scandals about the island institution broke in 1852, however, as Montagu's political opponents (members of the commercial middle class in Cape Town) criticized the management of the lunatic asylum in particular and proposed sweeping reforms. The ascendant colonial middle class in Cape Town used the old-fashioned custodial practices of the island asylum as a symbol of the backwardness of the old autocratic order represented by Montagu and his followers. Once the newly constituted colonial parliament sat in 1854, Birtwhistle, the first surgeon-superintendent on the island, was dismissed and a commitment was made to the humanitarian cure of the insane under a new psychological approach called 'moral management'.

The reforms of the island asylum were based on British asylum reforms designed to eliminate punishment-oriented treatment of the insane which had been gaining momentum since the beginning of the century as part of a broader humanitarian movement (see Scull 1993). In Britain these reforms were part of a new attitude towards labour among a new dominant class who attempted to reorganize industrial activity upon a free market in labour power (Russell 1983, 16). The humanitarian asylum is thought to have had a larger political role in disciplining the potentially useful worker and removing the 'useless' worker from the 'free' market in labour, distinguishing the employable from the unemployable. But the conditions surrounding reform were rather different at the Cape: the final emancipation of slave-apprentices in 1838 did not usher in a free labour system as black workers already within the colonial labour system were almost immediately subject to a harsh master-and-servant law. Montagu established the infirmary partly to remove disabled prisoners and patients from gaols which were to be turned into labour pools for public works. He thus made his major distinction between two groups of unfree labourers: the useful convict labourer (who could be used and reformed as a worker) and the incurable already-institutionalized pauper (who should be sent even further away from society – to Robben Island).

In the Cape the demand for asylum reform was less a response to the reorganization of 'industrial activity' (industrialization happened much later) than a symbolic gesture to the outside world, especially Britain, from a 'new class of persons' seeking greater local autonomy within the empire. Greene (1987, 214) has suggested that colonial elites of the nineteenth century found it necessary to employ a 'language of improvement' and an insistence on the standards of the mother country in order to bolster their poor status in the metropole. The Cape, with a lower status than other colonies such as India, was especially vulnerable — the Cape Town middle class in particular would have experienced a heightened insecurity *vis-à-vis* the standards of the metropole and the threat of the urban underclasses with the hope of representative government in the air (Bank 1991, 4–5; McKenzie 1991, 133–4). Reforming the island asylum along humanitarian lines became a demonstration of the colony's modernity and readiness for self-rule. It is not coincidental therefore that the main impetus for reform of the island asylum occurred between the granting to the

Cape of representative government from Britain in 1853 and responsible government in 1872.

The much older image of the island as a place of banishment did not fit well with its new role as a place of humanitarian cure. It was too isolated from society[5] and not sufficiently fertile to provide the leafy country-style atmosphere considered so essential for mental relaxation. After initial plans to remove the asylum failed, considerable resources were spent on changing the physical environment of the institution during the 1860s. Surgeon-superintendent William Edmunds, appointed in 1862, personified the scientific humanitarianism of the new reforms. Edmunds felt that the treatment of lunatics should be everywhere the same, i.e. the same as in Britain. By the early 1870s, when Edmunds died, the asylum had implemented moral management and non-restraint methods common in British asylums. It paid its staff three times the going wage for domestic servants in Cape Town and attracted sufficient applicants to staff the asylum with a ratio of one attendant to twelve patients (in contrast to a ratio of one in twenty-five which had existed in the 1850s). As a measure of his success, the number of middle-class female patients increased substantially.

By the late 1870s however the island's middle-class patients began to favour the new asylum in Grahamstown. More white patients were now considered by doctors to be amenable to psychological treatment and to be more curable (Biccard 1880, 9). Mainland asylums were felt to be more likely to provide the proper conditions for their treatment: green fields and controlled contact with good society. The Robben Island asylum was thought most suitable for the black insane because it provided opportunities for unsupervised freedom without the danger of escape, as the under colonial secretary, Captain Mills, explained (ibid., 3):

> With regard to the Kafir, the closer you can assimilate his condition to that of his normal state the better. I think it

would be a mistake to confine Kafirs to a house and tie them to one spot. For that reason I think the asylum on Robben Island is particularly suited for natives.

The Robben Island asylum was now conceived as part of a system where black and white lunatics required different treatment in separate asylums. The island, most suitable for the supposedly less curable black patients, was once again a place of banishment rather than cure.

Robben Island's tenacious associations with imprisonment and the racial segregation of asylum populations thus scuppered attempts in the mid-nineteenth century to recast it as a symbol of modernity through the reform of the lunatic asylum. The same reversal is unlikely to happen today because its dark history as a prison forms the very basis of its positive symbolic role as 'university' of the struggle, teacher of the past, and moral beacon for the future. This positive reconstruction may encourage some South Africans to feel that the shift from prison to museum on Robben Island cleanses us all of the horrors of apartheid. By making the island prison the focus of our memory of apartheid, we also run the risk, as with all memorials, of ossifying and simplifying the meaning of the past. It is indeed a gateway to the new democratic South Africa which symbolizes the moral strength of the anti-apartheid movement in the face of harsh repression, but it is not only that. A museum of apartheid may allow the erasure of personal memories as it tries to construct a public memory. As the island comes to stand for South Africa's transformation to modernity after apartheid – for its new focus on eco-tourism[6] from the 1970s or its new reputation as a shining example of human rights observance[7] in the 1990s – it should not absolve us of the duty to make this transformation happen.

Conclusion

There has been a fundamental shift in the symbolism of the island over the recent period of transition to democracy. Robben Island is no longer simply a repository of all that was considered negative in society ('communism and terrorism' on one hand or 'apartheid oppression' on the other). It is no longer a place for outcasts but houses what is at the heart of the new South Africa. It has been re-presented as a focus for remembering apartheid and a spearhead for national renewal. Its symbolic meaning has once again made the transition from negative to positive, its symbolic position from outside to inside. This shift, and the physical transition from high-security prison to a public and positive national monument, has only become possible after the release of political prisoners from the island and South Africa's transition to a democratic government. Through the public memories of high-profile island prisoners the history of Robben Island has become a marker of the broader transformation of South Africa as a whole. Like the Robben Islanders, the 'imprisoned society'[8] has been liberated from apartheid. The Robben Island story has thus become an important element in the construction of a new national identity around the observance of 'human rights'.

Although the Robben Island Museum project will clearly play a vital part in the construction of a national identity after apartheid, we should keep in mind, as the museum staff do, that any history or commemoration that it provides will necessarily be selective in its remembering and forgetting – precisely because of the island's vital role in national reconstruction. There is always a danger that the celebration of victory might exclude the individual memories of those who fell by the wayside during the anti-apartheid struggle as well as those who were always on the other side. Concentrating on the national symbolic role of the island may also unwittingly distract us from remembering individual activists, both on and off the island. The employment of ex-prisoners as tour guides around the island may help to ground visitors' experiences on the island in the personal suffering and heroism of individual prisoners.[9] Situated outside the country, in a place untouched by most South Africans until now, the island's story has to be related very concretely to South Africa's history, to ensure that visitors are encouraged to think deeply enough about their own parts in the dissonant symphony of apartheid and their role in the country's future. The island's story should also permit diversity: if it is to be a living monument for the new South Africa its great opportunity lies, as Huyssen (1994, 16) says of the Holocaust monument, in its opening outwards to other accounts of our past and our future. Ultimately, it will form just one (albeit important) part of a wider memorial culture instead of being a single, over-determined reference to one sorrow and one victory.

12

MARTIN HALL

Earth and stone: archaeology as memory

//Kabbo's account of his capture

We (that is, I) and my son, with my daughter's husband, we were three, when we were bound opposite to the wagon, while the wagon stood still. We went away bound to the Magistrate; we went to talk with him; we remained with him. We were in the jail. We put our legs into the stocks ... we came to roll stones at Victoria, while we worked on the road. We lifted stones with our chests; we rolled great stones. We again worked with earth. We carried earth, while the earth was upon the handbarrow. We carried earth; we loaded the wagon with earth; we pushed it. Other people walked along. We were pushing the wagon's wheels; we were pushing; we poured down the earth; we pushed it back. We again had our arms bound to the wagon chain; we walked along, while we were fastened to the wagon chain, as we came to Beaufort, while the sun was hot ... We walked, following the wagon, until we, being bound, came to the Breakwater.[1]

Library, Cape Town
August 23rd 1870

Sir,

The presence of twenty-eight Bushmen at the Breakwater
affords a rare opportunity for obtaining a knowledge of their
language. You are aware, Sir, of the importance of this
subject, totally distinct as the language is from that of any
other nation known in South Africa. Its affinities to other
languages are as yet unknown, but its apparently primitive
character promises to throw great light upon many important questions regarding the origin of development and
speech, that natural classification of languages, and other
points of philology, – to say nothing of the question regarding the origin of these tribes and all other ethnological problems connected with it ... I have every hope of gaining a
thorough insight into the character of the Bushman
language, if I have sufficient access to at least one of them.
This I find, is only practicable when I can keep him at my
own dwelling-place. As I now possess possibilities of keeping
a Bushman under proper surveillance such as I have never
had before...

I have the honour to be,

Sir,

yours faithfully

W. H. I. Bleek[2]

//Kabbo's dream of returning home

I must sit waiting for the Sundays on which I remain here,
on which I continue to teach thee ... I have sat waiting for
the boots, that I must put on to walk in; which are strong for
the road. For, the sun will go along, burning strongly. And
then, the earth becomes hot, while I am still going along

halfway. I must go together with the warm sun, while the ground is hot. For a little road it is not. For it is a great road; it is long. I should reach my place, where the trees are dry. For, I shall walk, letting the flowers become dry while I still follow the path.[3]

How are objects used to create traces through time – giving substance to memory? In Bleek's letter to the governor, despite the rectitude of language, we can sense the excitement of the academic alive with a new research obsession. For him, the recollections of his 'Bushman' subjects will be memory-as-transcript, a text to be looked at from all angles, dissected, analysed, and described in new language. But for //Kabbo, memories are recollections that define his identity as a man of the place where the trees are dry, one who has been brought to the Cape in chains, and who anticipates returning along the long, hot road. //Kabbo's words align objects – stones, wagons and chains, boots, trees, and flowers – to create a mesmerizing effect in language. In this chapter, I explore this relationship between language and objects – the material substance of the world – further. In particular, I want to show that objects have an elusive quality – a polyvalency of meaning which allows them to carry different meanings for different people at the same time. This quality gives objects – whether small things or public monuments – potency in the construction of memory.

//Kabbo, the other convicts at the Breakwater, and the San communities whose ancestors were once the sole inhabitants of the Cape had long been assigned to dusty archives, museum cabinets, and a brief mention in the history syllabus. But recently their histories have been recovered and are gaining an ever-widening and popular currency. In the confusing political swirl of identities in post-apartheid South Africa, new 'imagined communities' are being created, claiming collective memories in the roots of historical communities (Anderson 1991). //Kabbo, Bleek, and other protagonists are evoked in arguments about who has rights over history. These strands have collected around the 1996 exhibition 'Miscast' (itself a set of objects, and to which I will return later in this chapter), have parted again into a number of political movements, and will undoubtedly assemble again around other focal points. Central in these varied discourses is the continuing re-creation of memory and the play between words and the objects that come to signify such different things for different people.

Archaeology – the study of material forms or human expression – is all about memory. Whether, in the tradition of Bleek, the purpose is the construction of a narrative, or whether the enquiry is about the ways in which objects work as culture, archaeologists are trying to understand things in words. Consequently, the encounters between Bleek and //Kabbo, and the texts that resulted from it, have an archetypal quality that repays a closer look.

As a philologist, Wilhelm Bleek had a long-held interest in the 'Bushman' languages of southern Africa. In 1870, he persuaded the Cape government that selected San prisoners being held at Table Bay's Breakwater prison should be allowed to live at his home in the leafy suburb of Mowbray. Bleek believed that the language of the world's most primitive people held the key to the origins of all languages and, in common with other philologists, that language was the key to all human history and society. The tentativeness of Bleek's letter from his desk at Cape Town's library belies a gargantuan project – the search for the very essence of humanity.

Over the following fourteen years there was usually a small group of San living in the Bleek household. Wilhelm Bleek died in 1875 and the work was continued by his sister-in-law, Lucy Lloyd. By the time the last San informant left Mowbray in 1884 there was a stack of more than twelve hundred manuscript pages, often in phonetic script. Although Bleek's grand ambition was never realized – and philology has itself been abandoned as an academic discipline – Bleek and Lloyd's research has proved invaluable to a number of other academic enquiries.

Bleek's initial informants had little choice about their participation in the project. Incarcerated in the Breakwater on charges that were nominally criminal, but which were part of the systematic eradication of the San on the northern frontier, they were chained and put to work on the new harbour – a long finger of broken rock and soil stretching out into Table Bay. Many died. The degradation of those who survived is captured most poignantly in anatomical photographs taken at the time: naked, front and profile against a measuring stick.

Bleek was initially cautious – his new subjects were wild Bushmen, and he had the safety of his wife and children to consider. Accordingly, he retained the services of a pensioned policeman to guard the convicts and had them locked away securely at night. However, as the work progressed a relaxed intimacy grew up between the family and their strange lodgers, and the services of the policeman were discontinued. In some cases, prisoners elected to stay in Mowbray after their prison terms had ended. In other cases, informants left, and then returned to carry on working with Bleek, bringing others with them. //Kabbo, Bleek's most important informant, dictated both the painful memory of his initial incarceration and transportation to the Breakwater and his yearning to return north; to put on his boots and take the hot road to the drylands. Yet he elected to stay in Mowbray many months into his freedom and eventually left intending to return.

We know little of the intentions of //Kabbo, Diä!kwain, /A!kunta, !Kweiten ta //ken, and the other /Xam who spent time in Mowbray; their only traces are their stories recorded by Bleek and Lloyd and a small collection of faded photographs. But we can assume that they were motivated by an urgency as intense as Bleek and Lloyd's. They were all too aware of the life-and-death struggle for survival of communities who had seen their land taken by colonial stock-farmers, their game hunted out by frontiersmen, and their people slaughtered in retribution for retaliation. They knew the violence of colonialism as a personal brutalization. It would seem likely that their motivation for working with Bleek and Lloyd was to explain themselves and their people in the hope of intercession with their oppressors.

Despite the brutalities of these histories, and their particular places in the process of colonial expansion in southern Africa, there is something fascinating in Bleek and //Kabbo's sessions on the veranda of the quiet suburban villa. //Kabbo – ideal indigenous informant – presents complex, metaphoric accounts which are painstakingly recorded by Bleek, avatar of western inquiry. Looking back from a century on, there is also irony. Bleek, ever felicitous to his craft of philology, believes that language is everything, but //Kabbo, faithful to the form of his mythology, mobilizes elements of the everyday world in ways that cannot be reduced to language alone.

Time has shown that the greatest significance of Bleek's 'possibilities of keeping a Bushman under proper surveillance' lay not in the development of comparative grammar – not in the study of language alone – but in the painstaking recording of San mythology, particularly in the work continued by Lucy Lloyd after Bleek's death (Skotnes 1996). These stories, strange and difficult when rendered in English, arrange people, animals, and other elements of the world in complex relationships which express ideas about life, death, human relationships; a cosmology (Lewis-Williams 1981). Read against panels from the many thousands of southern African rock paintings, they show how words and objects, taken together, embed the material in highly complex expressions of meaning. //Kabbo's work in Mowbray demonstrated that, as an epistemology that claimed to be able to illuminate the core of the human experience, Bleek's philology was limited and pretentious.

The complex interplay of objects and words can be introduced through //Kabbo's account of his capture and imprisonment, the mnemonic sequence of the wagon, the stones, and the chain which provides the central coherence of the account. In //Kabbo's stories, the objects seem to stand outside the text, prior to the words, serving to recall them: the wagon and stocks, the huge stones on the road and barrows of earth, the chains, the road, the land itself, the trees and the boots. Together, the words and objects evoke the remembered landscape, sedimented and strati- fied; an archaeology of memory.

Although we appear to know a lot about Bleek, Lloyd, and the /Xam with whom they worked, there are at the same time many mysteries. What was the nature of the day-by-day relationship that grew up between Bleek and men like //Kabbo over the hours that they spent in each other's company? What did the /Xam do when they were not working with their patrons? Did they remain confined in the Mowbray villa, voluntary prisoners after physical constraints had been removed? Or were they tourists, perhaps visiting Cape Town and comparing the city with the arid beauty of the Bitterpits?[4] The contemporary records seem largely silent. Although family correspondence contains a few vignettes, Bleek and Lloyd confined themselves to scholarly discourse. The news- papers of the day – never shy to express an opinion about the savagery of the colony's native population at large – are silent about Mowbray's own San community. Memory-in-writing is selective, in this case serving general prejudice, academic interest, and practical administration, but neglecting the texture of daily urban life.

Such blank pages can be spaces for the imagination – for encounters which could have taken place, and which would show how words and objects create traces in time, and the substance of unequal interactions.

An imagined incident...

//Kabbo and Bleek stand side by side under the broad canopy of a tree in the Dutch East India Company Gardens, perhaps in June 1871. It is raining steadily and small pearls of water slide down the sides of Bleek's top hat to rest on his dark cape. //Kabbo, head-high to Bleek's chest, has his convict-issue greatcoat pulled up above his neck. They have come in from Mowbray by train so that Bleek can show his Bushman the fruits of civilization. The two men are contemplating the statue of Sir George Grey, recently erected, and behind it the portico of the library, Bleek's special responsibility and the repository of the manuscripts and books that are his life. //Kabbo reaches down and picks up a small object from the fresh earth. After a while, he opens his hand to reveal a small bead of ostrich eggshell, washed white by the rain ...

A statue, a colonial building, and a bead; how are they animated by the ligaments of power and language? In the first place, the staging of this imagined scenario is portentous. Sir George Grey, one-time governor of the Cape, was Bleek's patron and alter ego. Similarly fascinated by philology, Grey was egotistical, hungry for power, status, and recognition, and the promoter of grandiose imperial schemes today remembered for their disastrous consequences (Peires 1989). Bleek admired Sir George, unceasingly, from the day he first met him in 1855. Not surprisingly, Grey was anxious to secure a position in history, making sure that his ceremonial performances were captured in art and photography, that his patronage of the library was monumentalized, and that his own image was incorporated into the gardens as a suitable statue. Grey was power monumentalized, and Bleek's career – and his Bushman project – were a consequence of the governor's munificence.

Monuments serve to focus and direct the memory; both Bleek and Grey would have been the first to note that the word is derived from the Latin *monere*, to remind. Photographs, statues, and ceremonial facades achieve this in different, but complementary, ways. The allure of photography, as has often been noted, is its realism. In his considerable trouble in having his ceremonial acts as governor photographed, Grey was capturing the moment 'as it really was' so that it could be duplicated, distributed, albumized, and remembered long after his departure. Statues such as that of Grey erected in the gardens also make use of realism – the carving of a likeness – but also of an abstracted concept. Grey is portrayed in the posture of statesman; he is at once 'himself', but also a figure of grave nobility, the archetypal Englishman on whose capable shoulders civilization rests. Facades such as that of the library abstract the notion of civility still further by means of Palladianism's classic references to a notion of order vested in European high culture.

Together, these public artefacts inscribe an aspect of the colonial presence at the Cape through a manipulation of time. Both photograph and statue seize a moment – the governor at the climax of a ceremonial action or in a specific, statesmanlike posture – and then constantly reproduce it, as if time does not exist. The viewer looks at the same print – the same moment – over and over again, and the statue stands in the gardens for an intended eternity. The Palladian facade claims a different timelessness – an unchanging continuity between Greek culture as the fountainhead of civilization and British aristocracy as the custodian of civility.

Bleek would have celebrated the erection of his patron's statue and the library's grand facade. However, if he did ever stand in the gardens on a rainy day it is more than likely that he would have been thinking about the shelves of leather-bound volumes safe and dry inside, rather that the classical allusions of Palladian architecture.

In one sense, of course, the contents of the library were as monumental as its building, the mass and extent of arranged knowledge claiming an authority of experience and intellect.

Similarly, the written or printed word has a quality out of time, intended to be read and reread with a potential endlessness. When Sir George Grey gave his personal library to the Colony of the Cape of Good Hope, he was monumentalizing both his philological collection and his intellect, and would have delighted in the notion of the studious acolyte moving from the statesmanlike statue, then beneath the portico, to a bound volume lying open and ready for appreciation on a green baize table. But statue and book also have different qualities. Where, in the former, the sculptor has focused creative energy on eternalizing a moment – on holding time still – the narrator has concentrated on the opposite; on capturing a sequence of ideas and events in such a way that reveals the motion of logic or of an unfolding history.

//Kabbo's thoughts are likely to have been different. One of the particular qualities of material culture is polyvalency – its ability to mean different things to different people at the same time. Words, of course, have a similar quality of ambiguity; Sir George Grey's whole approach to administering the Cape colony had been predicated on interpreting and reinterpreting written instructions from London such that their intent was read to his advantage while remaining within the limits of their possible meanings. But, again, this quality of ambiguity depends on temporality. The meanings of words are negotiated as part of a process; their ambiguity lies in the complexity of discourse. Objects – things – are out of time by virtue of their substance, are available for any number of simultaneous discourses. For //Kabbo, then, Grey's statue would have been a different archetype – the oppressor who takes away the land rather than the epitome of civility. Similarly, the monumental facade could signify authority and retribution while the photograph would be a chilling reminder of humiliation – of the degrading anatomical photographs taken in the Breakwater prison.

And the bead? Bleek would have known what it was; ethnography and philology were closely connected. But it is not likely that he would have paid it much attention; what value would a single bead have? We can imagine a far greater significance for //Kabbo – a recollection of his life and family to the north, but also the indication of an earlier presence in colonial Cape Town; the herding communities who had brought their sheep and cattle to the shores of Table Bay for countless generations before their dispossession at the hands of the Dutch East India Company.

But there would have been another difference in the two men's private recollections. Bleek's philology was predicated on the concept of a universal human mind, and his fascination with the 'Bushmen' lay in his assumption that they were the most primitive living examples of humanity, allowing the philologist 'to connect that postlapsarian moment just after language's birth with the present, then to show how the dense web of relationships between language users is a secular reality from which the future will emerge' (Said 1984, 27–9). Subsequent scholarship has abandoned philology's grandiose claims, and today Bleek's epistemology can be seen as one among many epistemologies.

Rather than the talking fossil that Bleek took him for, //Kabbo was a person who organized knowledge differently. This is evident in his recollection of his journey to Cape Town and in his anticipation of his return home. In his memory of his capture and imprisonment, //Kabbo emphasized and re-emphasized the experience of hard labour at Victoria West; rolling and lifting stones; shifting earth. The journey to Victoria West, and from there to the Breakwater in Cape Town, are recounted with disproportionate brevity. In //Kabbo's 'dream' of his return to the north the quality of discontinuity is more pronounced. The anticipated journey comprises three stages: sitting in Mowbray with Bleek, the movement together of the sun, the boots, and the hot road, and the arrival 'where the trees are dry'. This system of temporality structures the mythology collected by Bleek and Lloyd, and seems to have organized aspects of the vast corpus of southern African rock art as well (Solomon 1992).

The imagined contemplation in the winter rain, then, encompasses two mnemonic systems. In the one, we could say that 'time lies in memory'. The sequence of objects – stocks, stones, earth, handbarrow – itself constitutes time. Similarly, in the projected memory of the dream, the sequence of boots, road, sun, and trees constitutes and contains the passage of time that will be spent on the journey. As a result, the distinction between subject and object becomes blurred; legs and stocks, chest and stone, body and wagon. In the other, we could say that 'memory is constituted in time'. Time is measured on a calibrated scale of days, months, and years which serves to locate human actions quite precisely. Monuments claim eternity by seizing moments and holding them still; Sir George Grey, statesman, caught by the sculptor in a statesmanlike gesture. In turn, this claim of timelessness permits the fantasy of eternal repetition, and draws a clear distinction between subject and object; Bleek admiring the memorial to his benefactor, invited by the statue to measure himself against the ideal.

After a while the rain eases and Bleek walks through the gardens with measured paces, //Kabbo following a short distance behind, cold beneath his skin. They pass by the governor's house and into Stalplein and to the door of a two-storeyed house where a brass plate announces 'Wilhelm Hermann. Photographer and Landscape Painter'. They are admitted, and pass through the photographic studio. A collection of prints hangs drying on a line; men – //Kabbo's people – taken naked in profile and front view, holding measuring sticks against their bodies. //Kabbo averts his eyes. They go up the stairs to where the artist is working at his easel. The canvas is of a forest clearing, framed by ancient, gnarled trees, through which flows a rapid stream ...

Bleek and Lloyd worked with more than words. Before the first /Xam convicts were delivered to his Mowbray villa, Bleek commissioned a set of anatomical photographs, following as closely as possible the instructions sent from London by Thomas

Huxley; //Kabbo, photographed naked in front view and profile, was one of his subjects (Godby 1996). Later, //Kabbo's portrait was drawn by Wilhelm Schroeder and a diverse range of studio photographs of the Mowbray Bushmen were taken by a number of professional photographers in Cape Town (Hall 1996). Writing many years later, Bleek's daughter used one of these photographs to help her recall her childhood:

> There stands before me an old photo of a Bushman. It is David, or Daud, as the Dutch called him. He is looking down with a happy smile at his best hat, which he holds gingerly, in order to display a brass ring on one finger. His best tie and suit have come out very well too. He holds his flute in his right hand. (Bleek and Bleek 1909, 40)

Wilhelm Hermann was one of the photographers who worked with Bleek and Lloyd, producing a range of Bushman studio photographs, many of which were sold as *cartes de visite* – fashionable collectibles in the Victorian world. Hermann was an accomplished polymath – probably by necessity, since photography in the 1870s and 1880s was uncertain. He practised at times as an architect – he designed his own studio on Stalplein – and was a formally trained landscape artist, that part of his work reported to be his passion. In its structure, the architecture of his studio seems to have reflected his interests – the portrait studio on the ground floor and the private atelier above, where Hermann could contemplate the mysteries of nature, aided by the rugged fastness of Table Mountain, seen from his window.

Looking through Hermann's surviving paintings, one is struck by the absence of human figures – strange at first, given the artist's downstairs work as a portrait photographer.[5] Some scenes of Cape Town, executed in the tradition of Thomas Bowler, have small human figures in the foreground, but the subject is clearly the city rather than its people. The landscape paintings are devoid of human subjects: forests, rushing streams, gnarled trees, and twisted crags. But, on deeper reflection, photographs and paintings seem more connected, focusing on the primitive subjects of the Bushmen and Africa. Both are icons of timelessness, and emphasize the timeliness of European culture. As monumental subjects, both Bushman and gnarled tree work in the same way as Grey's statue, representing a lack of change that highlights Europe's unfolding, advancing history. Both 'Bushman' and 'Forest' were essential primitives.

Time is ineluctably connected to space; together, time and space constitute landscape. //Kabbo's expression of temporality maps out journeys that connect the Bitterpits, Victoria West, and the Breakwater, and then Mowbray, the road, and the Bitterpits; time is in memory, and also in space. Bleek's contemplation of the timeless qualities claimed by Grey's statue and the library facade is within a system of organizing space that originated with the Renaissance; landscape as a 'way of seeing – in which some Europeans have represented to themselves and to others the world about them and their relationships with it, and through which they have commented on social relations' (Cosgrove 1984, 1).

Recent writing on landscape has stressed its existential qualities – its determination by actions and meanings – rejecting the notion of an empty frame waiting to be filled, an external, pristine 'nature' awaiting human agency (Bender 1993; Cosgrove 1984, 1993; Croll and Parkin 1992; Daniels and Cosgrove 1988; Parker Pearson and Richards 1994; Soja 1989). In this view, material objects can be seen as both within, and defining, time and space, and as playing between past and present, constantly defining and redefining memory. //Kabbo's dream of his return home uses the materiality of the tree as an icon for the qualities of the Bitterpits. Hermann's paintings use the tree in the Germanic tradition of the forest; the 'oak fetish' that characterized the search for an 'essential German character' (Schama 1995). Both //Kabbo's recollection of the thornveld of the northern frontier and Hermann's discovery of a Teutonic quality in Knysna's forests make use of the materiality of trees to evoke memory in, and by means of, landscapes.

Recent theorizing of the landscape has also stressed its contingency. Rather than being the universal, and inevitable, way of seeing, landscapes created by artists such as Hermann – and constructed in the city vistas of towns such as Cape Town – are now understood as specific inventions of the fourteenth and fifteenth centuries, based on mathematical principles and Albertian rules of perspective:

> The palladian landscape succeeds in uniting the two cultural streams out of which Venetian aristocratic ideology constructed its view of human life and landscape: rational humanism and aristocratic, pastoral *poesia*. Perspective and the concepts and techniques associated with it are inherent in the architectonic organization of the villa and the determination of particular angles of vision within and beyond it. The notion of a harmonious, almost mystical, interaction between the refined human soul and a nature drenched in the golden light of celestial love is articulated in the pure shapes of architectural space, in pastoral wall decoration and in the views from windows and loggias of a richly productive but carefully selected agrarian countryside. (Cosgrove 1984, 139–40)

This abandonment of the cultural superiority assumed by men such as Grey and Bleek in turn allows a restoration of /Xam humanity. Rather than being Bleek's fountainhead of primitive language, or a man with the childlike simplicity that comes from being close to nature (the imposed reputation of the 'Bushmen' in Bleek's time, and today: see Gordon 1992), //Kabbo can be seen to have constructed landscape within a different cosmology – a 'non-Albertian' system of time and space that nevertheless evokes memory by assembling objects which have multiplicities of meanings and associations. For Barbara Bender, this is the contrast between 'capitalist' and 'non-capitalist' notions of landscape; between 'landscapes *of* memory' – from which social and cultural relations can be read as 'inscriptions', and landscapes '*as* memory', in which social and cultural processes are made visual as they are enacted (Bender 1993, 11 – original emphasis).

Time and space in a landscape – whatever cosmological principles are employed – can be conceptualized together as 'place'; a concept developed by Henri Lefebvre and applied in a number of landscape studies. Places are the consequences of 'spatial practice' (and, because of the inevitable connection between space and time, of 'temporal practices' as well). They are

> the relationship of local to global; the representation of that relationship; actions and signs; the trivialized spaces of everyday life; and, in opposition to these last, spaces made special by symbolic means as desirable or undesirable, benevolent or malevolent, sanctioned or forbidden to particular groups. (Lefebvre 1991, 288)

For Lefebvre, places are given substance by their material quality, and are where the dialectics of domination and resistance are acted out. He sees objects – whether beads or statues – as the consequences of signifying practices, and therefore of language. But they are also much more – 'texture' rather than 'text'. Objects serve as 'anchors' – 'nexuses' – in spatial (and temporal) networks and, because of this, 'a spatial work ... attains a complexity fundamentally different from the complexity of a text'. Within these networks, 'the actions of social practice are expressible but not explicable through discourse; they are, precisely, acted – and not *read*.' Thus, and building on Lefebvre's analysis, each object – whether a monument or an everyday thing – has 'a *horizon of*

meaning: a specific or indefinite multiplicity of meanings, a shifting hierarchy in which now one, now another meaning comes
momentarily to the fore, by means of – and for the sake of – a
particular action' (ibid., 222 – original emphasis).

The city can be understood as a set of places; as spatial practices 'anchored' by buildings, streets, squares, statues, and other
material things; 'the city as artifact' (Kostof 1991, 9). Cape Town,
as a colonial city, was inevitably monumental, and the intent and
reception of Grey's statue and the library facade were replicated
over and over again from the slopes of Table Mountain to the
muddy beach of the bay. Each such monumentalization sought to
essentialize colonial domination by evoking the endless repetition
of moments or ideas – a continual call on memory. Such claims
for universality and eternity were also denials of the possibility of
other memories; the recollection of an eastern civility prior to
enslavement; of pre-colonial African kingdoms; or of the time
when San hunter-gatherers and Khoikhoi pastoralists camped
beside a sea uncluttered by colonial tunnage; the 'hidden transcripts of resistance' (Scott 1990).

Could the colonial project of 'symbolic domination' succeed?
Recent social and urban histories have stressed the power of resistance – the robust nature of underclass culture and its resilience to
eradication – and have shown how the bourgeoisie often lived
within an envelope of illusion, not seeing the ineffectuality of
civilizing projects. But there is also a structural weakness – a
contradiction that lies at the heart of the constitution of place in
material form. Because of the 'indefinite multiplicity of meanings' in objects – because artefacts can never be completely
reduced by words – the material world can never be completely
contained and controlled within text or discourse. In the course of
the imaginary outing from Mowbray to Cape Town, Bleek could
have attempted to impress //Kabbo – and could have demanded a
verbal indication of awe. But he could never know everything that
the other was thinking, or control the repossession and

reinterpretation of objects into subversive discourses. This particular quality of materiality is well demonstrated in the discourses that have swirled around the recollection of Bleek, //Kabbo, and others in 'Miscast', an exhibition opened in 1996 at the South African National Gallery, facing Cape Town's gardens and close to the place where Grey's statue still stands. 'Miscast' brought together both words and objects around the theme of the San and, particularly, Bleek and Lloyd's Mowbray project. The exhibition included bags, beads, arrows, and other artefacts, photographs – both those taken by Wilhelm Hermann and his contemporaries, and recent work – body casts made for museum collections early in the twentieth century, and extracts from the /Xam testimony recorded by Bleek and Lloyd. At the centre of the exhibition, surrounded by a ring of dismembered body casts, was a stark grey-brick cenotaph and a pyramid of rifles; a suitable monument to men such as George Grey, who advocated the eradication of the memory of other cultures in the name of British civilization.

Although it incorporated words, 'Miscast' was overwhelmingly texture, rather than text; a web of objects that evoked memories of discrimination, brutality, and genocide. With the exception of one small panel, the exhibition eschewed self-conscious explanation of its purpose and, with more than one entry point and no directional signposting, made no attempt to have its visitors 'read' its components in any linear fashion. Overall, then, 'Miscast' was more like a sculpture than a book – a monument within the monumental gallery.

Much has been written around, and about, 'Miscast'. The exhibition was accompanied by the publication of a substantial volume of essays (Skotnes 1996), and attracted fierce controversy, as have exhibitions in many parts of the world which have dealt with subjects such as ethnicity and genocide. This plethora of words – and the inscrutability of the exhibition itself – well demonstrates the life of the material world outside language. The politics of 'Miscast' were quite clear; this was no apology for colonialism, but a stark memory of the ways in which communities such as the /Xam were scattered and crushed by the juggernaut of colonial expansion.

Despite the clarity of its authorial signs – and in common with all material things – 'Miscast' could not contain or direct the verbal reactions to it which constantly spilled over – escaping the lofty ceilings and secure walls of the gallery.[6] At the exhibition's opening, for example, press photographers were diverted when a Bushman group from a nearby tourist resort arrived at the gallery dressed in animal skins, naked to the waist. Consequently, press reports played on the voyeuristic, perpetuating in words one of the themes that the exhibition was seeking to critique in objects. Others, claiming first nation status, demanded that the exhibition be closed because it insulted the memory of San victims, while others again objected to the public display of colonial photographs of naked subjects and museum casts of body parts. These critical voices were balanced by praise for the exhibition, and for the way in which it insisted on remembering those atrocities that were carried out in the name of progress and civilization.

'Miscast' challenged 'the image of the Bushmen as cast out of time, out of politics and out of history' (Skotnes 1996, 17). Its point was to prevent closure on a chapter of history, to contest the way in which the book of memory is closed in the name of forgetting the iniquities of the past. Its success lay in its very controversy – its ability to kindle fierce debates and claims on memory. In turn, this controversial quality lay in the exhibition's monumentality; its resistance to offering textual self-explanation; its insistence on allowing multiple meanings in its objects themselves.

Returning from 'Miscast' to Bleek's veranda a century earlier, the relationship between informant and scholarly scribe seems far from benign: one of the many places where the politics of domination and resistance were acted out. Bleek's listing of words and meanings – his dissection of grammatical structure, the neat pages between secure leather covers – appears as another form of imprisonment, more effective than the attentions of a pensioned policeman. Reduced into the components of language alone, //Kabbo's stories lose the force that they derive from the arrangements of images of objects.

//Kabbo and the other /Xam who came to Mowbray were no passive subjects of the anthropological gaze – not the expressionless respondents implied by the anatomical photographs taken of them. Their stories were performances which gave life to objects in the world, and which were brought to Cape Town as part of a desperate intercession in the politics of genocide. Rendering them in words alone, dismembering them as dictionary entries, stripped them of this power and enclosed /Xam mythologies within the secure boundaries of the book.

Sir George Grey – imperial politician to the tips of his manicured fingers – also knew the limitations of words. A man whose every utterance could be turned over and over to shake out its possible significances, he understood the necessity of marble, stone, and brick in securing a position in the vicissitudes of history, and the ways in which monuments were directed at securing 'profound agreement ... the presence of the city's people and their allegiance to their heroes and gods' (Lefebvre 1991, 222). He may also have known, perhaps in private moments of doubt, that he could never completely secure his version of history in material expression; that there was always the possibility of making his silent statue a player in a different script.

Memory may reside in the mind as the sum of recollections of the past, but recollection depends critically on the material world – on the elusive qualities of objects outside language – and on the place of words and objects in the politics of power. Objects and texts have a complex relationship: Grey's self-aggrandizement, //Kabbo's recollection of the northern frontier, and the colonial city within the global project of empire; modern assemblages of the artefacts of past genocide and the politics of the present. To adapt Edward Soja's comment on the materiality of space, this play between mind and object, between the transcripts of domination and resistance, results in a 'stressful ambivalence', 'an oxymoronic dance of destructive creativity' that prevents closure (Soja 1989, 158). Word, earth, and stone; an archaeology of memory.

13

KERRY WARD and
NIGEL WORDEN

Commemorating, suppressing, and invoking Cape slavery

IN EARLY 1995, one of us was approached by a travel operator specializing in African-American heritage tours. She wanted to organize a visit to South Africa which would enable her clients to 'discover their roots', and particularly the heritage of slavery so central to African-American identity. The tour never happened. This was only in part because slavery at the Cape bears no relation to the history of the trans-Atlantic African diaspora – Cape slaves were imported to Africa from the rest of the Indian Ocean. Once advised of this, the tourists were equally interested in visiting the slave sites of the region, meeting slave descendants, and hearing their memories and observing the practices and images of a slave past different from their own. The problem was that there was nobody in Cape Town who knew where to take them or to whom they could talk. For in striking contrast to the United States, images and representations of slavery had been firmly submerged in the Cape.

In part this was the result of the suppression of the history of South Africa's marginalized and working-class people which pervaded the public history of the apartheid era. Although there had been a thriving academic literature on the two hundred years of Cape slavery, none of it had penetrated into school curricula or public museums.[1] The curriculum in the apartheid era played down the significance of slavery in its desire to present a favourable view of white Cape colonists as brave pioneers and

bringers of civilization, rather than exploiters of slave labour.
When slavery was mentioned, the emphasis was on how well they
were treated, 'a good deal better, in fact, than was the case in
many other parts of the world at that time' (Lambrechts 1976,
103). Thus even slavery was used to present South African
colonists in a favourable light in comparison to those of other
parts of the world. A sub-text here was the oft-repeated statement
of apartheid apologists that racial discrimination and genocide
had been considerably worse in countries then critical of South
Africa, such as the United States.

Apartheid museums had nothing to say about slavery. The
South African Cultural History Museum (SACHM), a national
state-funded institution in Cape Town, represented a narrowly
white history which completely ignored the contribution of other
South Africans. This was particularly ironic since it is housed in
the building constructed by the Dutch East India Company in the
seventeenth century to accommodate its slaves. Not a single
mention was made of its original inhabitants. Up the road and
under the auspices of the SACHM is the Bo-Kaap Museum,
devoted to the 'history of the Malays', but here too slavery was
absent and the static displays of 'a typical Cape Malay house'
emphasized the dress, furniture, and cuisine of a wealthy Muslim
elite that had little to say about slave ancestry. The grand gabled
Cape Dutch mansions that grace wine estates of the south-
western Cape where the majority of the slaves once worked were
equally silent about the slave workers who had planted and
tended their vineyards for almost two hundred years. Of course
apartheid-era school history and museum representations were
firmly rejected by the majority of South Africans. But in the alternative popular histories and memories evoked in resistance to
apartheid, Cape slavery also played little part. For the descendants
of slaves at the Cape who were categorized as 'Coloured' and
'Malay' under apartheid legislation had repressed the history of
slavery as part of their perception of their heritage. This stood in

stark contrast to the African-American tourists for whom a slave past has been one of the main themes of identity politics and popular memory.

Constructing amnesia

It had not always been so. The Act ending slavery (but indenturing slaves for a further four years) was implemented on 1 December 1834. For several generations afterwards, the memory of slavery was maintained and its removal commemorated. A Swedish visitor in Cape Town on 1 December 1856 described how the day was marked 'by the former slaves and their descendants as a public holiday. It is celebrated with lively parties that often last an entire week.' Early in the morning he observed the local washerwomen, now wearing 'silk dresses with white waists and sleeves and ... shining silver arrows in their dark hair' being collected by a large wagon 'braided with leaves and ribbons. In the back flew a large red standard ... The entire coloured population of the Cape appeared to stream to the country ... only the white population appeared indifferent engaging in their daily pursuits and cares of acquisition as usual.'[2] A midnight march through the Camps Bay kloof and a midday family picnic with 'music, dancing, frolics and feasting' was reported on 1 December 1862, with countryside excursions now made by railway rather than wagon.[3] Street parades and picnic parties were still regular 1 December events in the 1880s, when *ghoemaliedjes* ('drum songs') satirizing the old masters may well have been sung by those who had been born slaves.[4] There were also more gendered commemorations. While male dock workers drank at the Queen's Hotel in 1886, because 'we were keeping up the first of December', women gathered at Platteklip Gorge, the site on the slopes of Table Mountain where slave washerwomen had worked, and 'made merry with song and dances under the trees'. Not all commemorations were so public.

Lydia, an ex-slave who lived in District Six, held an annual prayer meeting at her 'cottage' on 1 December at which she recounted the stories of her sufferings as a slave to her friends and neighbours (Bickford-Smith 1994, 303–5). But by the early twentieth century these popular celebrations of the ending of slavery were disappearing. In part they were giving way to other festivities, notably New Year, as those born in slavery died out and the immediacy of the slave past faded. In contrast to the United States and the Caribbean, there were no written slave testimonies by ex-slaves at the Cape. Such narratives were usually encouraged by missionaries and abolitionists; neither paid attention to Cape slaves. A belated recognition of the passing of the memories of this generation was made when in 1910 the newspaper of the African People's Organization (despite its name, a political organization representing Coloured interests) published an interview with Katie Jacobs, a 96-year-old inhabitant of District Six who was one of the last surviving ex-slaves. Despite recalling the pain of being separated from first her mother and then her husband, her interview is suffused with a nostalgia that reflects the passing years since emancipation: 'There was more love in the old slave days ... it was more peaceful. Now the electric trams pass my door from early morning till late at night, and the whole day long people shout at each other.'[5]

But there were other reasons why the descendants of the first generation of slaves neglected, or suppressed, their past in the early twentieth century. This was the era of segregation, when African Capetonians were being forcibly removed from the centre of the city, and Coloured inhabitants were struggling to identify themselves with the privileged whites rather than the black South Africans who at the time of union were being increasingly discriminated against and excluded from political and social position.[6] The suppression of a distinctive slave past for political and economic advantage was caustically noted by 'Uithaalder', the pseudonym of the author of the colloquial 'Straatpraatjes' column of the APO newspaper on 4 December 1909:

> Dit speit mij dat ons s'mense so min dink van die eerste
> December. Op die dag soes alga weet het die slave vrij
> gekom. Hoe kom kan ons nie die dag op hou nie, net soes
> Koning's verjaarsdag en Boxing day... Da was e tijd waner die
> Kaaps' bruine mense die dag op gehou het. Ma nou hou te
> veel van hulle vir hulle wit. Hulle 'play white' so lang as
> hulle geld het...
>
> [trans: I regret that our people think so little of 1
> December. On that day, as everyone knows, the slaves were
> freed. Why is it that we don't commemorate that day, like
> the king's birthday or Boxing Day... There was a time when
> the Cape brown people did remember it. But now too many
> of them want to be white. They 'play white' when they have
> money...]

The elite among Coloured Capetonians were thus distancing
themselves from their slave past in order to claim a more privileged position in the colony than indigenous Africans who were
being increasingly marginalized. Although the APO organized
political meetings on 1 December at 'The Stone' meeting ground
above District Six, public celebration of emancipation was fading.

The centenary of emancipation on 1 December 1934 was
marked not by trips to the countryside, but by a number of
midnight church services. At one, held at the Bethel African
Methodist Episcopal Church in Hanover Street, Jacoba Titus, aged
80 and the daughter of a Mozambican slave, told the congregation
how 'her father had been sold by auction on the seashore where
Adderley Street now ends'. At midnight the chanting congregation
processed through the streets of District Six: 'as they walked, the
Signal Hill gun boomed out ... nothing could have been more
impressive than their deep sincerity and obvious devotion' ('Slaves'
Descendants Give Thanks', *Cape Times*, 1 December 1934).

The Bethel church procession was led by its minister, Dr Francis Gow, a leading member of the APO (he became its president in 1940) as well as a renowned musician. It was Gow who organized a 'grand floodlit pageant' at the Green Point track the following January to celebrate slave emancipation. This 'greatest performance in non-European history',[7] consisting of a series of tableaux, songs, and dancing by over five hundred 'coloured folk from all parts of the Cape',[8] sought, in Gow's words, 'less to show individual historical happenings than to show what these happenings mean to the spirit of the non-European and what they mean today in his awakening consciousness of nationhood'.[9] But the nationhood of Gow's pageant was one that bore little relation to the earlier spontaneous popular celebrations of 1 December. Supported by the white political elite (the souvenir programme contained messages from the lord mayor of Cape Town, Countess Labia, and Jan Smuts), it was a paean of praise to the achievements of the British empire and the saving grace of Christianity. The '2,000 Europeans' who 'watched attentively' saw a slave on the auction block, but little was said about his own experiences of enslavement in Cape colonial society. Emphasis lay rather on the 'great humanitarians who stung the conscience of the world' and in particular 'the gentle Wilberforce who, with Pitt behind him, raised his voice for so long and with such eloquent appeal in the British Parliament that £20,000,000 was voted for the emancipation of the slaves'. As the figure of a 'sick Wilberforce seeing the triumph of his campaign' appeared on stage, the assembled choir sang 'Let my people go' while the pageant orchestra played a new composition entitled 'Malay Quarter'. The pageant ended with a (Coloured) Queen Victoria presenting a Bible to King Khama in reply to his question 'On what does the might of the British Empire rest?'[10]

The pageant's representation of slavery thus reflected the politics of the APO in the mid-1930s. This organizaton desperately wished to identify itself with the imperial mission, and was concerned not to alienate the white rulers of South Africa, seeking only an equal place with them in the face of exclusion under Hertzog's 'civilized labour policy'. But it was also a time of division within Coloured politics as more radical voices rejected the moderation and collaboration of the APO with an increasingly segregationalist state (Lewis 1987, chap. 7). At the gates of the Green Point track, in the words of the *Cape Argus*, 'Communists distributed leaflets to performers and audience alike as they streamed from the pageant illustrating the loyalty of the coloured people a century after freedom. The pamphlets, issued by the "Lenin Club" cried "A hundred years of liberty!" The very words are a mockery ... Today you are wage-slaves, the slaves of capitalism.'[11]

This association of slavery with capitalist (and racial) oppression in general was also apparent in the launching in Cape Town on the following 1 December of the National Liberation League, a militant organization which used as its emblem 'a black slave with severed chains, holding aloft a flaming torch, with the slogan, "For Equality, Land and Freedom"' (Van Heyningen 1977). Its successor, the Non-European Unity Movement, followed the example. In reaction against the 1952 Van Riebeeck Festival, a number of Unity Movement publications reminded people of the links between slavery and oppression under apartheid (for instance Jaffe 1952, chaps. 6, 9, and 10) and at public rallies on the Parade Ground in 1952 Unity Movement leaders used 'slave' as an appellation for all acts of colonial conquest and dispossession, such as the 1910 Act of Union (Witz 1997, 230). At the same time, the exclusion of Cape slave emancipation from the 1952 pageant was condemned by the Communist Party Cape Town councillor Sam Khan, as well as by some of the students at the University of Cape Town (ibid., 170, 217).

But the suppression of slavery was not only the action of the new apartheid state. It was also 'forgotten' by many of the slave descendants themselves. In the course of the 1940s and 1950s, the

distancing of the urban Coloured elite from popular commemorations of a slave past was furthered by the construction of a
'Malay' identity. 'Malayism' gave an identity for Cape Town's
Muslims with Islamic and South-East Asian origins but neglected
the slave roots of such a culture. It was given a particular boost in
the 1940s and 1950s when I. D. du Plessis, Afrikaner academic and
poet who later became director of the Coloured Affairs
Department, promoted the notion of a specific 'Malay culture'
marked by choirs, cuisine, and a distinctive residential quarter in
the 'Bo-Kaap' district of Cape Town. This found a remarkable
degree of acceptance, not least for the distance it imposed
between a 'respectable Malay' heritage and the bastardized
culture of the 'Cape Coloureds' who were rapidly being excluded
from political and social status in the apartheid state (Jeppie 1986).
During the apartheid years it found many supporters among
those resident in the Bo-Kaap district which was saved from
destruction under the Group Areas Act by being declared a Malay
Group Area. In the process it played down the commonalities of a
slave past in place of an emphasis on the origins of Cape Muslims
as political exiles from Dutch Batavia, or as specialist artisan slaves
who had little in common with non-Muslim field-worker slaves.[12]
During the 'struggle years' which began with the Soweto school
revolt of 1976 and continued with the campaigns of the United
Democratic Front and the Mass Democratic Movement in the
1980s, slavery was also absent. There were good political reasons
for this. Chattel slavery had been confined to one region of the
country, the Western Cape. The Cape-based Unity Movement
images of the 1950s were giving way to other resistance histories.
Cape slavery had little to offer South Africans elsewhere in the
country who were seeking to recapture a past that white rule had
denied them. And in the Western Cape itself, slavery was now also
seen as divisive; a history that separated 'Coloured' South
Africans from their brothers and sisters in the struggle who were
descended from indigenous inhabitants of the land. At a time

when Africanist political rhetoric identified the enemy as the 'settlers', epitomized in the Pan Africanist Congress' slogan of 'One settler, one bullet', to claim descent from slaves who were also 'settlers' from outside gave no solidarity in the struggle against apartheid. One of us participated in a heated debate at a trade union workshop in Cape Town in 1989 when some shop stewards argued that the historical experience of slavery explained the passivity of Western Cape farm workers while others pointed out the divisiveness of recalling a history in which descendants of indigenous African workers had no part.[13] In place of a slave ancestry, a popular claim in the 1980s was descent from the indigenous Khoikhoi and San pastoralists and hunter-gatherers, who had been driven out of their herding and hunting lands by white settlers and whose experience of serfdom and genocide gave a greater identity with the indigenous population of the rest of the country. Benny Alexander, leading politician in the Pan Africanist Congress, changed his name in 1989 to '!Khoisan X' to show, like Malcolm X, that the name of his ancestors had been stolen from him by the experience of colonialism. But, unlike Malcolm X, it was not slavery that he associated himself with, but the indigenous 'KhoiSan'. And in the 1990s as land claims on the basis of original ownership became a possibility, to claim descent from original inhabitants rather than imported slaves was a distinct advantage.[14]

Forgetting slavery in Mamre

This identification with Khoi rather than slave ancestors was also apparent in an extended oral history project which one of us participated in at Mamre (Ward 1992). Mamre was a Moravian mission station founded about fifty kilometres from Cape Town in 1808. Its specific purpose was to provide homes for the families of free 'Hottentot' (KhoiSan) soldiers who were part of the Cape

Corps under the newly established British government at the Cape (Krüger 1966). Mamre grew slowly with the incorporation and conversion of a neighbouring Khoi community who were still largely independent from the local colonists, unlike most indigenous KhoiSan people who were virtually indistinguishable from slaves on white farms throughout the Cape. But it was during the decade following the emancipation of slaves in 1834 that Mamre's population expanded most rapidly. The influx of several hundred ex-slaves from around the neighbouring district was prompted largely by their desire to reconstitute their kinship networks as resident family groups under the protection of the mission station (Ludlow 1992). But by the end of the nineteenth century distinctions between those who were of slave origin and those who were part of the original families had largely disappeared (Ward 1994). One of the core myths of Mamre's history revealed in the life stories told by its residents in the early 1990s involved the fusion of a written history of the origins of the village with residents' own perceptions of their family origins. One of the first novels published in Afrikaans was *Benigna van Groenekloof of Mamre*, written by the Moravian missionary W. F. Bechler and published in 1873. It outlines the conversion story of Benigna, a Khoi woman who had lived with a neighbouring white farmer until his marriage to a white woman, upon which he sent Benigna and their children to live in Mamre. There is a tension between the received written version of Mamre's history, symbolized by *Benigna*, and Mamre's oral history. Isabel Hofmeyr (1991, 633–53) suggests that 'for some people writing has an authority that relieves them from the necessity of remembering'. Mamriers had a perception of their history which gave greater value to the history contained in the written word than to reminiscing about their own lives. Yet nobody interviewed in 1990 had read *Benigna*; they recited it as a story told to them about the meaning of belonging to the Mamre community. But part of the Mamre family history was suppressed in this process, that is the community's links with slavery. When asked about their family history and the origins of Mamre, people often referred to *Benigna* as the best source of knowledge. They had either forgotten or didn't know that their grandparents or great-grandparents had been slaves. As Amalia Collins said in response to questions about what her parents told her about themselves and about Mamre's history: 'Mmmm-mm... you know [laughs], the parents of the olden times, they didn't tell us nothing... they didn't speak with us. Our parents didn't tell us things.'[15]

One of the oldest members of Mamre, Adam Pick, who had a reputation of being someone who knows about Mamre's history, related the story he tells to young Mamriers:

> There was a hotnot, a Hottentot er captain. He used to stay at Louwskloof ... a kraal was there ... And when Mamre started, the missionary started here in Mamre, a lot of people stays in Louwskloof ... And so those days, then you've got the Hottentots, and then, the Boesmans. Die Strandlopers was hier. In the Western Province, they were here when, when ... this whites came here ... So my people, my, our Hottentot people, they were here. They're from South Africa. And we are intermarriage ... my father's mother, she was from St Helena. And my oupa was a hotnot ... In those days, there was a mix children ... There was a whole intermarriage business. That's why we're Coloured today! Ja, my oupa told me. The hotnots, that was the history. They stayed all over, and then when Mamre opened, all the people come together here, and they live here ... They wanted the word of God, and to be under that blanket ... The Moravian Church, I can say today, they were the people that teaches the people everything.[16]

Certain issues in the collective memory of Mamre had been forgotten. There was a level of denial among Mamriers that was manifest in people's amnesia about the community's slave origins, although they clearly recognized descent from indigenous KhoiSan. An acknowledgement of Mamriers' heritage of slavery was not part of the popular memory of Mamre. The transformation of the written text of *Benigna* into a story of the origins of Mamre had rendered silent people's own family histories of slavery. While slavery had not become part of Mamre's usable past, the moral and religious lessons contained in the story of Benigna, that of conversion and belonging to the community were core concepts of being a Mamrier. Slavery played no part in such an identity; it was an experience shaken off, denied.

Recovering memory of a slave past

But in the past few years, the slave heritage of the Western Cape is beginning to be recovered in ways that reflect the new realities of the post-apartheid era. At one level this is apparent in the use of the recent work of slave historians and archaeologists in school curricula and in the beginnings of a reorientation of museum displays to incorporate the slave past.[17] But it is also apparent in a new public awareness of a slave heritage, harnessed to current needs and concerns.

Most striking has been the reorientation of a Muslim identity in Cape Town. From an elite movement in the Bo-Kaap quarter of town, Islam has become a rallying point of identification for a much broader sector of the city's population. This was apparent on the eve of the April 1994 election which coincided with the organization of the 'Sheikh Yusuf Tricentenary Commemoration'. A co-ordinating committee with representatives from a number of different Muslim organizations was set up specifically for the purpose of co-ordinating the celebrations. Sheikh Yusuf was a religious leader in the independent polity of Banten, Java, in the 1690s who was exiled to the Cape as a political prisoner by the

Dutch East India Company and accompanied by his family, slaves, and followers, constituting an entourage of 49. But Sheikh Yusuf is not remembered in Cape Town as a slave owner: quite the opposite. He is hailed as a spiritual liberator of slaves through the propagation of Islam. He is honoured as a Muslim saint and acknowledged as one of the main founders of Islam at the Cape; his tomb just outside Cape Town is a local pilgrimage site (Da Costa and Davids 1994). The timing of the tricentenary celebration was fortuitous but not entirely coincidental. It was planned to culminate just weeks before the election. One of the main events of the tricentenary was the organization of a 'Muslim arts and crafts' exhibition at the Castle of Good Hope in the centre of Cape Town. The Castle itself is a powerful symbol of white rule in South Africa and has been a military headquarters since its inception. It also houses one of the main museum collections in South Africa devoted to artefacts depicting European civilization at the tip of Africa. This exhibition challenged the use of space at the Castle and reclaimed the Castle itself for Cape Muslim history specifically within a slave heritage (Ward 1995, 96–131). One of the tricentenary organizers commented on the way that Muslim people visiting the exhibition were using the Castle space for their own recreation by saying: 'I said to Lalou [Meltzer – chief curator of the William Fehr Collection] one day when people were running around the Castle grounds and up on the ramparts: "The slaves have taken over!"'[18]

Approximately 15 000 people attended the exhibition, the majority being local Muslims. Although it was only one of the tricentenary events, it was the most sustained event of the celebrations. The organizers had presented the tricentenary as '300 years of Islam in South Africa' but it quickly became a local Cape Town affair. Even within Cape Town, the tricentenary highlighted the re-emergence of a 'Malay' identity which was presented as part of a 'Malay diaspora' that had taken place with the forced migration of 'Malay' exiles and slaves during the Dutch East India

Company rule of the Cape from 1652 to the 1795. This notion of a 'Malay diaspora' was enthusiastically embraced both by the tricentenary organizers and by the Malaysian government sponsors of the tricentenary. At the opening ceremony, visiting Malaysian dignitaries embraced their long-lost brothers at the Cape. More to the point, the Malaysian government had sponsored the tricentenary for half a million rand, while the Indonesian delegation were much more circumspect in their support. Geo-political rivalry in South-East Asia between Malaysia and Indonesia played itself out within the dynamics of the tricentenary. Prominent Cape Town Muslims who were members of the tricentenary co-ordinating committee appeared on stage dressed in distinctively Malaysian-style outfits imitating those worn by the Malaysian delegation.

The irony of this situation is that, historically, only a tiny fraction of slaves and exiles to the Cape came from what is now Malaysia; the majority of people sent to the Cape from the Indies came from the Indonesian archipelago. Slaves from the Indies were themselves a minority; India and Madagascar were the main sources of supply for Cape slaves yet this heritage, little suited to the politics of Islam in the 1990s, has been forgotten by Muslim Capetonians (Worden 1996b). In its place is the allure of links to the emerging 'tiger economies' of South-East Asia. The tricentenary was soon followed by a Malaysian business delegation which proclaimed that 'the people of Malay descent in Cape Town are of some interest to us – it is good to re-establish the links broken many years ago'.[19]

The increasing awareness of Muslim links with a slave past was also marked by cultural activities. A new musical, *Rosa*, performed to packed audiences at one of Cape Town's main theatres in April–May 1996. *Rosa* presented as Malaysian the 'traditional dance, songs, stories and an entire culture of celebration [that] goes back to the slave days and [which] has been manipulated and ultimately lost'.[20] And in late 1996 protests against the development of a new housing estate on the Atlantic seaboard slopes of Table Mountain at Oudekraal mobilized Muslim objections to the desecration of grave sites, many of which belonged to Muslim slaves who had escaped and lived on the mountain.[21] For the first time a slave heritage was being mobilized to address land issues.

The recognition of a 'Malay' slave past was given particular impetus by Deputy President Thabo Mbeki's address to the nation at the adoption of a new constitution in September 1996. In his powerful rhetorical plea for unity, he included among those past South Africans to whom he 'owed my soul':

> In my veins courses the blood of the Malay slaves who came from the East. Their proud dignity informs my bearing, their culture a part of my essence. The stripes they bore on their bodies from the lash of the slave master are a reminder embossed on my consciousness of what should not be done.[22]

Such an identity ignores the past of the large number of slaves who were not 'Malay', and stresses the Muslim identification with a slave past that is overwhelmingly urban and has recently been channelled into cultural, political, and economic strategies. But his words have also been invoked by a new grouping which began to take shape in late 1996 and which attempts to broaden its appeal to all Coloureds. Throughout 1995 and 1996 there had been calls for a new political organization to represent Coloured interests, arising from the rejection of the ANC that many Coloured voters had shown in both national and municipal elections.[23] The 1 December Movement was founded by a group of middle-class Coloureds (clergy, academics, and politicians) in frustration at the lack of a forum for political and economic issues faced by Coloureds in the Western Cape region.[24] But in attempting to mobilize widespread support, it has overtly evoked the slave past. Stating that the 'coloured community needed a movement which recognised that the particular slave experiences and history of

coloured people had ongoing consequences in the way the
coloured community perceived itself and how it responded to key
moments in its history', it named itself after the day commemorated by freed slaves throughout the nineteenth century but
subsequently forgotten. For 'December 1 … is a remembrance of
the worst that could be done by people to other people, and could
serve to unlock the door of memory and knowledge of who we
[Coloured people] truly are, where we come from and where we
belong'.[25] On 1 December 1996 its launch was accompanied by the
laying of a wreath at the site in central Cape Town where slave
auctions were held and a meeting at the nearby South African
Cultural History Museum, the building where slaves were housed
in the eighteenth century.

The 1 December movement is a manifestation of a growing
sense of a unified Coloured identity which was suppressed both in
the 'going for white' strategies of the early twentieth century and
in the call for unity with the oppressed of South Africa in the liberation struggles of the 1980s. At its launching Trevor Oosterwyk,
member of the steering committee, described it as 'not just
another coloured grouping in search of a homeland. It sought full
participation in the new democracy and had faith in the future of
the country.'[26] But it has attracted criticism for evoking a separatist ethnic identity which divides 'our own blood brothers and
comrades' of the recent past,[27] and its supporters have 'been
labelled reactionaries, racists and gravy-train wannabes'.[28] 'Given
the enforced racial divisions and oppression of apartheid, it would
not be surprising if there is some suspicion of a reinvention of the
December 1 tradition' commented one historian.[29] It remains to
be seen how much support the movement will attract and how
powerfully it can harness a slave heritage to a new politics of
Coloured identity.

Current attempts by a group of local tour operators and
community leaders to construct a Western Cape 'slave route' as
part of the UNESCO-sponsored international 'slave route' project

are consciously trying to promote rural communities in accordance with the government's Reconstruction and Development Programme.[30] Some progress has been made at Elim, a Moravian mission station in the southern Cape, where the prospect of income from tourism is helping to overcome the kind of amnesia about a slave past that was so evident in Mamre. There is also strong political pressure to recover the African slave past of the Cape in order to benefit from the Africanist emphasis of central government tourism and heritage policy, although comments at one 'slave route' workshop from the deputy mayor of Cape Town that this requires awareness of the 'glories of the Ashante kings' are not exactly encouraging to historical accuracy. Such a representation might well appeal to the Afro-American tour operator who approached us in 1995. But the tourists expecting to find a united bond in the evocation of a common slave heritage would be little prepared for the tensions that surround the mobilization of the slave past by the 1 December movement. As yet there has been little support for the 'slave route' from the state and such contestations over the contemporary meaning of a slave past are likely to grow in the near future.

PART IV

Inscribing the past

14

EVE BERTELSEN

Ads and amnesia: black advertising in the new South Africa

'Forgetting' the struggle

AFTER SOME DECADES of promoting a quasi-socialist critique of class society, South Africa's political leadership has, since the elections of 1994, enthusiastically embraced the philosophy of the late capitalist 'free market'. This about-turn has been effected rapidly. Mandela himself announced to international forums that privatization is now the policy of the ANC. We have the daily spectacle of erstwhile communist ministers promoting a macro-economic plan which will ensure a reduction of the budget deficit to the Maastricht target of 3 per cent of GDP, issuing in widespread public spending cuts and inadequate budgets for housing, health, welfare, and education. Work is 'outsourced', workforces 'rationalized', and the authority of the trade unions eroded, while affirmative action policies are used to create and reproduce a new black elite. Even liberal commentators feel obliged to point out that primary accumulation and class formation form the coercive subtext of these moves. While R. W. Johnson (1996, 20–3) asserts that all this 'is economically more conservative than anything the NP was willing to try', and that disparities within the black community are escalating, creating 'an absolute, not a relative increase in inequality', Heribert Adam (1997, B3) offers a challenging overview:

> When former activists turn into instant millionaires, they
> not only *bury their own history* but confirm the triumph of
> non-racial capitalism ... Was the anti-apartheid struggle
> never more than getting a larger slice of the pie? Was it
> merely a materialistic fight against racist exclusion from
> capitalist spoils rather than creating an alternative, more
> humane and equal social order? (my italics)

These are large questions, which cannot be satisfactorily
addressed here. For the purposes of the present discussion, what I
would like to take from these critiques is the key dynamic of a
'forgetting'. Since there appears to be no embarrassment at leadership level about these reversals, no sense of any need to admit
past errors or offer an explanation for this thorough and fundamental shift in thinking, it must be assumed that government
feels it can rely on the fabled persuasive forces of the market itself
to bring constituents into line.

My argument will be that this crucial project of erasure and
forgetting has been enthusiastically taken up by the institutions
and agents of consumer culture who are admirably equipped for
the task, indeed, whose armoury is replete with weapons
designed, honed, and ready for just such a contingency. Current
ads targeted at the new market of black consumers operate in the
classical mode of ideology as outlined by Stuart Hall, namely, to
unsettle (disarticulate) the terms of existing discourses in order to
realign them with new imperatives (Hall 1988, 35–57). Scrutiny of
a recent run of 'black' magazines yields evidence of this strategy.
In both their editorial copy and ads they mobilize the cultural
power of the South African democratic struggle by appropriating
its respected signifiers and rerouting them to a vigorously propagated discourse of consumerism and the 'free market'. The ads, in
particular, erase the logic, context, and history of such terms,
'forgetting' their origin in a critique of class society (its economic,
political, and gender relations), and invite us to embrace them as a

newly assembled currency of commodity signs.

This is not to exaggerate the power of ads. To support such a case one might of course cut into the culture at any point: parliamentary papers, the discourse of education, press, and television, or the 'gravy train' rhetoric of the new elite. Ads are perhaps best seen as a concentrated, readily accessible, and highly influential instance of a general shift. I will try to show how this discursive shift is effected. I will also contend that, as an important part of consumerist discourse more generally, such ads contribute to the construction of new historical subjects.

Consumerism, ads, and subjectivity

While space does not permit a full discussion of current debates around consumerism and its role in the construction of new social identities, a brief reference to some of the proposals being made around the commodity, the subject, and the text will have to serve as frame for this discussion.

Two influential studies of the changing nature of the commodity and socialization are David Harvey's *The Condition of Postmodernity* (1992) and Fredric Jameson's *Postmodernism: Or, the Cultural Logic of Late Capitalism* (1991). Both use the term 'postmodernism' to speak of late 'consumer' capitalism; 'consumption' designates a set of social, cultural, and economic practices, and 'consumerism' its extraordinarily successful ideology, which serves to legitimize the system in the eyes of ordinary people. Jameson, invoking Raymond Williams, identifies a changed 'structure of feeling'. New forms of practice and social and mental habits follow from a profound modification of the political economy, issuing in a more plastic and 'performative' sense of the self. Consumer capitalism creates its 'necessary subjects' by eroding occupation and class as determinants of identity, and ensuring that distinction is increasingly conferred by possessions and appearances. Robert Bocock puts it strongly: 'Consumption [has] become established as the characteristic socio-cultural activity *par excellence* of late twentieth-century post-modern capitalism... Consumption is *a*, or even *the*, major characteristic of postmodernity' (1993, 77). While the world's (or indeed South Africa's) poor and unemployed may not be able to afford to buy, their desire for commodities is just as great, and their 'interpellation' by the discourse of consumerism is no less achieved.

While these arguments persuasively situate advertising discourse in the broad project of late capitalism, 'post-Marxists' Stuart Hall (1988, 35–79) and Chantal Mouffe (1988, 89–101) usefully theorize the subject of this new consumer culture. Offering a lucid revision of categories of the commodity, the subject, and the text, they propose a historical subject, constituted at the intersection of discourses which are available at any historical moment, with 'new historical subjects' produced when new discourses which contradict the old become widely dispersed. This formulation allows us to account for change.

Since the events of 1990, the identity of both white and black South Africans has been radically destabilized. Settled meanings that had informed identities throughout the 1970s and 1980s became again subject to competing ideological forces during the crisis culminating in 1990. At such moments all those taken-for-granted couplings, which through repetition have acquired the authority of habit, are loosened and again rendered open and available for reconstitution.

I will argue that South African ads of the 1980s and 1990s make a significant contribution to the production of new subjects and the development of an organic ideology adequate to late capitalist demands as they raid for their raw materials every major discourse of our contemporary culture (high and popular artistic forms, family values, sexuality, politics, social mobility, racial and gender issues) and align these with 'free market' thinking. Of particular interest here will be the way the terms of a discourse of popular 'struggle' are redeployed, as these texts free signifiers (words and images) from their signified in the political discourse (a shared social good) and attach them to new signifieds (consumer goods and the transformative power of the market). By transforming notions of equity and political choice into the freedom to choose between products, such texts exploit the aspirational power of the political discourse while simultaneously defusing its oppositional potential.

What remains is to scrutinize a sample of current South African ads. In doing so I would hope to support these general claims: I will read them as shifting the co-ordinates of systems of shared and individual meanings, and suggest how they may contribute to the construction of new identities.

Promises, promises

During South Africa's first democratic election of 1994 the two main contenders, the African National Congress (ANC) and National Party (NP), conducted a lively dialogue through their political advertising campaigns. This was a battle of the Titans, with ANC ads planned by the organizers of Bill Clinton's successful 1992 presidential campaign and the NP packaged by Saatchi & Saatchi, the marketers of Margaret Thatcher. 'Change' was the commodity on offer, and their challenge was persuasively to package and market variants of massive social and political change. I have covered these campaigns in some detail elsewhere (Bertelsen 1996, 225–52). Here I will simply identify one major dynamic at work: the parasitic double-take. Ads habitually operate in a mode of combative dialogue which involves compulsive intertextual borrowing as rivals freely 'steal' terms and images and cohesively ally these with their own interests. In this case the ANC were first off the mark, with their slogan which ran as a strapline under all their ads: '*Sekunjalo!*/Now is the time!', glossed as 'A better life for all. Working together for jobs, peace and freedom'. The NP responded with 'Now is the time' and 'Be sure of a better life', its point being that the ANC's promises were hollow; only the NP had the experience and the ability to deliver. These were the promises that addressed the hopes and needs of the electorate and delivered votes, and we will return to them in due course.

The behaviour of commodity advertisers during the election offered an interesting preview of how they would proceed in the years to follow. They entered into the spirit of the occasion by, in their turn, running ads that fed off the political rhetoric of the main contenders, particularly the discourse of the ANC. Volkswagen ('For the people, By the people') lined up its cars in formation to depict the new flag; BP glossed its staple 'We like to keep you moving' by adding 'The future of South Africa is written with one letter: x'; trainer shoes gave us 'When a new nation stands on its feet, HiTec take the step'; hamburger chains offered a 'multi-party party' and 'voters' rolls', and Beacon sweetly punned 'It takes allsorts to make a new South Africa'. An ad for Bonnita milk summed up the commercial mood. An opened milk carton enters the frame from above left, spilling a huge white cross against a black ground. 'Why cry over spilt milk' runs the copy 'when we can build a healthy nation. The past is just that ... past. It's the future that's important'. The frame is made up of repeated red hearts and 'South Africa we love you' slogans. Here four decades of apartheid are written off in a mollifying cliché as an unfortunate mistake which is best forgotten, followed up with the promise that all the spilt milk of our past will be effectively mopped up by market forces.

All of these texts employ the standard (and by now international) strategies of ads as a distinct discourse type. They are parasitic (ads have no unique discourse of their own, they are intensely intertextual and completely dependent on other discourses); opportunistic (ads habitually seize upon whatever powerful idiom

happens to be situationally available to promote their products);
they make intense use of codeplay (metaphors, riddles, puns, and
jokes), and are highly cohesive texts, making dense use of inter-
modal parallelism and repetition. These general features of ads as
discourse have been clearly described by Guy Cook (1992, 214–30),
who also insists that we can only make sense of advertising texts if
we pay equal attention to their formal linguistic properties (their
choice and rhetorical ordering of materials) and the cycle of
communication (in which the materials that make up the text and
their decoding by readers both occur within a specific social and
cultural context). He demonstrates that ads offer a shared vernacular of rituals, aphorisms, and stories, which serve to confirm our
social identity, and stresses advertising's ability constantly to adapt
and even reverse its tactics in response to readers' moods or social
and market pressures. Goldman, a Marxist, further sees ads as
perfectly reproducing the commodity form, as they detach signifiers from their signifieds in prior referent systems and reroute

them to enrich the appeal of consumer items, with serious social and psychological consequences. He shows, for example (1992, 37–60), how recent ads directed at women (as to be seen, for example, in Virginia Slims' famous 'You've come a long way, baby!') 'pun' the victories of a whole generation of feminists into commodity signs through iconic and verbal play.

As my focus here is on current South African advertising targeted at new black consumers, what will particularly interest me is the articulation between these standard ploys of advertising discourse and specifically South African intertexts. My thesis is that current black ads form part of a process at present under way in the many sites of South African culture generally, in which once well-secured discourses are systematically being dismantled, and their terms rearticulated to those of new social and political projects. This takes the form of a double movement. On the one hand progressive forces set about the task of 'undoing' the discourses of the apartheid era and naturalizing in their place ideas of non-racism and equity. But as quickly as this is achieved, we observe a contrary movement, as the vigorously propagated discourses of consumerism and the 'free market' in their turn move in to displace the quasi-socialist (or at least social-democratic) terms of inherited discourses of 'struggle', redefining democracy as individual freedom and, especially, the freedom to consume. On the assumption that ads carefully research and then forcefully represent attitudes and desires, and so dramatize the many conflicting voices of the society in which they occur, my aim will be to discover whether a sample of current South African ads may serve as an index for the discursive contest of post-apartheid South Africa, and to consider some of the implications of this process for the emergence of new South African subjects.

'A better life: ... jobs, peace and freedom'

This study forms part of a larger project which will look at advertising in the South African media generally. Here I concentrate on ads in magazines targeted at the market of black magazine readers. Research by McGrath and Whiteford (1995) shows that the African share of total personal income increased over the period 1970 to 1991 from about 20 per cent to roughly 28 per cent. They qualify this by stressing that almost all of this has flowed into the richest 20 per cent of black households (a tendency which has grown dramatically since 1994). This nonetheless indicates a steady growth in disposable income which has stimulated local markets and increased circulation of 'black' magazines which serve as a prime vehicle for advertising and fostering a desire for consumer goods. My sources are the following magazines (*AMPS* 1995 readership figures in brackets): the women's magazines *Thandi* (130 000) and *True Love* (245 000); the family magazine *Bona* (915 000); *Pace* (405 000) and *Drum* (447 000), which have recently adopted a sensational 'tabloid' style, and the more upmarket *Tribute* (72 000) and *Ebony* (150 000). These are all rival monthlies, with *Bona* taking the largest slice of the market with roughly one-third of total black readership. In terms of race and gender, they are mainly read by Africans (average 97 per cent), but unlike their 'white' counterparts, all are read by both sexes (the largest differential, for *Thandi* and *True Love*, is only 15 per cent). With low cover prices, readership is also remarkably even across income groups (average differential 10 per cent). While some of these magazines publish African-language editions alongside their English issues (*Drum*: Zulu; *Bona*: Zulu, Xhosa, and Sotho), the rest use the medium of English. It might also be noted here that as 'white' magazines at present tend to have a more diversified readership than their 'black' counterparts, many black readers would also read these. My sample here is limited to titles explicitly targeted at a 'black' readership.

While I am not closely concerned with editorial copy here, some brief comments on the general ambience of these publications may help to contextualize their advertising content. The longest established are *Drum* (1951) and *Bona* (1956), published respectively by Nasionale Pers and Republican Press. Trading on their success in the general market, each introduced a 'sister' magazine with Nasionale's *True Love* launched in 1984 and Republican's *Thandi* in 1985. *Pace* (Caxton Publications) entered the market in 1978 as a direct rival to *Drum*. And *Tribute* (Penta, 1985) and *Ebony* (EBCO and Johnson, USA, 1995) are the latest entries, specifically catering to the emerging black middle class. Most offer an eclectic mix of features: current events, political issues and social problems, celebrities, and sport, with the women's imprints emphasizing fashion, home, and child care. A peculiarly South African addition is the direct educational content of all but the 'prestige' magazines, in the shape of literacy and learning features. These are only partially altruistic, since in this instance extending literacy goes hand in hand with moulding the attitudes that will, in time, stimulate demand for just such publications and the norms and commodities they promote. My general comments are confirmed by a study of three complete runs, those of January, July, and December 1996, while my cited examples are drawn from the July 1996 editions.

An overview of advertising copy shows that ads in *Thandi* and *True Love* feature largely 'women's' products: cosmetics, clothing, and a sprinkling of household goods (baby products and food). *Bona* inverts this pattern, carrying general domestic products. *Pace* and *Drum* have an eclectic mix of items aimed at both sexes and a range of income groups. *Tribute* and *Ebony* duplicate the profile of upmarket 'white' journals, featuring ads for fashion, banking, luxury items, and cars not carried at all by the other black magazines. On average half of the advertising texts use black models, and about two-thirds explicitly angle their copy at black readers. While constraints of space and my choice of focus will restrict my present discussion to what might be termed a 'vertical' reading of these texts (that is, I am interested in a strategy that I perceive to be global, cutting across significant class and gender variables clearly evident here), I am aware that this needs to be complemented by 'horizontal' work which will identify important variations as advertisers address class, gender, and other social sub-groups.

One could classify the advertising texts to be discussed here in a number of ways. I have chosen to employ the categories suggested by the ANC's election slogan 'A better life for all. Working together for jobs, peace and freedom', since this formulation succinctly expresses the aspirations of the South African majority at the time of the 1994 elections. My argument is that current ads absorb the tensions of transition in a very suggestive way, speaking to these basic needs while simultaneously operating a sleight of hand, as they set about uncoupling the terms of the political discourse of 'struggle' (especially the 'working together' element, the communal or collaborative dynamic) and recoupling its potent signifiers (of black pride and accomplishment, democratic choice, civil rights, the right to a better life) with the discourse of consumerism (the individual, entrepreneurialism, and the drive to unrestrained acquisition). In the process, the desire for a shared social good is replaced by the desire for consumer goods or commodities.

The headings 'jobs', 'peace', and 'freedom' yield three useful categories for us to address the signification in these ads: occupation, mobility, and status (framed by notions of social success); 'normal' life in the nuclear family, and homes with mod cons and security (framed by an ideology of satisfactory personal relations); and a modified version of 'freedom' (redefined as the freedom to choose between products). In each case I will try to show how advertising discourse effects this transformation as the residual charge of well-secured political idiom is brought under the sign of the market.

Jobs

Set as it was against the constraints and coercions of apartheid, the discourse of the struggle put a very particular gloss on 'jobs'. Political oppression and economic exploitation were conceived as cognate and inseparable obstacles: the goal was a universal franchise (involving participatory democracy) coupled with an equitable distribution of wealth (jobs for all replacing unemployment; unions securing workers' interests, which were conceived of as structurally opposed to those of capital and management). The heroic figures (role models) of the anti-apartheid narrative were accordingly principled political and union leaders who lived frugally and stoically battled for the cause. In the organizing narrative here collaborative endeavour ensures the betterment of the whole community. This discourse serves current advertising as a most fertile intertext, as the real achievements of the struggle are appropriated and transformed.

What one notices immediately on scanning the range of social roles depicted in the ads is the absence of 'ordinary' occupations: workers, factory hands, artisans, street traders, domestics (the staple of black employment) are all absent. (While some beer ads on television use romanticized labourers, these are not run in the magazines.) In their place we have a very skewed picture of the labour market, exclusively represented by glamorous models and executive or entrepreneurial types. (Though a fascinating example of discursive crossover is *Bona*'s cooking special in the July issue, which offers 'Special Winter Recipes from Parliament', in which female M Ps – the deputy speaker, senators, deputy ministers – team up with Rama margarine, Tastic rice, Snowflake flour, and Rainbow chickens to pass on their culinary secrets to the ordinary voter.) Copywriters, of course, will point out that ads are in the 'dreams and aspirations' business, and do not aim for realism, which is absolutely true. Mundane images cannot create excess value for products. So let us leave aside for the moment the extraordinary cast, and look at the construction of those aspirations.

In these ads positive social identity is strictly tied to the acquisition of commodities in the form of credit cards and 'lifestyle' products. Foschini is brazen: 'You've won your freedom. Now use it. Get a Foschini's credit card today'; Edgars' challenge is 'Want it? charge it!', and Totalsports', 'You deserve some credit. Get it'. The banks take up the siren call with (First National) 'Get a life. Get a bank. Get the edge', and (Standard), 'With us you can go so much further'. Opel 'puts you in the fast lane'. Old Mutual insurance asks 'Why let your dreams run on two cylinders?' when with unit trusts you can replace the old banger with a luxury imported model. Power trainers explicitly tie their product to politics with a mock news cutting: 'Evidence of huge growth from reconstruction and development programme. Power. It's not a game any more'. Revlon's black hair products, with crimson banners streaming, offer a 'Special Feeling' that is 'Revolutionary'; and Swankie Look will 'Seize the day!'.

These slogans all serve to anchor visual images of proud, assertive, and beautiful black figures. A run of Caivil haircare ads places its executive women against dramatic backdrops: 'Defy the political wasteland' (the desert); 'A woman for president, why not?' (Mount Rushmore); and 'Daughter of the earth. Mother of the nation' (magnified sunflowers). And role models drawn from the struggle are replaced by their commercial understudies, such as entrepreneurs Dali Tambo and Felicia Mabuza-Suttle. In the Black Like Me (hair relaxer) ad in which they alternate, Dali and Felicia pun on election jargon with 'I've made my choice. Perfect choice. Black like me. Embracing black dignity and beauty. Giving you freedom of choice'. In a similar vein, the magical name of Mandela now, via his daughter, graces a promotions company, and Tambo, via his son, a designer label.

The ad for the newly launched South African edition of *Ebony* might usefully be added to this set. It reads simply:

EBONY
SOUTH AFRICA
BACK BY POPULAR DEMAND

It is run as a double-page spread, using bold lettering in white on a stark black ground, with the first two lines boxed in red. Here codeplay takes the form of a pun, which operates a multiple action: it foregrounds the magazine's title (the colloquial use of 'ebony' as a simile for intense blackness), identifies South Africa itself as 'black' by popular political choice (the election), and plays on *Ebony*'s return ('back' after the American edition was withdrawn some years ago). Then, through the showbiz connotations of the shared phrase 'popular demand', it absorbs all of these connotations back into the brandname. Again, signifiers of democratic choice are cunningly freed from their place in the political discourse and serve to promote a commodity.

While these texts obviously employ the stock-in-trade of advertising tricks, what makes them peculiarly South African is their parasitism upon local and situated agendas and terms of value. Signifiers of choice, freedom, change, and confrontation have an undeniable local charge, and here these are detached from their place in a discourse of collaborative struggle with its critique of unequal economic, political, racial, and gender relations, and rerouted to promote a discourse of individual entrepreneurialism and consumption. This induces a selective amnesia, as readers are required to recognize the aspirational power of this rhetorical set while abandoning its context and history.

Peace

Under this heading we consider the image of 'normal' life as it is constructed in these ads. The image of settled domestic life offered by the discourse of the struggle was inescapably the antithesis of the black apartheid experience. Offensive racial classification, restriction to 'group areas', and the degree of state violence used to enforce these engendered a counter-project which placed high value on mutual support, group identity, and 'solidarity' with the extended community, who could be relied upon to share core principles and goals. The ads see this communal project displaced by the highly individualized 'romance' of atomized loving couples, blushing brides, and the self-contained two-parent, two-child nuclear family. To harp on 'realism' once more, we may note that this model in no way represents the reality of black family life, whose fragmentation manifests the legacy of migrant labour and other depredations of apartheid. While a set of down-to-earth generic ads stand out here in directly addressing basic domestic needs (Telkom for phones; Eskom for electricity; Huletts for sugar; Sasko for flour) let us again allow that ads express not-really-existing conditions but equally 'real' dreams and aspirations, and study their interested construction of gender and personal relations in the home and the family. Here we will focus on representations of women.

Thandi and *True Love* specialize in personal relations. True to the general codes of women's magazines, they first present women as preternaturally slim and glamorous through the models for fashion and beauty products, and then, in the home-care pages, as more substantial nurturers, mothers, and cooks. In their overall format such magazines are organized by a well-established narrative which moves in classic mode from the nubile glamour of the opening pages (the precipitating enigma or danger) through a series of tasks and obstacles (aided by the magic of consumer goods) to its resolution in marriage, mother-hood, and domesticity. In the final sections there is invariably massive promotion of extravagant weddings (Bride of the Month competitions abound), closely followed by babies and baby-care products. This compelling narrative of woman's life with its contradictory constructions of femininity is of course overdeter-mined; it derives from many social sources, and is grist to the global advertising mill.

But again I would like to contextualize advertising strategy in this area as it engages new black South African readers and consumers. While we must take as an axiom that magazines are primarily a vehicle for selling consumer products, my argument concentrates on the cultural implications of this 'selling' moment. Ads sell not only commodities but desires and aspira-tions. They operate ideologically as they persuasively inscribe readers in a limited range of cultural options. The form this strat-egy takes in addressing female readers is stunning in its simplicity, and while it serves as a model for the mode of address adopted by advertising generally, its effect on recently urbanized black women must prove to be fairly dramatic.

Thandi and *True Love* perfectly exemplify the method of women's magazines, whose stock-in-trade is the myth of the 'problem' female body. This is initiated in the editorial copy with features on personal relations: 'The Truth about Sexual Desire: Pepping up a Low Libido'; 'Talking Straight about Mistresses', or 'When You Change and Your Husband Stays the Same', in which the task of sustaining a partnership falls to the woman. These are closely followed up by pieces that establish the female body as a minefield of 'problems': pieces on hair, skin, and weight prob-lems, and combating bodily odours. No surface or orifice escapes attention. This is the initial move, which undermines and subverts the reader's confidence in her own body and her ability to control it. Into this vacuum of confidence is then introduced a captivating array of products, which promise to correct this imbalance: Revlon's 'Revolutionary' hair relaxer and Felicia's Perfect Choice; New Youth vanishing cream or Pond's Lasting Oil Control for oily black skins; Weigh-Less – 'Changing the Shape of the Nation', and then Dior's Dolce Vita, 'the spirit of happiness'.

These products are 'fetishized' in advertising text, that is, made replete with excessive cultural meanings, offering far more than mere physical redress. As Goldman (1992) puts it, they function to alienate from the subject any worth her everyday identity may be assumed to possess, to replace this with the more desirable attitudes, norms, and dispositions supposedly 'possessed' by consumer commodities. Goffman (1979, 1–27) has shown how restricted are the physical and emotional codes of gender representation in ads. For example, while men may adopt active and vertical postures, women are invariably presented off the vertical, in submissive postures of bending and canting, and allowed to express a limited range of emotions, from slightly 'sexy' glances to the 'mollifying' smile. None of the ads in *Thandi* and *True Love* offers an exception to this rule. Through this strategy of subversion and fetishization the female subject is rendered vulnerable and open to inscription by a predefined set of acceptable social norms of womanhood, which find their apotheosis in the many pages on the appropriate conduct of weddings and obligatory Bride of the Month competitions.

The men, alas, must suffer neglect here due to constraints of space. Suffice it to say that whereas women in ads always present themselves as objects of the gaze, the men are invariably depicted acting on the world, for example, in executive or sporting situations, and are always handsome, well groomed, and virile. Natruboost, 'the ultimate stiff drink for men', says it all by asking: 'Do you remember the days when you could hang three wet towels from it!'.

It seems redundant to point out that the model of gender and family relations propagated by these texts directly serves the interests of the market. While terms such as 'freedom', 'pride', and 'empowerment' are widely deployed, these terms are detached from their place in a discourse of mutual support and communal endeavour, and attached to the new consumerist narrative in which isolated individuals must struggle not only against the constraints of 'nature', but also against social and sexual rivals, assisted only as they may be able to purchase transforming commodities.

Freedom

South Africans tend to be rather complacent at present as we bask in the freedom of our new-found liberal democracy. Yet the way market discourse is currently raiding and redefining this 'freedom' must surely compel attention. Mouffe (1988, 102) points out that historically the concept of democracy (political equality) was articulated to liberalism (with its individual freedoms and defence of private property) through concrete struggles. And while the idea of democracy has subsequently been incorporated and disarmed, the notion of equality nevertheless remains potentially subversive. The discourse of the South African democratic struggle saw a radical reassertion of the 'democratic' strand within this coupling, which issued in the bold vision of a non-sexist, non-racist, and egalitarian society. Market forces have been quick to recognize this, and have energetically set about the task of undoing what they see as a threat to 'natural' social stratification and unfettered consumption. Mouffe sees the general tendency of the market as rearticulating liberalism without democracy, or at least working to disarm democracy as a radical and participatory social force.

I asserted earlier that advertising discourse is parasitic, that it voraciously absorbs and incorporates other discourses to realign them with the imperatives of the market. I have tried to identify the 'ideological' moment in which the notion of democratic choice is transmuted into consumer choice and political freedom into the freedom to choose between products. Current South African ads freely employ phrases drawn from political discourse, and copywriters would probably argue that in most cases these are simply used as facile puns or jokes. I have taken a different view, insisting that the charge of such texts is stronger than this. While I am by no means claiming that ads unilaterally reconstruct social subjects, it would seem that, together with other texts generated in opinion-forming sites (I have mentioned Parliament, education, and the media generally), they have an important function in redefining and naturalizing the co-ordinates of popular understanding. Apart from their independent ideological efficacy, they serve as a suggestive index of a broad cultural shift, as consumer capitalism energetically campaigns to produce its 'necessary subjects'.

The importance of this recognition for the production of new historical subjects should be clear enough. The black South African subject of the 1990s bears very little resemblance to the fêted 'revolutionary worker' of the struggle as s/he hurries home fitted out by Sales House, in an entrepreneurial taxi, to watch *The Bold and the Beautiful* on television. To put it baldly, the newly available and energetically distributed discourses of libertarian democracy, upward mobility, and the free market are a volatile mix. And if one takes into account a residue of tribal culture, the new mood of our mass media, and our government's own recent enthralment by free market ideas, black South Africans in particular have much to contend with. Any notion of essential or historically guaranteed orientation (e.g. of class, race, or gender) is thrown into doubt. Nothing can be taken for granted. This new subject is 'contradictorily interpellated' with a vengeance.

In Gramscian terms, the prize in this discursive contest is the naturalization of a new and widely shared South African 'commonsense' (Gramsci 1971, 181–2). The election slogan offered South Africans 'A better life for all. Working together for jobs, peace and freedom'. Whether we will retain those terms that the advertisers set out to erase (for it is precisely the items 'all' and 'together' that render democratic the whole idea of change) is, of course, still moot. But in the meantime, the atomized consumer subject favoured by the market does seem a feeble substitute for that democratic ideal.

15

SINFREE MAKONI

African languages as European scripts: the shaping of communal memory

IN THIS CHAPTER I EXPLORE the impact of the invention and use of standardized African languages on the form and substance of African communal memory. I look at this particularly in the context of the current entrenchment of language rights in South Africa's new constitution, and the kinds of 'past' to which such policy implicitly makes an appeal.

'Invention' is a notion that has won widespread recognition, especially through the work of Terence Ranger (1989), but which is currently under stress. Arguing from a social constructivist perspective, Ranger and others are now adamant that 'invention' does not forcefully enough capture the involvement of Africans in their own history. In spite of this, I want to argue that 'invention' remains a robust concept, foregrounding, as it does, the artificiality of ethnicity, and the assumptions of primordialism upon which it is based. As such, it remains a useful way of discussing some of the vagaries of current South African discourses of multilingualism, the linguistic equivalent of the 'rainbow nation'.

In South Africa, missionaries played an active role in the invention of African languages. They drew the linguistic boundaries, determining what was to be regarded as constituting a specific language. The linguistic processes they set in motion had clear political dimensions and implied particular forms of social relations between Africans and Europeans and among Africans themselves. Isabel Hofmeyr (1993, 48) argues that Africans actively took advantage of the presence of missionaries to articulate their dissatisfaction with existing political systems:

> Both among commoners and within the royal caste itself, then, there existed cause for dissatisfaction against the ruling lineage. The dissatisfaction was expressed by entering into a loose association with missionaries. For commoners, the mission and its schools which used a lot of Sesotho remained a source of attraction.

Hofmeyr does not, in my view, examine adequately what was happening to Africans in the process of entering into an alliance with the missionaries, however. She does not emphasize strongly enough how the discourse missionaries were creating limited what could be said 'about', 'to', and discussed 'with' Africans – the extent to which the construction of African languages was designed not only to restrict the universe of discourse entered into with Africans, but their participation in that discourse as well (Jeater 1994, 2).

The major objective of missionaries was to comprehend African cosmology in their own terms, and only those terms that could facilitate that process were included in the vernacular language. They were passing judgement about the society they were operating in (Cameron 1995, 33–47). Jeater (1994, 4) shows how in translation exercises, Africans who preferred to find alternative sources of cash were regarded as dishonest and lazy because they were not making themselves available for exploitation as colonial labour. The inventions were structured in a way that encouraged Africans to internalize European epistemology about themselves, creating a new view about their current affairs and superimposing new values on their past. The new values distanced the African convert elite from the conceptual worldview of the vernacular population, and by implication distanced Africans from their own past.

The construction of African languages reflected, in many cases, evangelical rivalry more than existing linguistic reality (Harries 1995, 154). For example, the emergence of a single standard for Zulu and Xhosa was prevented by the competing interests of different missionaries (Herbert 1992). The recent distinction between Zulu and siSwati was motivated first and foremost by political considerations reflecting the inadequacy of a linguistic definition of language (Le Page and Tabouret-Keller 1985; Pennycook 1994, 167). This involved splitting African speech forms into separate languages. Previously African speech forms had constituted a continuum 'stretching across Africa from the Atlantic to the Indian ocean' (Le Page and Tabouret-Keller 1982, 161–93). The idea of African languages as constituting an array of separate boxes or, as Fardon and Furniss (1994, 3) call it, 'bound-aries discourse', was based on the belief that different languages constitute mutually exclusive categories.

The discourse of African languages as separate categories, then, had its genesis in concepts in colonial thinking. An ideology of 'linguistic fixity', as Paul Gilroy (1987) has termed it, was useful for social classification. Moreover, literacy and language education are as much tools for social control as means of social emancipation. Current constitutional provisions about language can be seen as a retrospective legitimization of a particular view about the past. Emerging discourses about multilingualism derive their strength and vitality through a deliberate refusal to recollect that in the past multilingualism has always been used to facilitate exploitation of Africans. Memory is as much about what people would like to recall as it is about what they would like to unremember (I prefer the term unremember because it underscores that forgetting is as much an active process as remembering). Discourses about the promotion of African languages are likely to be received with scepticism unless stan-dardized written forms can be recast through a process of an active and egalitarian reinvention.

Current discourses about multilingualism anxious to reverse the inequalities between languages as part of the apartheid legacy do not engage with the differences within each linguistic label operating under the guise of an African language. Proponents of multilingualism thus become ideological captives of the system they are seeking to challenge. Brink, in chapter 2 of this volume, comments that if we are to transcend the legacy of the past, language itself has to be reimagined:

> The past cannot be corrected by bringing to it the procedures and mechanisms and mind-sets that originally produced our very perception of that past. After all, it is not the past as such that has produced the present or poses the conditions for the future... but the way we think about it. Or, even more pertinently, the way in which we deal with it in language.

This is as true in the more metaphorical sense in which Brink uses it as it is in a more literal, linguistic, sense.

All languages are fictions. Pennycook (1994, 28) illustrates the fictionality of English when he says that 'English is fragmented, struggled over, resisted, rejected, diverse, broken, centrifugal and even incommensurable with itself'. If English is a fiction, then African languages are even more highly fictionalized. Xhosa, for example, has many spoken varieties. Speakers of Hlubi and Bhaca from the Eastern Cape may experience problems when writing standard Xhosa, which is closer to a variety spoken by the Ngquka, derived from Rharhade. The situation is not peculiar to Xhosa. There is such great diversity within the box labelled 'Northern Sotho' that no dialect has successfully served as a standard. Non-standardized Zulu differs so much from the standardized version that Zulu students in urban areas feel alienated from the very language that has been attributed to them as their mother tongue.

The labelling process has led to a construction of idealized languages which has begun to create substantial problems for language teaching. Some teachers compare the teaching of standard Zulu to urbanized Zulu speakers with teaching a foreign language (Herbert 1992, 4). In some situations Zulu language teachers find themselves having to resort to the use of Iscamtho (an urban anti-language) to explain aspects of Zulu (Ntshangase 1995, 291). Recently published research suggests that the mixed African pan-ethnic varieties are now being used in the classroom not only as a last resort by teachers; pupils themselves frequently use these varieties as the unmarked norm for interaction within the classroom (Calteaux 1996). If a Zulu teacher has to resort to another language in order to explain aspects of Zulu, it means the students do not have the necessary expertise in the language attributed to them as their 'mother tongue'. Perhaps the three-way distinction that Rampton (1990, 98) proposes between 'affiliation', 'inheritance', and 'expertise' may be significant. The term 'language expertise' refers to the question of how proficient one is in a language; 'language affiliation' refers to the attachment or identification a person feels for a language, whether or not that person nominally belongs to the social group customarily associated with that language; 'language inheritance' refers to the ways in which individuals can be born into a language tradition that is prominent within the family and/or community setting, whether or not they claim expertise in or affiliation to that language. Language teachers need to ask, with reference to each language nominally said to exist in a particular learner's linguistic repertoire, whether the learner's relationship with his or her language is based on expertise, on inheritance, on affiliation, or on a combination of all three.

The triad of concepts Rampton has introduced is of great assistance in explaining the phenomenon Ntshangase describes. The students Ntshangase has in mind may be affiliated to Zulu ethnically, and possibly have inherited some Zulu, but do not have demonstrable expertise in it. Their expertise may lie in another language which because of the constitution's orientation towards language history is not recognized because it has not acquired historical longevity and does not possess the weight of tradition in order to acquire constitutional legitimacy.

> A major problem with the strategy is the artificiality of mother tongue. Young children living in urban townships may find themselves living next door to Nguni speakers, across the road from Sesotho, whilst their parents derive variously from Xhosa or other language groups.
> (Street 1993, 34)

Widespread use of pan-ethnic varieties reflects ways in which individual speakers can construct their own individual pasts. Language may be used to reveal certain identities, and to mask others. For example, the use of Pretoria Sotho by people who have migrated to urban areas enables them to conceal or distance themselves from their rural pasts (Malimbe 1990, 13). The use of pan-ethnic forms such as Pretoria Sotho also enables Africans to hide their ethnic origins. Language creates the space to forge a new past.

Language debates in African languages between language purists and those adopting a *laissez faire* attitude towards pan-ethnic varieties are potentially acrimonious. Usually, the purists are on the offensive, describing pan-ethnic forms as corrupt, bastardized, and impure linguistic behaviour (Zungu 1995, 108). Concern about the health of languages, or apprehension that the health of a particular language is declining are, however, not at all peculiar to African languages. The use of split infinitives in English has frequently been cited by some users of English as signifying the declining health of English. Linguists for the most part agree, however, that languages do not fall sick. Calteaux (1996, 50–1) points out that non-standardized varieties are increasingly beginning to replace standardized varieties in formal settings. She cites exciting evidence of the use of these varieties in domains previously restricted to standardized languages. For example, there is an increasing use of these varieties in traditional ceremonies such as marriages, celebrations of birth, and funerals. The ceremonies are perceived as a marker of the society's link with its past in the present. The use of emerging varieties is often construed as constituting a threat to that continuation, or creating a disjuncture with that past. It does not matter whether that threat is real or imagined. What is important is that language is seen as symptomatic of that threat. Language in such contexts is regarded not only as a form but as constituting the actual substance of that ritual, which in itself is representative of a community's past (Connerton 1989, 41–72).

Conclusion

In this chapter, I have examined the effects of the invention of African languages on the values Africans have attached to their new past. I have also argued that concern about the restandardization of African languages is much more than a linguistic debate. It reflects a concern on the part of the purists about the possible establishment of a disjuncture between their past and present: an expression of fear that they no longer control the future evolution of their practices.

My main argument is that the process of reinvention should involve introducing pan-ethnic speech forms into ordinary institutional discourse as a replacement of an often archaic discourse traumatically out of step with ordinary usage. It is only through the process of egalitarian reinvention that African languages can be made more malleable. Societies, like individuals, may reinvent their past, by assuming new ways of speaking, distancing themselves from one past and creating a new one.

16

EDUARD FAGAN

The constitutional entrenchment of memory

Introduction

CONSTITUTIONS ESTABLISH THE RULES of government. Constitutions such as the South African one, which derive their pedigree from the United States constitution, control the way in which governments exercise power in two distinct ways. The first is by prescribing the manner in which power is to be divided, on both a horizontal and a vertical axis. On the horizontal axis, the constitution will delimit the functions of the legislature, the executive, and the judiciary. On the vertical axis, power might be allocated variously to the central government and to the provincial and local governments. The second way in which the exercise of governmental power is controlled is through limiting the actions of the legislature and the executive in order to ensure that they do not infringe unduly upon individual freedoms. Governmental power is therefore both diffused and curtailed.

Constitutions are therefore intended to regulate the future conduct of government. It is inevitable, however, that constitutions carry within them the history of their creation. So, the United States constitution famously contains a provision that distinguishes between 'free Persons', 'Indians', and 'other Persons' (article 1, section 2), the last-mentioned category counting three-fifths of the first-mentioned in calculating the apportionment of political representatives among the states. Nor is it coincidental that the Fourteenth Amendment, ensuring the equal protection of the laws to all the citizens of the various states, was introduced at the conclusion of the Civil War. Wary of a recurrence of a situation like the rise of Nazism during the Weimar period, the German Basic Law (article 18) provides for the forfeiture of a number of rights, including freedom of expression, assembly, and association, by anyone seeking to undermine the free democratic basic order. The Canadian Charter of Rights and Freedoms, which is otherwise quite a concise document, contains lengthy provisions, pertaining among other things to language rights, aimed at ensuring the acquiescence of Quebec to the promulgation of the charter (sections 16–23, 33).

I wish to suggest that the South African constitution[1] differs from constitutions such as these in an important respect. With all constitutions traces of the history of their making, of the context in which they came into being, are implicit in their choice of, and way of formulating, constitutional provisions. The South African constitution, however, in a number of provisions seeks expressly to capture the history and the context. It regulates the future conduct of government, of course, but it also contains a number of unusual provisions which are best explained as deliberate attempts constantly to remind the interpreter of the constitution of the unequal society that forms the backdrop to the text.

There are numerous examples of this. I shall limit my discussion to four instances. The first is the preamble; the second the provision dealing with languages; the third the provision pertaining to the application of the bill of rights; and the fourth the sections providing for what are known as socio-economic rights.

Preamble

Although the preamble is largely rhetorical in form, it does serve an interpretative function. Reference may be made to it in order to discover the meaning of a constitutional provision which is unclear (Basson 1994, 1; Kentridge and Spitz 1996, 11–12). Already, in interpreting the interim constitution,[2] the Constitutional Court on a number of occasions has referred to the preamble of that document.[3] The role of the preamble is particularly pronounced where, as here, the court adopts a so-called purposive approach to interpretation, which requires the court to find what might be termed the moral values underlying the constitution, and to interpret the constitution in the light of those values. The preamble, being rhetorical in tone, is a good place to begin the search for such values. It begins:

> We, the people of South Africa,
> Recognise the injustices of our past;
> Honour those who suffered for justice
>   and freedom in our land;
> Respect those who have worked to build
>   and develop our country; and
> Believe that South Africa belongs to all
>   who live in it, united in our diversity.

The entrenchment of the past is readily apparent. It is against the background of apartheid in the short term and a general history of injustice in the longer term that the constitution is adopted. Indeed, the first aim of the constitution is expressly to 'heal the divisions of the past'.

As has been said, the constitution is primarily a document that sets out the structures of a democratic government, limited in their operation firstly to the areas of competence accorded them by the constitution and secondly by the restrictions placed on the exercise of their powers by the bill of rights.[4] The extent to which the preambles of both the interim and the final constitutions are concerned with the constitution as an instrument for healing the ills of the past, an instrument of transformation, is therefore striking. One might usefully compare these preambles with the preamble of the United States constitution, also born of conflict:

> We the People of the United States, in Order to form a more perfect Union, establish Justice, insure domestic Tranquility, provide for the common defence, promote the general Welfare, and secure the Blessings of Liberty to ourselves and our Posterity, do ordain and establish this Constitution for the United States of America.

The preamble of the German Basic Law, adopted in 1949, is similarly forward looking:

> Conscious of their responsibility before God and humankind, Animated by the resolve to serve world peace as an equal part of a united Europe, The German people have adopted, by virtue of their constituent power, this Basic Law.

It is not surprising in the circumstances that some judges have seen fit to interpret the provisions of the constitution fairly robustly, taking as their cue textual references to the iniquitous past and the need for redress. As an example of such an approach:

> In some countries the Constitution only formalises, in a legal instrument, a historical consensus of values and aspirations evolved incrementally from a stable and unbroken past to accommodate the needs of the future. The South African Constitution is different: it retains from the past only what is defensible and represents a decisive break from, and a ringing rejection of, that part of the past which is disgracefully racist, authoritarian, insular, and repressive, and a vigorous identification of and commitment to a democratic, universalistic, caring and aspirationally egalitarian ethos expressly articulated in the Constitution. The contrast

between the past which it repudiates and the future to which
it seeks to commit the nation is stark and dramatic. The past
institutionalised and legitimised racism.[5]

Languages

The language provision, contained in section 6 of the constitution, is a long one. By it no fewer than eleven languages are recognized as official. These languages are stated as being Sepedi,
Sesotho, Setswana, siSwati, Tshivenda, Xitsonga, Afrikaans,
English, isiNdebele, isiXhosa, and isiZulu. In addition, the Khoi,
Nama, and San languages, sign language, 'all languages commonly used by communities in South Africa, including German,
Greek, Gujarati, Hindi, Portuguese, Tamil, Telegu and Urdu', as
well as 'Arabic, Hebrew, Sanskrit and other languages used for religious purposes in South Africa' are to be promoted by a Pan
South African Language Board. If taken at face value, the
language provision raises a number of intractable difficulties. It
has been estimated that at least 40 per cent of the European
Union's administrative budget goes to paying for its policy of
multilingualism.[6] Furthermore, it is at least arguable that in developing countries multilingualism tends to slow down moderniza-
tion, for it impedes economic integration and delays the dissemi-
nation of basic knowledge.[7] For fiscal and developmental reasons,
therefore, one must assume that Venda, used as a home language
by less than 2 per cent of the South African population (Mesthrie
1995, xvii), will never enjoy a position commensurate with its official status. It is unlikely, for example, that even national legislation
will be translated into Venda in any but the most exceptional
cases.

   Pedi is included as an official language. It takes the place of
Sesotho sa Leboa in the interim constitution (section 3(1)). Pedi is
the major dialect of Northern Sotho (Bailey 1995, 30), for which

Sesotho sa Leboa is an alternative name. This illustrates the fact that the African languages listed have for a variety of historical reasons not been delineated and formalized to the same extent as Afrikaans and English. Indeed, the present deputy chairperson of the Pan South African Language Board has come out in favour of a standardization of the written varieties of the Nguni and Sotho languages.[8] Save for Richtersveld Nama, there is no extant Khoi language. The only remaining San language in South Africa is spoken probably by fewer than ten people (Traill 1995, 1–2). So the obligation placed on the Pan South African Language Board in this regard by the constitution makes very little sense in the real world. The same goes for the 'languages commonly used by communities in South Africa', with the strong emphasis that is placed in the list on Indic languages. Telugu, according to one study (Mesthrie 1995, xvi), is spoken by 762 people in South Africa, considerably fewer than the almost 9 000 speakers of Italian, which is not a listed language.

Clearly the language provision is not intended to be read too literally. The reasons for the decision to follow what is pretty much an all-inclusive constitutional language policy should be sought in a South African colonial history that marginalized languages without a European pedigree. The inclusion of Khoi and San languages is a poignant reminder of marginalization to the point of extinction. It seems to serve no other function. So, too, the reference to religious languages reminds us that a certain form of Calvinism became during the period of National Party rule a virtual state religion. A more practical option was ready to hand. Despite the small percentage of first-language English speakers in Namibia, the constitution of that country, drafted not long before the South African constitution, makes English the only official language (article 3(1)). But the drafters here were concerned less with practicalities[9] than with making the point that the divisions of the past are to be overcome, that we are 'united in our diversity', as the preamble would have it. It is from the symbolism, again, that some judges have drawn their inspiration: 'The principle of inclusivity shines through the language provisions.'[10]

Application

A fraught area is the application of the bill of rights. Does it apply vertically or horizontally? In other words, does it bind only organs of state, or also private persons in their legal relationships with one another? Clearly the state may not discriminate on the grounds of, say, sexual orientation in its employment policies. May companies? May individuals?

As a general rule,[11] it is the state that is obliged in its conduct to conform to the constitutional rules contained in the bill of rights.[12] This is in line with one of the main purposes of having a written constitution, which is to curtail what might otherwise be an unbridled exercise of state power. For this reason the tendency is to speak, in the constitutional context, only of individual rights (*vis-á-vis* the state), not of individual obligations (which would be entailed if private persons had constitutional rights *vis-á-vis* one another). A good example of this is the extensive publicity campaign that surrounded the drafting by the Constitutional Assembly of the final constitution, part of which involved calling for public participation in the process. Never, to my knowledge, was it intimated to the public that they might acquire anything other than rights from the constitution.[13]

It is obviously so, however, that white people, including corporations controlled by white people, derived enormous benefit from the racist policies of pre-democratic governments in South Africa. Furthermore, it has been forcefully argued that the membrane whose existence lawyers assume between the public and private spheres is in fact fairly porous (Cockrell 1993, 227), particularly in industrial and post-industrial economies where large corporations play a dominant part in the ordering of society. There is accordingly a fairly widely held view that a bill of rights that is purely vertical in operation would be indicative of a failure to recognize the invidious influence that 'privatized apartheid' has had on the shaping of South African society.[14]

This view appears to result in part from an interesting confusion, in which the role of the constitution as blueprint for future government behaviour becomes entwined with its status as historical (or historic) document. As an illustration of this confusion one might take a statement by Kader Asmal and Ronald Roberts (*Cape Times*, 2 June 1995) to the effect that a vertical bill of rights would permit private persons to engage in forced labour practices. This is obviously wrong, for the authors forget that ordinary legislation and indeed the common law can be used to prevent forced labour.[15] Forced labour is a little unusual as an example. The focus in debates about horizontality generally falls on the equality provision, where the point about privatized apartheid comes most readily to the fore. A universal franchise and a democratically elected legislature should however suffice to ensure that laws similar to the civil rights legislation of the United States are passed to prevent discrimination in the private sphere. Such laws have the advantage over the bill of rights of being able to target with some precision the persons and institutions who should not be permitted to discriminate, leaving untouched the individual's right to make choices, even discriminatory ones, in what is sometimes referred to as the intimate sphere. Even without such laws, the values of the constitution are expected to permeate the common law through the process known as indirect horizontality[16] and should suffice to strike down the more egregious examples of privatized apartheid.[17]

Aware of these arguments, and being wary of the unforeseen impact that direct horizontality might have on the existing common law and of the legal uncertainty that might result, the drafters ended up with what is probably best described as a nebulous compromise. The bill of rights binds private persons, but only 'if, and to the extent that, it is applicable' (section 8(2)).[18] Even this is exceptional among constitutions of the world. Other countries have tended to recognize direct horizontality only rarely and in truncated form.[19] I would suggest that the stronger form of it which appears to have been introduced by the final constitution is again a response to a history of social inequality. I do not wish to suggest that the application provision serves only a symbolic function. On the contrary, it seems to me that there are a number of rights in respect of which direct horizontality might well be applicable. But that its inclusion is a response to a historical situation, that the provision is to be read in the first place historically and only thereafter functionally, seems equally to be undeniable. Were this not so, were it intended to operate simply and truly as a functional provision, the qualifications with which the provision is ringed about would be inexplicable.[20]

Socio-economic rights

The fourth and last example of the dual role intended for the constitution may be found in the provisions pertaining to socio-economic rights. Briefly, rights are handily divided into first-, second-, and third-generation rights (although there is no bright line between them). The division reflects the historical development of a human rights culture. First-generation rights are the civil and political rights: the right to equality before the law, the right to free speech, the freedom to assemble and to associate. Second-generation rights are primarily social and economic rights, such as the right to housing and to education, but also include cultural rights. And third-generation rights include the rights to self-determination, peace, and a protected environment.[21] A bill of rights would hardly qualify for the appellation were it not to include the principal civil and political rights. It is however considerably less self-evident that socio-economic rights, which are not universally accepted fundamental rights,[22] should be entrenched.[23] The enforcement of socio-economic rights involves the courts in decisions about the allocation of the national budget.[24] It is not apparent that judges, their only training law and life's little knocks, possess the requisite expertise to make such decisions. It is also, parenthetically, not a role much desired by judges.[25] Furthermore, judges are not elected, but appointed, and from a very small and unrepresentative sector of society. The way in which the budget is allocated is an issue about which the people of a democratic country should have a say, which they have, at least in principle, through their elected representatives.[26] In the South African context, one would have thought that the redistribution of wealth through appropriate taxation and budgetary allocations is precisely what a majoritarian legislature is in a position to ensure.

Much was made during the drafting process by liberationists,[27] including leading members of the African National Congress, of the fact that South African society was dramatically skewed at all levels. The official policy of apartheid went hand in hand with the economic deprivation of those discriminated against. It was in the circumstances not sufficient for the constitution merely to entrench civil and political rights. The state should be placed under a constitutional obligation also to redress social and economic disparities (De Villiers 1994, 599). The right to vote, the reasoning goes, is relatively meaningless to someone who has no food (see Sachs 1990, 8). Even so, the liberationists were generally well aware of the fact that it is at best a highly problematic proposition that the courts should play any role whatsoever in controlling the fiscus.[28]

The upshot of this ambivalence has been a number of provisions which are ambiguous in the extreme. The provision pertaining to housing, a paradigm example, might be best described as giving the right with one hand and taking it away with the other.

The right is firstly not to housing, but, considerably less clearly, to 'access to adequate housing'. In addition, the right itself is phrased in such a way as to make it apparent that it is not a vested right, but an aspiration at best. It also provides the state with a ready excuse for any failure to provide housing: 'The state must take reasonable legislative and other measures, within its available resources, to achieve the progressive realisation of this right' (section 26 (2)).[29] The right as phrased again will be of little use as far as constitutional litigation is concerned. Its alternative role is a twofold one. It reminds the government that the country requires substantial social and economic transformation.[30] And it informs the court, exercising the function of primary interpreter of the document, that the constitution is an instrument of transformation.

Seeking reasons

Why does the South African constitution contain such provisions, and so many of them? The answer should be sought, I would suggest, in the unique way in which South Africa has gone in the space of a few years from being a white oligarchy to having a democratically elected majoritarian government. The unusual thing about this changeover has been the fact that an entrenched minority has given up power more or less voluntarily,[31] through negotiated settlement, rather than as the direct result of a successful revolution.

The settlement negotiations revolved around the process of drafting a new South African constitution. The initial stages, known as the Convention for a Democratic South Africa (CODESA I and II), took place between December 1991 and May 1992. The important substantive work was however done between May 1993 and the end of 1993, during the so-called Multi-Party Negotiating Process (MPNP) (see Corder 1994, 131–70; Du Plessis 1994, 706; Klug 1996, chap. 2).

The essence of negotiated settlements is compromise. In return for giving up its long-held control of political power in the country, the National Party was to have a major say in the formulation of a new South African constitution. The constitutional process resolved upon at the MPNP was an ingenious two-stage one. The first stage involved the drafting, by the 26 parties involved in negotiations, of a transitional constitution. This constitution would among other things establish the ground-rules for the staging of South Africa's first democratic election. The persons elected as members of the two new houses of Parliament, the National Assembly and the Senate, would make up the membership also of the Constitutional Assembly, the *sui generis* body responsible for the single task of drafting a second, or final, constitution.

The two-stage process in large part obviated the difficulty of having a final constitution drafted by 26 political groups whose respective levels of popular support in the country could at that stage only be guessed at. It also permitted the existing tricameral Parliament, which lacked the legitimacy necessary for the formulation of a final constitution, effectively to vote itself out of power and embrace the new democratic order through adopting the transitional constitution as an item of ordinary legislation. The risk to the National Party, however, was the loss of all control over the process of drafting the final constitution, for it obviously knew that it was unlikely to provide the majority of members of the Constitutional Assembly. As part of the compromise, therefore, the interim constitution had annexed to it a list of 34 constitutional principles, agreed upon by the parties participating at the MPNP.[32] It was a requirement, inscribed into the interim constitution (section 71(1)), that the constitutional text drafted by the Constitutional Assembly was to comply with the constitutional principles. To that extent, therefore, the National Party had succeeded in retaining a fair measure of control over the contents of the final constitution.

The constitution represents and embodies within it the fundamental transformation of South African society. It replaces the policy of apartheid and introduces, for the first time in the history of the country, a democratic order based on a universal franchise. As such, it should have been written by the newly liberated oppressed; it should have been a Freedom Charter. But it is not: it was co-written by the oppressed and the oppressors. This was the quid pro quo for the National Party's surrendering power. In the result the constitution would be typified as a liberal-democratic rather than a social-democratic one. The emphasis is on individual rights, with limited scope for an African National Congress government to redistribute wealth[33] (or, for that matter, to exercise its newly acquired legislative powers generally).

Compare this with what might have been. The Freedom Charter[34] provides that 'the mineral wealth beneath the soil, the banks and monopoly industry shall be transferred to the ownership of the people as a whole', and that 'all other industries and trades shall be controlled to assist the well-being of the people'. In its *Constitutional Guidelines for a Democratic South Africa*, published in 1988, the African National Congress maintained much of the centralized economic planning of the charter. The first three provisions under the 'Economy' subheading read:

(n) The state shall ensure that the entire economy serves the interests and well-being of all sections of the population.

(o) The state shall have the right to determine the general context in which economic life takes place and define and limit the rights and obligations attaching to the ownership and use of productive capacity.

(p) The private sector of the economy shall be obliged to co-operate with the state in realising the objectives of the Freedom Charter in promoting social well-being.

The ANC produced a working draft called *A Bill of Rights for a Democratic South Africa* in 1990, as a contribution to the negotiation process. By now the provisions on economic rights and the economy were little more than an extended version of what appears in the final constitution. The socio-economic rights are aspirational in form, and existing property and mineral rights are strongly entrenched. Thus the ANC was obliged to compromise its own history and the history of the struggle in South Africa, in which human rights had always been linked inextricably with guaranteed economic empowerment.[35] The constitution is the pre-eminent document in South Africa now, and its substance is, as I have said, liberal democratic. In the shoring of fragments of memory, though, there has been no compromise. The fragments act as reminders, constitutionally entrenched reminders, of an unpleasant past and an unequal present. As such, the courts will not be permitted altogether to forget that past when interpreting and applying the provisions of the constitution. One might therefore aptly quote, in conclusion, the first chief justice to hold office under the new South African constitution:

> The constitution of a nation is not simply a statute which mechanically defines the structures of government and the relations between the government and the governed. It is a 'mirror reflecting the national soul', the identification of the ideals and aspirations of a nation; the articulation of the values bonding its people and disciplining its government. The spirit and tenor of the constitution must therefore preside and permeate the processes of judicial interpretation and judicial discretion.[36]

Notes

3 Forgiving and forgetting: the Truth and Reconciliation Commission

1 All subsequent references to this work will be given by way of bracketed numbers, corresponding to Wittgenstein's numbering of his remark.
2 The doctrine is most plainly set out and defended in the *Meno*.

4 Cracked heirlooms: memory on exhibition

In an earlier form, this was first given as a keynote address to the Fourth International Conference on Adult Education and the Arts at St Andrews University, 10–14 July 1995, under the title 'Memory and Representation: The Arts and Social Change in South Africa'. It also incorporates points made in my paper 'The Fault Lines Initiative: Inquiries into Truth and Reconciliation', *West Coast Line* 20 (30/20). Special edition, ed. J. Penberthy, 1996, 107–10.

5 Telling 'free' stories? Memory and democracy in South African autobiography since 1994

My thanks to Carli Coetzee, Rob Nixon, Mahmood Mamdani, and Kate Flint for discussions which contributed to some of the thoughts in this chapter.

6 Orality, memory, and social history in South Africa

1 At the time La Hausse, a South African social historian, was a research officer at the African Studies Institute (now known as the Institute for Advanced Social Research) under the directorship of Charles van Onselen. This was perhaps the foremost oral history documentation centre in South Africa.
2 *A Place in the City: The Rand on the Eve of Apartheid* (1993); and more generally her popular history series produced on behalf of the History Workshop, *A People's History of South Africa*, so far in three volumes: *Gold and Workers, 1886–1924* (1981); and *Working Life, 1886–1940: Factories, Townships and Popular Culture on the Rand* (1987) being the first two volumes respectively.
3 'Assessment'. 1988. People's History Programme. Cape Town: University of the Western Cape.
4 Schudson argues that there is no such thing as individual memory and that all memory is social.
5 *See* Callinicos' three volumes in the *People's History of South Africa* series; *Natal Worker History Project Annual Report* (1991); Fairbairn (1990).

264   NEGOTIATING THE PAST

6   There is a range of articles and published works, but Bonner et al., eds. (1993),
    provides a useful recent compilation. More generally the *Journal of Southern
    African Studies (JSAS)*, the *South African Historical Journal (SAHJ)*, and sometimes
    Transformation, *Social Dynamics*, and, more recently, *Kronos*, carry much of
    this new work; as have the edited collections by B. Bozzoli and P. Bonner et al.
    of the four triennial Wits History Workshop conferences, and S. Marks et al.
    of three edited collections based on research into South African history
    grouped around the themes pre-colonial societies, industrialization, and race,
    class, and nationalism.
7   It is interesting to note at this stage the issues raised by these authorship
    designations. The relational word 'with' does not imply co-authorship.
    Indeed, Nkotsoe's (and Ndatshe's) ambiguous place in the authorship of these
    works is beginning to result in their omission. *See*, for example, the references
    to *Women of Phokeng* in Van Onselen 1993, 514 and 1996, 549.

7   Memory and history in William Kentridge's *History of the Main Complaint*

My thanks to William Kentridge for generously making a copy of his film available,
for providing the illustrations, and for commenting on a draft of this chapter.
As always, I am grateful to Sandra Klopper for many helpful suggestions.

1   For a study of the phenomenon of anamnesis in contemporary South African
    art, *see* Rosengarten (1996).
2   Jay Winter (1995) describes the process of coming to terms with catastrophes
    such as the Great War as a tension between forgetting and remembering.
    I am grateful to Sarah Nuttall for bringing this book to my attention.

8   Krotoä remembered: a mother of unity, a mother of sorrows?

1   So, for example, Wanda Smit (1995, 40) writes, about the possible return of
    the body of Saartje Baartman to South Africa, that it 'heralds the return of the
    moon (or feminine principle) to a country wounded by too harsh a sun (or
    masculine principle)'.
2   'Soos die doop geen waarborg is van Christelikheid nie, so is die beskawing
    geen waarborg van sedelikheid nie. By Eva was sowel Christelikheid as
    sedelikheid baie oppervlakkig, bloot 'n lagie vernis. Telkens verval sy weer in
    haar oorspronklike staat van barbarisme' (1942, 6).
3   'gewoontes en karaktereienskappe van die gekleurdes en nie van ingebore
    vooroordeel van die blankes nie' (ibid., 7).
4   'Eva as 'n vroulike Quisling' (ibid., 64).
5   The work of Elphick (1985) and Malherbe (1990) forms the basis of much
    of the later work on Krotoä.

9 Silence in my father's house: memory, nationalism, and narratives of the body

1 Indian historian Shahid Amin observes that Hindi collective memories of Muslim conquest have since the late nineteenth century produced a 'communalisation of history' that has resulted in the narrow religio-sectarian loyalties of Hindi majoritarians who identify the Muslim minority as the villains of the Indian past and present. The official histories of the Indian nation written by secular historians over the past fifty years have not therefore resonated with the needs and desires of the Hindu majority. In response to the ineffectiveness of objectivist secular histories, Amin calls for the crafting of New Hindu History, which 'poses afresh the relationship between memory and history, between oral and written, between the transmitted and the inscribed, between stereotypicality and lived history' (Amin 1997, 3–4).

2 South African scholars such as David Bunn, Carli Coetzee, Shawn Field, Heidi Grünebaum-Ralph, Patricia Hayes, Gary Minkley, Ciraj Rassool, Leslie Witz, and the contributors to this volume have contributed to a growing body of work on the question of memory, identity, and narratives of the body.

3 Driving through Kreuzberg in search of the apartment of my late uncle Siegfried, a German historian friend of mine expressed surprise that he had such a German name. He was somewhat embarrassed when I pointed out that my father had seen himself very much rooted in German culture, and it was therefore not surprising to me that his brother should have a typically German name.

4 This temporal bias is also evident in the fact that the land claims courts will only deal with claims based on land dispossession during the latter half of this century.

5 The following quotation is from the director of the DEHOMAG (Deutsche Holleroth Maschinen Gesellschaft), a subsidiary of IBM that manufactured the 'Holleroth Machine', a punch-card tabulator used in Nazi population census exercises and to monitor large numbers of prisoners shipped in and out of concentration camps. The machine also enabled the SS to distinguish between the categories 'Jews' and 'Jewish mixed breeds' and 'Aryans' and aliens':

We are recording the individual characteristics of every single member of the nation on a little card ... We are proud that we can contribute to such a task, a task that provides the physician of our German body politic with the material [he needs] for his examination so that our physician can determine whether from the standpoint of the nation's health, the data thus arrived at correlate in a harmonious, that is, healthy relationship – or whether diseased conditions must be cured by corrective interventions. We have confidence in our physician and will follow his orders blindly, for we know that he will lead our nation toward a great future. Heil to our German people and their Leader!

(Willy Heidinger, managing director of DEHOMAG, 8 January 1934)

6 The connections between the racial studies of Jews, Roma (Gypsies), KhoiSan, and Herero are particularly interesting given the fact that German scholars such as Dr Eugen Fischer, a senior Nazi Party official, appear to have been involved in such comparative studies. It seems likely that Fischer was drawn to studying these 'nomadic peoples' precisely because they appeared to be 'wanderers' without loyalty to any particular territory or national state. It is therefore perhaps not that surprising that the 'Miscast' exhibition displayed a letter from Dr Fischer in which he describes the correct procedure for cutting and displaying 'Bushman' genitalia.

7 Skotnes responded that her aim was not to represent the San but to explore material cultural remains that embody diverse European and San interactions ranging from the genocidal to the redemptive. She wanted to reveal the cold and objectifying scientific gaze of the anthropocentric photography as well as the more humane interactions and ethnographic encounters between the /Xam San and Lloyd and Bleek. 'Miscast' indeed highlighted questionable museum practices that resulted in the objectification and dehumanization of KhoiSan bodies through photographs, resin casts of naked bodies, and trophy heads. These museum artefacts told a powerful story of the excesses of European science, colonialism, and genocide.

8 Given the variety of ways in which Holocaust memory has been appropriated, it may seem futile to attempt to control and restrict these appropriations. In response to this dilemma, Young concludes that it is better to borrow from the 'emotional reserves' of the Holocaust memory than to censure 'inappropriate appropriations' and thereby unwittingly play into the hands of those seeking to bury all traces of the Nazi past.

9 Mahongo was not alone in his desire for the Bushman bodies to be clothed and covered. Christian cultural attitudes towards the body appear to have been at the heart of the numerous objections to the display of nakedness in 'Miscast'. Since the arrival of missionaries in southern Africa, the African body has been seen as a privileged site for the cultivation of Christian moral values and self-improvement. Missionaries sought to cover African nakedness, which they believed spoke of savage degeneracy, darkness, disorder, pollution, carnal urges, and diabolical desires (Comaroff 1993, 3–4). Western dress was seen as both the sign and instrument of the transformation necessary for African bodies to undergo 'to become vessels of the Spirit'.

10 When the *Mail & Guardian* reproduced illustrations of the naked body of Saartje Baartman, readers complained that the newspaper was complicit in perpetuating racial imagery of sexualized black bodies that have circulated since nineteenth-century Europe discovered its fascination with the 'primitive' genitalia and buttocks of Baartman the 'Hottentot' (*see* Gilman 1995). 'Miscast' encountered similar criticisms of its casts of naked bodies. The casts, which were originally made in the early decades of the twentieth century for scientific study, were displayed in order to draw public attention to the dehuman-

ization and objectification of KhoiSan bodies in the name of science but ended up being seen by some members of the public as yet another manifestation of this legacy of racist representation.

11 I would like to thank Heidi Grünebaum-Ralph for alerting me to the relevance of the Maki Skosana testimony for this chapter. I have found her work on Holocaust memory, language, identity, and the body extremely provocative and instructive.

12 While it remains to be seen how the state, museum curators, historians, and future generations of South Africans will re-present the collective memories of the apartheid era, it seems likely that the state will concentrate its limited resources on a few flagship national projects of memory, such as the Robben Island Museum. These nationalist projects of memory will probably be at the expense of local museums such as the District Six Museum, which testify to the devastation of the Group Areas Act. Given the priorities of the ANC government and its nationalist agenda, everyday experiences and memories of apartheid will probably be marginalized in future projects of public history.

10 Museums and the reshaping of memory

1 The SAM was founded in 1825. It was originally a general museum including natural history and cultural history, but since 1964 it has covered only natural history and anthropology. 'Bushman, Whale and Dinosaur', title of a book on the work of James Drury who was responsible for casting and modelling at the SAM from 1902 to 1942, accurately sums up popular perceptions of the SAM.

2 'Miscast' was presented at the SANG in association with the SAM and the University of Cape Town, from April to September 1996.

3 In July 1996 a workshop on the proposed slave route posed the telling question to the heritage sector, 'What's in it for you?' The control of such projects and who stands to benefit are contested issues.

4 In mid-1996 new councils of trustees for national museums were appointed by the ministry, and the Arts, Culture and Heritage White Paper emphasized redressing past inequities. As Dickerson (1991) notes for museum practice in the USA, a convergence of concerns – ethical, political, financial, and social – motivates strategies for bringing the margins into the mainstream.

5 The Bo-Kaap Museum and the Islamic holdings of the SACHM anomalously became part of a white Own Affairs institution.

6 Papers from the controversial 1987 SAMA Conference were published in the *Southern African Museums Association Bulletin* (1987, vol. 17). Papers by Stuckenburg, and Wright and Mazel reflect the critical edge of the meeting. The late John Kinard, director of the Anacostia Museum in Washington, DC, caused a walkout when he urged the profession to confront racial prejudice. In the past five years many defenders of the status quo have seemingly changed, chameleon like, in line with the shifting balance of power.

7 Thulamela is situated in the northern section of the Kruger Park; archaeologically it relates to the Zimbabwe culture within the southern African Iron Age. It was opened on Heritage Day in 1996 by the Minister for the Environment and Tourism.

8 The Wits History Workshop, 'Myths, Monuments and Museums: New Premises' conference at the University of the Witwatersrand, July 1992, exemplifies this trend.

9 The new National Museum of the American Indian in New York City has pioneered this approach, and also revealed the difficulties inherent in postmodern museum practice. *See* Arieff 1995.

10 Responsibility for Robben Island has been transferred from the Department of Correctional Services to the Department of Arts, Culture, Science and Technology.

11 At the forum held on 7 September 1996, the director of the SANG publicly apologized to individuals and groups who were hurt and angered by 'Miscast'.

12 Alex La Guma, born in 1925, was the son of Jimmy La Guma, president of the Coloured People's Congress. As well as being a journalist and novelist, he was a political activist and Communist ideologue. He was accused of treason and banned in South Africa. He died in exile in Cuba. I am grateful to Tony Voss for drawing my attention to this reference.

11 Remembering tragedy, constructing modernity: Robben Island as a national monument

1 Bodnar (1992, 14) makes this point about public memory in general.

2 Accepting the Jawaharlal Nehru Award for International Understanding in New Delhi, 1980, on behalf of Nelson Mandela who was then imprisoned on Robben Island (Tambo 1987, 199).

3 The figures include votes that linked the casino and hotel to the resort.

4 *See* the film *Robben Island, Our University*; Mbeki 1991, 1992.

5 Report, Select Committee of 1854, CPP, A37–55, iv.

6 Although this is a particularly narrow form of eco-tourism which positions nature as separate from human society, it is an example of the way in which the South African right has appealed to an internationally acceptable model of ecological morality.

7 The human rights reputation associated in particular with Mandela has been more enthusiastically applauded by the west than by other African countries.

8 The term comes from Cook (1974).

9 *See*, for example, 'Grim tour of the island is a living history lesson', *Sunday Independent*, 26 January 1997.

12 Earth and stone: archaeology as memory

1 //Kabbo's capture and journey to Cape Town: first account (Bleek and Lloyd 1911, 295).
2 Draft of a letter from W. H. I. Bleek to the governor, Sir Henry Barkly. UCT/BCI51/CII.6.
3 //Kabbo's intended return home (Bleek and Lloyd 1911, 315).
4 The Bitterpits was identified by //Kabbo as his home; it lies in the area between Kenhardt, Brandvlei, and Vanwyksvlei in the Northern Cape (Deacon 1996).
5 A portfolio of Hermann's paintings was acquired by the South African National Gallery in 1995, and I am grateful for permission to examine this material.
6 I am indebted to David Chidester for this insight.

13 Commemorating, suppressing, and invoking Cape slavery

1 Academics working on slavery were especially influenced by North American historiography: *see* Southey (1992); Cuthbertson (1992).
2 Wiborg in *Tidning för litteratur, handel och ekonomi*, 30 January 1857, trans. Thomas Lindblad. I am grateful to Robert Ross for this reference.
3 *Cape Argus*, 2 December 1862. I am grateful to Vivian Bickford-Smith for this reference.
4 Bickford-Smith (1994). On the *ghoemaliedjes*, *see* Winberg (1992).
5 *Die Banier*, 2 June 1963; repr. of original article in *APO* newspaper, 1910.
6 The forced removal of Africans took place in 1901. For Coloured identity politics in the years around union, *see* Lewis (1987), chap. 2.
7 Advertisement in *Cape Times*, 7 January 1935. We are grateful to Vivian Bickford-Smith for drawing our attention to the pageant.
8 '"Satan's Mad and I Am Glad": Coloured Folk's Pageant at the Track', *Argus*, 11 January 1935.
9 'To-night's Centenary Pageant', *Argus*, 10 January 1935. Gow had lived in the United States and was much influenced by Booker Washington's notions of 'Negro upliftment' to prove loyalty to the state.
10 '"Satan's Mad and I Am Glad": Coloured folk's pageant at the track', *Cape Argus*, 11 January 1935; *Souvenir Brochure of Historical Pageant 1834–1934 held at the Green Point Track, 10–11 January 1935* (Cape Town, 1935).
11 '"Satan's Mad and I Am Glad": Coloured folk's pageant at the track', *Cape Argus*, 11 January 1935.
12 For further discussion of the dichotomy of urban 'Malayism' and rural African slavery *see* Worden (1996).
13 The workshop was held in Cape Town by FAWU in May 1989.
14 For instance, the *Weekend Argus* of 17/18 June 1995 reported that Cecil Cornelius Koopman, 'who will soon Xoi-Xoianise his own name', planned to

found a movement to 'become part of the world-wide groups of indigenous peoples who are claiming the right of full citizenship and rights to their land, culture and identity': 'Xoi-Xoi set to reclaim their place in the sun', 16.

15 Amalia Collins (b.1908), unpubl. interview with Kerry Ward, 4 March 1991, 13–14.

16 Adam Pick (b.1927), unpubl. interview with Kerry Ward, 10 July 1991, 49–50.

17 New history school textbooks that incorporate the findings of new academic work on Cape slavery include Beck et al. (1995), Potenza and Faris (1994), Worden (1996a). The South African Cultural History Museum is planning new displays that will feature the history of the building as the Dutch East India Company slave lodge, and Vergelegen farm near Somerset West exhibits a slave archaeology project.

18 Interview with Dr C. D. D'Arcy, Penlyn Estate, 28 June 1994.

19 'Malaysia rediscovers links with SA Malays', Weekly Mail & Guardian, 25–31 August 1995.

20 'Passionate song and dance about the bad old slave days', Cape Times, 22 May 1996, Arts and Entertainment supplement.

21 'Moslems versper pad by Oudekraal', Die Burger, 16 September 1996.

22 'Response to dilemma of identity', Cape Times, 16 October 1996.

23 For instance, 'Coloureds go for splinter groups', Weekend Argus, 16/17 September 1995; 'New party needed for W Cape', Cape Times, 19 February 1996. On analysis of Coloured rejection of the ANC, see especially Mattes, Giliomee, and James (1994), 108–67.

24 'December 1st movement reveals plans', Cape Times, 21 October 1996.

25 'New group out to woo Coloureds', Cape Times, 9 October 1996.

26 'Gang bosses and poets turn out as new Coloured group meets', Argus, 2 December 1996.

27 Letter from Geoffrey Mamputa to Cape Times, 23 October 1996.

28 'The "children of slaves" gather together', Weekly Mail & Guardian, 18–24 October 1996.

29 Letter from Vivian Bickford-Smith to Cape Times, 2 December 1996.

30 The project has been particularly promoted by Shareen Parker of the Development Agency for Tourism Advancement and Farieda Khan of the Environmental Advisory Unit, University of Cape Town.

16 The constitutional entrenchment of memory

I am indebted to Hugh Corder for his helpful comments on this chapter.

1 The Constitution of the Republic of South Africa, 1996, Act 108 of 1996.

2 The Constitution of the Republic of South Africa, 1993, Act 200 of 1993. The relationship between the 1993 ('interim') constitution and the 1996 ('final') constitution is discussed hereunder.

3 S v Makwanyane and Another 1995 (3) SA 391 (CC) at 488A, para. [262], 514E–F,

para. [363]; *S v Mhlungu and Others* 1995 (3) SA 867 (CC) at 913H, para. [112]
('[The preamble] connects up, reinforces and underlies all of the text that
follows. It helps to establish the basic design of the Constitution and indicate
its fundamental purpose'); *Du Plessis and Others v De Klerk and Another* 1996 (3)
SA 850 (CC) at 892G, para. [75], 910D, para. [123], 911F–912B, paras. [125], [126].

4 The bill of rights is contained in chapter 2 of the constitution.

5 *Makwanyane* (*see* n. 3) at 487H–J, para. [262] (per Mahomed J). Compare
also the following:

> The way I read the preamble and the postscript, the framers unequivocally
> proclaimed much more sweeping aims than those ... apparently accepted by
> some of my Colleagues. Our past is not merely one of repressive use of State
> power. It is one of persistent, institutionalised subjugation and exploitation of
> a voiceless and largely defenceless majority by a determined and privileged
> minority (*Du Plessis* (*see* n. 3) at 911F–G, para. [125] (per Kriegler J).

6 Coulmas (1992, 117). One should, however, take into account the fact that the
EU budget is more heavily skewed towards administrative costs than would
normally be the case with a country's national budget.

7 Ibid., 120. *See* in this regard also Ernest Gellner's (1983) analysis of the development of the nation state, typified by monolingualism, as a response to
industrialization. Some recent studies have suggested that the promotion of a
minority language might have positive effects for regional economic development. The studies are, however, very preliminary, and deal with the promotion of a single minor language. *See* Sproull (1996, 93) and Grin (1996, 24).

8 Alexander (1989), esp. at 64. What is envisaged is a situation analogous to that
of Germany, which has a single standard German and many dialects. 'Nguni'
and 'Sotho' would be used in formal situations, including education. A major
disadvantage of such a project is that Tsonga and Venda, the only two of the
nine languages not falling within either of these groups, would become even
more marginalized.

9 One of the reasons why the Namibian approach could not be adopted in
South Africa was, however, a practical one: the resistance of the National
Party to the idea of giving up the position of Afrikaans as an official language.
But this does not provide a full answer, for it fails to explain the all-inclusive
nature of the language provision.

10 *Makwanyane* (*see* n. 3) at 514F, para. [363].

11 For a brief overview of the position in a number of other jurisdictions,
see Woolman (1996, 10–15, n. 3).

12 If it fails so to conform, it must justify to a court why it should in that instance
be permitted to infringe upon an entrenched right. If it is unable to show, in
accordance with section 36 of the constitution, that the infringement is
reasonable and justifiable in an open and democratic society based on human

dignity, equality, and freedom, the state's act will be ruled invalid.

13 *See* also the judgment of Ackermann J in *Du Plessis* (*see* n. 3) at 906G, para. [112].

14 *See* the judgment of Madala J in *Du Plessis* (*see* n. 3) at 922E, para. [154], 927B, para. [163] and of Kriegler J in the same case at 911F–912A, para. [125], 918G–H, para. [145]. *See*, too, Woolman and Davis (1996, 361).

15 Were it correct, one would have to ask why there is no forced labour in the numerous countries in the world where bills of rights operate vertically only.

16 For a succinct discussion, *see* Cockrell (1996, paras. 3E3–3E5).

17 *See* the judgment of Ackermann J in *Du Plessis* (*see* n. 3) at 905E–906E, para. [110].

18 This is, of course, little different to saying that the bill of rights applies to private persons if it applies to private persons. Adding to the confusion is the retention, in section 8(3) and elsewhere, of the common law as the first port of call for the courts when applying a provision of the bill of rights to a private person.

19 The best-known example of this is the United States Supreme Court judgement in the case of *Shelley v Kraemer* 334 US 1 (1948), concerning a racially restrictive covenant in a title deed. But even this judgement has come in for a great deal of academic criticism, and stands more or less alone in the United States jurisprudence. *See* Wechsler (1959) esp. at 29–31; Henkin (1962); and Tribe (1988), chap. 18.

20 A further clear indication of the lack of faith the drafters have in their own horizontality provision is the inclusion in the formulation of certain of the rights, and notably of the right to equality (section 9), of direct horizontality provisions. These would, of course, be unnecessary were section 8, which is applicable to the entire bill of rights, to be taken as itself ensuring direct horizontality.

21 For a useful overview, *see* De Villiers (1994, 599–628).

22 *Ex parte Chairperson of the Constitutional Assembly: in re Certification of the Constitution of the Republic of South Africa, 1996* 1996 (4) SA 744 (CC) at 800H, para. [78].

23 For the South African debate, *see* Haysom (1992, 451); Mureinik (1992, 464); and Davis (1992, 475). Cf. also Scott and Macklem (1992, 1).

24 The point has been made often enough, and correctly, that the enforcement of first-generation rights might also have budgetary implications. *See* for example the *Certification* judgement (*see* n. 22) at 800I, para. [78]. Such enforcement will not, however, as a general rule involve the courts in deciding about welfare trade-offs, about balancing the cost of housing against the cost of education. *See* in this regard Stephan Malherbe, 'Dealing with social welfare in the South African Constitution' (unpublished paper, 1995).

25 *See* the views of Judge Didcott in SA Law Commission (1991, 533).

26 *See* in this regard the useful distinction between choice-sensitive and choice-insensitive matters that Ronald Dworkin (1987, 1) draws.

27 For a useful discussion of the meaning of the term in the context of the

negotiations, *see* Du Plessis and Corder (1994, 33–5).

28 *See* for example the transcript of the proceedings of the Mini-Conference on Social and Economic Rights held on 21 June 1995 in the Good Hope Chamber, Parliament, Cape Town, under the auspices of the Institute for Democracy in South Africa.

29 The formulation follows that of article 2 of the International Covenant on Economic, Social, and Cultural Rights. International human rights instruments tend by their nature to be aspirational.

30 In this it might be said to be fulfilling the function of a directive principle, outlining desirable social policy for the government, albeit contained within the body of the bill of rights rather than in an annexure thereto, as is usually the case with directive principles.

31 Of course, historians will continue to debate the extent to which the National Party really could have clung to power in the face of economic sanctions, internal uprising, and military defeat in Angola. But there can be no doubt that it could have clung to power for a considerable number of years yet.

32 A number of the principles are very broadly stated, such as 'The Constitution shall be the supreme law of the land. It shall be binding on all organs of state at all levels of government' (CP IV). Others are very specific: 'The independence and impartiality of a Public Service Commission, a Reserve Bank, an Auditor-General and a Public Protector shall be provided for and safeguarded by the Constitution in the interests of the maintenance of effective public finance and administration and a high standard of professional ethics in the public service' (CP XXIX).

33 Most telling in this regard is the provision entrenching the right to property, section 25 of the final constitution, for it largely serves to ensure that property is regarded as a fundamental first-generation right. In an excellent analysis of the equivalent provision in the interim constitution, Theunis Roux argues that a better alternative would have been to follow the German constitutional provision, which provides: 'Property entails obligations. Its use should also serve the public interest' (art 14(2) GG). *See* Roux (1995a; also 1995b).

34 Adopted by the ANC at the Congress of the People in 1955. It has been called the most socialist of all liberationist declarations. *See* Dugard (1978, 213–14).

35 No doubt events in Eastern Europe made it somewhat easier for the ANC to surrender its socialist programme.

36 *S v Acheson* 1991 (2) SA 805 (NmHC) at 813A–B (per Mahomed AJ).

Bibliography

Introduction

ASMAL, K., L. ASMAL, and R. ROBERTS. 1996. *Reconciliation through Truth: A Reckoning of Apartheid's Criminal Governance*. Cape Town: David Philip.

COETZEE J. M. 1988. *White Writing: On the Culture of Letters in South Africa*. New Haven: Radix.

NDEBELE, N. 1991. *Rediscovery of the Ordinary*. Johannesburg: COSAW.

PLAATJE, S. [1916] 1982. *Native Life in South Africa*. Johannesburg: Ravan.

VAN ONSELEN, C. 1996. *The Seed Is Mine: The Life of Kas Maine, a South African Sharecropper 1894–1985*. Cape Town: David Philip.

1 Memory, metaphor, and the triumph of narrative

BEHR, M. 1995. *The Smell of Apples*. London: Abacus.

GOOSEN, J. 1992. *Not All of Us*, trans. A. Brink. Strand: Queillerie.

MOYANA, T. 1976. 'Problems of a Creative Writer in South Africa', in *Aspects of South African Literature*, ed. C. Heywood. London: Heinemann.

SCHOEMAN, K. 1982. *Promised Land*, trans. Marion Valerie Friedmann. London: Jonathan Ball.

2 Stories of history: reimagining the past in post-apartheid narrative

ATWOOD, M. 1996. *Alias Grace*. London: Bloomsbury.

BRINK, A. 1974. *Looking on Darkness*. London: Allen & Unwin.

— 1988. *States of Emergency*. London: Faber & Faber.

— 1993a. *The First Life of Adamastor*. London: Secker & Warburg.

— 1993b. *On the Contrary*. London: Secker & Warburg.

— 1996. *Imaginings of Sand*. London: Reed Books.

DERRIDA, J. [1967] 1976. *Of Grammatology*, trans. G. S. Spivak. Baltimore and London: Johns Hopkins University Press.

HOMER. 1996. *The Odyssey*, trans. R. Fagles. New York: Viking.

JAMESON, F. 1981. *The Political Unconscious. Narrative as a Socially Symbolic Act*. London: Methuen.

JOYCE, J. 1955. *Ulysses*. London: The Bodley Head.

LOFTUS, E. and K. KETCHAM. 1994. *The Myth of Repressed Memory*. New York: St Martin's Press.

MACHEREY, P. [1966] 1978. *A Theory of Literary Production*, trans. G. Wall. London: Routledge & Kegan Paul.

RAY, W. 1990. *Story and History*. Oxford: Blackwell.

SZCZYPIORSKI, A. [1955] 1994. *Self-portrait with Woman*, trans. B. Johnson. New York: Grove Press.

VAN ONSELEN, C. 1996. *The Seed Is Mine: The Life of Kas Maine, a South African Sharecropper 1894–1985*. Cape Town: David Philip.

WHITE, H. 1978. *Tropics of Discourse*. Baltimore and London: Johns Hopkins University Press.

3 Forgiving and forgetting: the Truth and Reconciliation Commission

Government Gazette. 1995. Pretoria: Government Printers. 26 July.

HACKER, P.M.S. 1990. *Wittgenstein: Meaning and Mind*. Oxford: Blackwell.

LOCKE, J. 1959. *An Essay Concerning Human Understanding*, ed. A. Campbell Fraser. New York: Dover Publications.

PARRY, B. 1995. 'Reconciliation and Remembrance'. *Pretexts* 5 (1–2).

TRUTH AND RECONCILIATION COMMISSION. 1995. *Explanatory Memorandum to the Parliamentary Bill*. TRC home page, Internet.

WITTGENSTEIN, L. 1958. *Philosophical Investigations*, trans. G. Anscombe. Oxford: Blackwell.

4 Cracked heirlooms: memory on exhibition

MAMDANI, M. 1996. 'Reconciliation without Justice'. *Southern African Review of Books* 46. November/December.

MEREWETHER, C. 1993. 'Naming Violence in the Work of Doris Salcedo'. *Third Text: Third World Perspectives on Contemporary Art and Culture* 24. Autumn.

REYNOLDS, P. 1996. *Traditional Healers and Childhood in Zimbabwe*. Athens, OH: Ohio University Press.

SACKS, P. M. 1985. *The English Elegy: Studies in the Genre from Spenser to Yeats*. Baltimore and London: Johns Hopkins University Press.

WALCOTT, D. 1993. *The Antilles: Fragments of Epic Memory*. New York: Farrar, Strauss, & Giroux.

5 Telling 'free stories'? Memory and democracy in South African autobiography since 1994

ANDREWS, W. 1986. *To Tell a Free Story: The First Century of Afro-American Autobiography 1760–1865*. Urbana and Chicago: University of Illinois Press.

BEHR, M. 1995. *The Smell of Apples*. London: Abacus.

— 1996. 'Living in the Faultlines'. Paper delivered at the Faultlines Conference, UCT Business School, 4–5 July.

BORAIN, N. 1996. 'The smell of rotten apples'. *Mail & Guardian*, 12–18 July.

COETZEE, J. M. 1992. 'Confession and Double Thoughts: Tolstoy, Rousseau,

Dostoevsky', in *J. M. Coetzee: Doubling the Point – Essays and Interviews*, ed. David Atwell. Cambridge, Mass.: Harvard University Press.

GORDIMER, N. 1995. Extract from 'Writing and Being'. *Southern African Review of Books* 39, 40. September–December.

GREGORY, J. 1995. *Goodbye Bafana: Nelson Mandela, My Prisoner, My Friend*. London: Headline.

HEPWORTH, M. and B. TURNER. 1982. *Confession: Studies in Deviance and Religion*. London: Routledge & Kegan Paul.

JAY, M. (forthcoming). 'Walter Benjamin, Remembrance and the First World War' in *War and Remembrance*, ed. E. Sivan and J. Winter.

MALRAUX, A. 1934. *Man's Fate*. New York: The Modern Library.

MANDELA, N. 1994. *Long Walk to Freedom*. Randburg: Macdonald Purnell.

MODISANE, B. [1963] 1986. *Blame Me on History*. Parklands: Ad Donker.

RAMPHELE, M. 1995. *A Life*. Cape Town: David Philip.

SCHUDSON, M. 1995. 'Dynamics of Distortion in Collective Memory', in *Memory Distortion: How Minds, Brains and Societies Reconstruct the Past*, ed. D. Schacter. Cambridge, Mass.: Harvard University Press.

SIVAN, E. and J. WINTER (forthcoming). *War and Remembrance*.

WINTER, J. 1995. *Sites of Memory, Sites of Mourning: The Great War in European Cultural History*. Cambridge: Cambridge University Press.

WOLPE, A. 1994. *The Long Way Home*. Cape Town: David Philip.

6 Orality, memory, and social history in South Africa

Assessment, People's History Programme. 1988. Unpublished, Cape Town: University of the Western Cape.

BONNER, P. et al., eds. 1993. *Apartheid's Genesis*. Johannesburg: Ravan/Wits University Press.

— 1994. 'New Nation: New History – History Workshop Conference, Democracy: Popular Precedents, Practice, Culture', 13–15 July.

BOZZOLI, B. with M. NKOTSOE. 1991. *Women of Phokeng*. Johannesburg: Ravan.

BROWN, J. et al., eds. 1991. *History from South Africa*. Philadelphia: Temple University Press.

CALLINICOS, L. 1981. *Gold and Workers 1886–1924*. Johannesburg: Ravan.

— 1987. *Working Life 1886–1940: Factories, Townships and Popular Culture on the Rand*. Johannesburg: Ravan.

— 1993. *A Place in the City: The Rand on the Eve of Apartheid*. Johannesburg and Cape Town: Ravan/Maskew Miller Longman.

FAIRBAIRN, J. 1992. *Flashes in Her Soul: The Life and Times of Jabu Ndlovu*. Cape Town: Buchu.

HARRIES, P. 1994. 'Histories New and Old'. *South African Historical Journal* 30. May.

HOFMEYR, I. 1994. *'We Spend Our Years as a Tale That Is Told': Oral Historical Narrative in a South African Chiefdom*. Johannesburg: Wits University Press.

JEWSIEWICKI, B. and V. Y. MUDIMBE. 1993. 'Africans, Memories and Contemporary History of Africa'. *History and Theory* 32 (4).

KEEGAN, T. 1988. *Facing the Storm: Portraits of Black Lives in Rural South Africa*. Cape Town: David Philip.

LA HAUSSE, P. 1990. 'Oral History and South African Historians'. *Radical History Review* 46/47. Winter.

LAZAR, J. 1987. 'Conformity and Conflict: Afrikaner Nationalist Politics 1948–1961'. Unpublished Ph.D. thesis. Oxford University, Oxford.

MINKLEY G. and N. ROUSSEAU. 1995. 'The "Native Crisis" in Cape Town in the 1940s: Life Histories, Official Representations and Academic Discourse'. Paper delivered at the 15th Biennial Conference of the South African Historical Society, 'The Written Past in Transforming Society: Trends and Directions in South African History', Rhodes University, 2–5 July.

MOODIE, T. D. with V. NDATSHE. 1994. *Going for Gold: Men, Mines and Migration*. Johannesburg: Wits University Press.

NASSON, B. 1990. 'Oral History and the Reconstruction of District Six', in *The Struggle For District Six, Past and Present*, ed. S. Jeppie and C. Soudien. Cape Town: Buchu.

— 1991. *Abraham Essau's War: A Black South African in the Cape 1899–1902*. Cambridge: Cambridge University Press.

— 1996. 'A Sharecropper's Life'. *Southern African Review of Books*. March/April.

POSEL, D. 1991. *The Making of Apartheid 1948–1961*. Oxford: Clarendon Press.

QOTOLE, M. and L. VAN SITTERT. 1994. Cape Town Oral History Project, 'Hostels'. *Southern African Review of Books*. January/February.

ROUSSEAU, N. 1994. 'Popular History in South Africa in the 1980s: The Politics of Production'. MA thesis. University of the Western Cape, Cape Town.

SCHUDSON, M. 1995. 'Dynamics of Distortion in Collective Memory', in *Memory Distortion: How Minds, Brains and Societies Reconstruct the Past*, ed. D. Schacter. Cambridge, Mass.: Harvard University Press.

VAN ONSELEN, C. 1993. 'The Reconstruction of a Rural Life from Oral Testimony: Critical Notes on the Methodology Employed in the Study of a Black South African Sharecropper'. *Journal of Peasant Studies* 20 (3).

— 1996. *The Seed Is Mine: The Life of Kas Maine, a South African Sharecropper 1894–1985*. Cape Town: David Philip.

WITZ, L. 1988. *Write Your Own History*. Johannesburg: Ravan.

— 1990. 'The "Write Your Own History" Project'. *Radical History Review* 46 (7).

7 Memory and history in William Kentridge's *History of the Main Complaint*

BURKE, P. 1991. 'History of Events and the Revival of Narrative', in *New Perspectives on Historical Writing*, ed. Peter Burke. Cambridge: Polity Press.

FOUCAULT, M. 1986. 'Of Other Spaces'. *Diacritics*. Spring.

KENTRIDGE, W. 1988. 'Landscape in a State of Siege'. *Stet* 5 (3).

ROSENGARTEN, R. 1996. *Don't Mess with Mr. In-between: 15 Artistas da Africa do Sul*. Lisbon: Culturgest.

WINTER, J. 1995. *Sites of Memory, Sites of Mourning: The Great War in European Cultural History*. Cambridge: Cambridge University Press.

8 Krotoä remembered: a mother of unity, a mother of sorrows?

ABRAHAMS, Y. 1996. 'Was Eva Raped? An Exercise in Speculative History'. *Kronos* 23.

ALARCON, N. 1983. 'Chicana's Feminist Literature: A Re-Vision Through Malintzin / or Malintzin: Putting Flesh Back on the Object', in Moraga and Anzaldua, eds., *This Bridge Called My Back*.

BOSMAN, D. 1942. 'Uit die biografie van 'n Hottentottin: 'n Eksperiment in beskawing'. *Huisgenoot*, 3 July and 10 July.

BOSMAN, D., ed. 1952. *Daghregister gehouden by den opperkoopman Jan Anthonisz. van Riebeeck*, 3 vols. Cape Town: A. A. Balkema.

BRINK, A. 1997. *Imaginings of Sand*. London: Reed Books.

BRINK, E. 1990. 'Man-made Women: Gender, Class and the Ideology of the *Volksmoeder*', in *Women and Gender in South Africa to 1945*, ed. C. Walker. Cape Town: David Philip.

COETZEE, C. 1994. 'Visions of Disorder and Profit: The Khoikhoi and the First Years of the Dutch East India Company at the Cape'. *Social Dynamics* 20 (2).

— 1996. 'Early Afrikaans Theatre and the Erasure of the Black Face: Some Notes on *Susanna Reyniers*'. *Tijdschrift voor Afrikaans en Nederlands*.

DEACON, H., ed. 1996. *The Island: A History of Robben Island 1488–1990*. Cape Town: Mayibuye Books and David Philip.

ELPHICK, R. 1985. *Khoikhoi and the Founding of White South Africa*. Johannesburg: Ravan.

FRANCKEN, A. 1908. *Susanna Reyniers: 'n Blijspel*. Amsterdam and Pretoria: J. H. De Bussy.

GAITSKELL, D. and E. UNTERHALTER. 1989. 'Mothers of the Nation: A Comparative Analysis of Nation, Race and Motherhood in Afrikaner Nationalism and the African National Congress', in *Woman-Nation-State*, ed. N. Yuvel-Davis and F. Anthias. Basingstoke: Macmillan.

HEESE, H. F. 1979. 'Identiteitsprobleme Gedurende die 17de Eeu'. *Kronos* 1.

HEESE, J. A. 1971. *Die Herkoms van die Afrikaner, 1657–1867*. Cape Town: Balkema.

KRÜGER, L. M. 1991. 'Gender, Community and Identity: Women and Afrikaner Nationalism in the *Volksmoeder* Discourse of *Die Boerevrou*'. Unpublished MA thesis. University of Cape Town, Cape Town.

MALHERBE, V. C. 1990. *Krotoä, Called Eva: A Woman Between*. Cape Town: Centre for African Studies.

MC CLINTOCK, A. 1991. '"No Longer in a Future Heaven": Women and Nationalism in South Africa'. *Transition* 51.

— 1993. 'Family Feuds: Gender, Nationalism and the Family'. *Feminist Review* 44.

MORAGA, C. 1986. 'From a Long Line of Vendidas: Chicanas and Feminism', in *Feminist Studies / Critical Studies*, ed. T. De Lauretis. Bloomington: Indiana University Press.

MORAGA, C. and G. ANZALDUA, eds. 1983. *This Bridge Called My Back: Writings by Radical Women of Color.* Watertown: Persephone Press.

PAZ, O. 1985. *The Labyrinth of Solitude*, trans. Lysander Kemp. Harmondsworth: Penguin.

PRESS, K. 1990a. *Bird Heart Stoning the Sea.* Cape Town: Buchu.

— 1990b. *Krotoä.* Pietermaritzburg: Centaur.

SMIT, W. 1995. 'Return of the Hottentot Venus'. *Die Suid-Afrikaan.* Spring.

STOLER, A. 1992. 'Sexual Affronts and Racial Frontiers: European Identities and the Cultural Politics of Exclusion in Southeast Africa', in *Gender at the Crossroads of Knowledge: Feminist Anthropology in the Postmodern Era,* ed. M. Di Leonardo. Berkeley: University of California Press.

THOM, H., ed. 1952a. *Journal of Jan van Riebeeck*, 3 vols. Cape Town / Amsterdam: A. A. Balkema.

— 1952b. 'Historiese Aantekeninge' in Bosman, ed., *Daghregister gehouden by den oppercoopman Jan Anthonisz. van Riebeeck.*

9 Silence in my father's house: memory, nationalism, and narratives of the body

AMIN, S. 1997. 'On Retailing Muslim Conquest in India'. Paper presented at the Cultural Transformations in Africa Conference, 11–13 March. Cape Town: Centre for African Studies, University of Cape Town.

BOONZAIER, E. and J. SHARP. 1994. 'Ethnic Identity and Performance: Lessons from Namaqualand'. *Journal of Southern African Studies* 20 (3).

BOYARIN, J. 1994. 'Introduction' and 'Space, Time and the Politics of Memory', in *Remapping Memory: The Politics of TimeSpace*, ed. J. Boyarin. Minneapolis and London: University of Minnesota Press.

BUNN, D. (forthcoming). *Land Acts: Representation, Modernity and the Making of South African Space.* Durham, N.C.: Duke University Press.

COMAROFF, J. 1993. 'The Empire's Old Clothes: Fashioning the Colonial Subject'. Paper delivered at the Institute for Historical Research and Department of History, South African and Contemporary History Seminar, University of the Western Cape.

COMAROFF, J. and J. COMAROFF, 1992. 'Home-Made Hegemony: Modernity, Domesticity, and Colonialism in South Africa', in *African Encounters with Domesticity*, ed. K. Hansen. New Brunswick, N.J.: Rutgers University Press.

DEACON, H., ed. 1996. *The Island: A History of Robben Island 1488–1992*. Cape Town: David Philip.

DEACON, J. 1996. 'A Tale of Two Families: Wilhelm Bleek, Lucy Lloyd and the /Xam of the Northern Cape', in *Miscast: Negotiating the Presence of the Bushmen*, ed. Pippa Skotnes. Cape Town: UCT Press.

DOUGLAS, M. 1970. *Natural Symbols*. New York: Pantheon Books.

FELDMAN, A. 1991. *Formations and Violence: The Narratives of the Body and Political Terror in Northern Ireland*. Chicago: University of Chicago Press.

FRIEDLANDER, S. 1993. *Memory, History and the Extermination of the Jews of Europe*. Bloomington and Indianapolis: Indiana University Press.

GILMAN, S. 1982. *On Blackness without Blacks*. London: G. K. Hall.

— 1985. *Difference and Pathology*. Ithaca: Cornell University Press.

HUYSSEN, A. 1995. *Twilight Memories: Marking Time in a Culture of Amnesia*. New York and London: Routledge.

KAPLAN, H. 1994. *Conscience and Memory: Meditation in a Museum of the Holocaust*. Chicago and London: University of Chicago Press.

KRAMER, J. 1995. 'Letter from Germany: The Politics of Memory'. *The New Yorker*, 14 August.

RICHARDS, C. 1996. 'A Bad Memory: Telling Tales'. Paper delivered at the Faultlines Conference, UCT Business School, 4–5 July.

ROBINS, S. 1997. 'Transgressing the Borderlands of Tradition and Modernity: Identity, Cultural Hybridity and Land Struggles in Namaqualand (1980–94)'. *Journal of Contemporary African Studies* 15 (1).

SAMUEL, R. and P. THOMPSON, eds. 1990. *The Myths We Live By*. London: Routledge.

STIER, O. 1993. 'The Propriety of Holocaust Memory: Rereading the "Master Narrative" in Emily Prager's *Eve's Tattoo*'. Paper delivered at the annual meeting of the Association for Jewish Studies, 13 December, Boston.

WELLS, J. 1997. 'The Story of Eva and Pieter: Transcultural Marriage on the Road to Success in Van Riebeeck's Colonial Outpost'. Paper delivered at the Gender and Colonialism Conference, University of the Western Cape, Cape Town. January.

YOUNG, J. E. 1988. *Writing and Rewriting the Holocaust*. Bloomington and Indianapolis: Indiana University Press.

10 Museums and the reshaping of history

ARIEFF, A. 1995. 'A Different Sort of (P)Reservation: Some Thoughts on the National Museum of the American Indian'. *Museum Anthropology* 19 (2).

BODNAR, J. 1992. *Remaking America: Public Memory, Commemoration and Patriotism in the Twentieth Century*. Princeton: Princeton University Press.

DAVISON, P. 1991. 'Material Culture, Context and Meaning. A Critical Investigation of Museum Practice, with Particular Reference to the South

African Museum'. Ph.D. thesis. University of Cape Town, Cape Town.

— 1993. 'Human Subjects as Museum Objects: A Project to Make Life-casts of "Bushmen" and "Hottentots", 1907–1924'. *Annals of the South African Museum* 102 (5).

DEACON, J. 1993. 'Archaeological Sites as National Monuments in South Africa: A Review of Sites Declared since 1936'. *South African Historical Journal* 29.

DICKERSON, A. 1991. 'Redressing the Balance'. *Museums Journal* 91 (2).

HAMILTON, C. 1994. 'Against the Museum as Chameleon'. *South African Historical Journal* 31.

HUDSON, K. and A. NICHOLLS. 1975. *The Directory of Museums*. London: Macmillan Press.

KARP, L. and S. LAVINE, eds. 1991. *Exhibiting Cultures: The Poetics and Politics of Museum Display*. Washington, D.C.: Smithsonian Institution Press.

KLOPPER, S. 1996. 'Whose Heritage? The Politics of Cultural Ownership in Contemporary South Africa'. *NKA Journal of Contemporary African Art*. Fall / Winter.

KRAFCHIK, B. 1994. 'Adventurous Changes'. *Museums Journal* 94 (4).

KUSEL, U. 1994. 'No Building, No Problem'. *Museums Journal* 94 (4).

LANE, P. 1996. 'Breaking the Mould? Exhibiting Khoisan in Southern African Museums'. *Anthropology Today* 12 (5).

LOWENTHAL, D. 1985. *The Past Is a Foreign Country*. Cambridge: Cambridge University Press.

MARTIN, M. 1996. 'Bringing the Past into the Present – Facing and Negotiating History, Memory, Redress and Reconciliation at the South African National Gallery'. Paper delivered at the Faultlines Conference, UCT Business School, 4–5 July.

ODENDAAL, A. 1994. 'Let It Return!' *Museums Journal* 94 (4).

STEINER, C. 1995. 'Museums and the Politics of Nationalism'. *Museum Anthropology* 19 (2).

VOSS, A. 1990. 'Die Bushie is Dood: Long Live the Bushie'. *African Studies* 49 (1).

WEBB, D. 1994. 'Winds of Change'. *Museums Journal* 94 (4).

11 Remembering tragedy, constructing modernity: Robben Island as a national monument

BANK, A. 1991. 'Slavery in Cape Town, 1806–1843'. Unpublished MA thesis. University of Cape Town, Cape Town.

BICCARD, 'Minutes of Evidence: Report of the Commission Appointed to Inquire into and Report upon the Best Means of Moving the Asylum at Robben Island to the Mainland'. CPP, G64-1880.

BODNAR, J. 1992. *Remaking America: Public Memory, Commemoration and Patriotism in the Twentieth Century*. Princeton: Princeton University Press.

COOK, A. 1974. *South Africa: The Imprisoned Society*. London: International

Defence and Aid Fund.

GREENE, J. P. 1987. 'Changing Identity in the British Caribbean: Barbados as a
    Case Study', in *Colonial Identity in the Atlantic World 1500–1800*, ed. N. Canny
    and A. Pagden. Princeton: Princeton University Press.

HUYSSEN, A. 1994. 'Monument and Memory in a Post-modern Age', in *The Art of
    Memory: Holocaust Memorials in History*, ed. J. E. Young. New York: Prestel.

JACOBS, J. H. 1992. 'Narrating the Island: Robben Island in South African
    Literature'. *Current Writing* 4.

LUBBE, G. 1987. 'Robben Island: The Early Years of Muslim Resistance'. *Kronos* 12.

MBEKI, G. 1991. *Learning from Robben Island*. Cape Town: David Philip.

— 1992. 'Robben Island retold'. *Staffrider* 10 (3).

MCKENZIE, K. 1991. 'The *South African Commercial Advertiser* and the Making of
    Middle-class Identity in Early Nineteenth Century Cape Town'. Unpublished
    MA thesis. University of Cape Town, Cape Town.

RUSSELL, R. 1983. 'Mental Physicians and Their Patients: Psychological Medicine
    in the English Pauper Lunatic Asylums of the Later Nineteenth Century'.
    Unpublished Ph.D. thesis, University of Sheffield, Sheffield.

SCULL, A. 1993. *The Most Solitary of Afflictions: Madness and Society in Britain
    1700–1900*. London: Yale University Press.

TAMBO, O. 1987. *Preparing for Power*. London: Heinemann.

YOUNG, J. E., ed. 1994. *The Art of Memory: Holocaust Memorials in History*.
    New York: Prestel.

12 Earth and stone: archaeology as memory

ANDERSON, B. 1991. *Imagined Communities: Reflections on the Origin and Spread of
    Nationalism*. London: Verso.

BENDER, B. 1993. 'Landscape – Meaning and Action', in *Landscape: Politics and
    Perspectives*, ed. B. Bender. London: Berg.

BLEEK, E. and D. BLEEK. 1909. 'Notes on the Bushmen' in *Bushman Paintings*,
    ed. M. Tongue. London: Clarendon Press.

BLEEK, W. H. I. and L. C. LLOYD. 1911. *Specimens of Bushman Folklore*. London:
    George Allen.

COSGROVE, D. 1984. *Social Formation and Symbolic Landscape*. London:
    Croom Helm.

— 1993. *The Palladian Landscape: Geographical Change and Its Cultural
    Representation in Sixteenth-century Italy*. Leicester: Leicester University Press.

CROLL, E. and D. PARKIN. 1992. 'Anthropology, the Environment and
    Development', in E.Croll and D. Parkin, *Bush Base: Forest Farm.
    Culture, Environment and Development*. London: Routledge.

DANIELS, S. and D. COSGROVE. 1988. 'Introduction: Iconography and Landscape',
    in *The Iconography of Landscape: Essays on the Symbolic Representation, Design
    and Use of Past Environments*, ed. D. Cosgrove and S. Daniels. Cambridge:

Cambridge University Press.

DEACON, J. 1996. 'A Tale of Two Families: Wilhelm Bleek, Lucy Lloyd and the /Xam San of the Northern Cape' in Skotness, ed., *Miscast*.

GODBY, M. 1996. 'Images of //Kabbo', in Skotnes, ed., *Miscast*.

GORDON, R. J. 1992. *The Bushman Myth: The Making of a Namibian Underclass*. Boulder: Westview Press.

HALL, M. 1996. 'The Proximity of Dr Bleek's Bushman' in Skotnes, ed., *Miscast*.

KOSTOF, S. 1991. *The City Shaped: Urban Patterns and Meanings through History*. London: Thames & Hudson.

LEFEBVRE, H. 1991. *The Production of Space*. Oxford: Blackwell.

LEWIS-WILLIAMS, J. D. 1981. *Believing and Seeing. Symbolic Meanings in Southern San Rock Paintings*. London: Academic Press.

PARKER PEARSON, M. and C. RICHARDS. 1994. 'Ordering the World: Perceptions of Architecture, Space and Time', in *Architecture and Order: Approaches to Social Space*, ed. M. Parker Pearson and C. Richards. London: Routledge.

PEIRES, J. B. 1989. *The Dead Will Arise. Nongqawuse and the Great Xhosa Cattle-killing Movement of 1856–7*. Johannesburg: Ravan.

SAID, E. W. 1984. *The World, the Text, and the Critic*. London: Faber & Faber.

SCHAMA, S. 1995. *Landscape and Memory*. London: HarperCollins.

SCOTT, J. C. 1990. *Domination and the Arts of Resistance: Hidden Transcripts*. New Haven: Yale University Press.

SKOTNES, P. 1996. 'Introduction', *Miscast: Negotiating the Presence of the Bushmen*, ed. P. Skotnes. Cape Town: UCT Press.

SOJA, E. W. 1989. *Postmodern Geographies: The Reassertion of Space in Critical Social Theory*. London: Verso.

SOLOMON, A. 1992. 'Gender, Representation, and Power in San Ethnography and Rock Art'. *Journal of Anthropological Archaeology* 11.

13 Commemorating, suppressing, and invoking Cape slavery

ADHIKARI, M., ed. 1996. *Straatpraatjes: Language, Politics and Popular Culture in Cape Town 1909–1922*. Cape Town: Van Schaik.

BECHLER, W. F. 1873. *Benigna van Groenekloof of Mamre*. Genadendal: Moravian Press.

BECK, L. et al., eds. 1995. *In Search of History: Primary 1*, Cape Town: Oxford University Press.

BICKFORD-SMITH, V. 1994. 'Meanings of Freedom: Social Position and Identity amongst Ex-slaves and Their Descendants in Cape Town, 1875–1910', in Worden and Crais, eds., *Breaking the Chains*.

CUTHBERTSON, G. 1992. 'Cape Slave Historiography and the Question of Intellectual Dependence'. *South African Historical Journal* 27.

DA COSTA, Y. and A. DAVIDS. 1994. *Pages from Cape Muslim History*. Pietermaritzburg: Shuter & Shooter.

HOFMEYR, I. 1991. 'Jonah and the Swallowing Monster: Orality and Literacy on a Berlin Mission Station in the Transvaal'. *Journal of Southern African Studies* 14 (4).

JAFFE, H. 1952. 'Mnguni', in *Three Hundred Years*, Unity Movement History Series. Cape Town: Ardust.

JEPPIE, M. S. 1986. 'Historical Process and the Constitution of Subjects: I.D. du Plessis and the Reinvention of the "Malay"'. BA Honours thesis. University of Cape Town, Cape Town.

KRÜGER, B. 1966. *The Pear Tree Blossoms: The History of the Moravian Church in South Africa 1737–1869*. Genadendal: Moravian Book Depot.

LAMBRECHTS, H. 1976. *New History for Standard 5*. Cape Town: Nasou Limited.

LEWIS, G. 1987. *Between the Wire and the Wall*. Cape Town: David Philip.

LUDLOW, H. 1992. 'Missions and Emancipation in the South-Western Cape: A Case Study of Groenekloof (Mamre), 1838–1852'. MA thesis. University of Cape Town, Cape Town.

MATTES, R. H. GILIOMEE, and W. JAMES. 1994. 'The Election in the Western Cape', in *Launching Democracy in South Africa: The First Open Election*, ed. R. Johnson and L. Schlemmer. New Haven: Yale University Press.

POTENZA, E. and D. FARIS. 1994. *Hands-On History*. Cape Town: Maskew Miller Longman.

SOUTHEY, N. 1992. 'From Periphery to Core: The Treatment of Cape Slavery in South African Historiography'. *Historia* 37.

VAN HEYNINGEN, E. 1997. 'The Emergence of the Modern City, 1919–1945', in *Cape Town: A Social History*, ed. V. Bickford-Smith, E. Van Heyningen, and N. Worden. Cape Town: David Philip.

WARD, K. 1992. 'The Road to Mamre: Migration, Memory and the Meaning of Community, c.1900–1992'. MA thesis. University of Cape Town, Cape Town.

— 1994. 'Links in the Chain: Community, Identity and Migration in Mamre 1838–1938', in *Breaking the Chains*, ed. N. Worden and C. Crais.

— 1995. 'The "300 Years: Making of Cape Muslim Culture" Exhibition, Cape Town, April 1994: Liberating the Caste?' *Social Dynamics* 21 (1).

WINBERG, C. 1992. 'The Ghoemaliedjes of the Cape Muslims: Remnants of a Slave Culture'. Unpublished paper, University of Cape Town.

WITZ, L. 1997. 'Commemorations and Conflicts in the Production of South African National Pasts: The 1952 Jan Van Riebeeck Tercentenary Festival'. Ph.D. thesis. University of Cape Town, Cape Town.

WORDEN, N. 1996a. *The Chains That Bind Us*. Cape Town: Juta.

— 1996b. 'Slavery and Amnesia: Towards a Recovery of Malagasy Heritage in Representations of Cape Slavery'. Paper delivered at Fanandevozana ou esclavage – colloque international à l'occasion du centenaire de l'esclavage à Madagascar, Antananarivo. 24–28 September.

WORDEN, N. and C. CRAIS, eds. 1994. *Breaking the Chains: Slavery and Its Legacy in the Nineteenth Century Cape Colony*. Johannesburg: Wits University Press.

14 Ads and amnesia: black advertising in the new South Africa

ADAM, H. 1997. 'Embarrassment of "filthy riches"'. *Mail & Guardian*, 6–13 March.

All Media Products Survey (AMPS). 1995. Johannesburg: South African
    Advertising Research Foundation.

BERTELSEN, E. 1996. 'Selling Change: Advertisements for the 1994 South African
    Election'. *African Affairs* 95 (379).

BOCOCK, R. 1993. *Consumption*. London: Routledge.

COOK, G. 1992. *The Discourse of Advertising*. London: Routledge.

GOFFMAN, E. 1979. *Gender Advertisements*. London: Macmillan.

GOLDMAN, R. 1992. *Reading Ads Socially*. London: Routledge.

GRAMSCI, A. 1971. *Selections from the Prison Notebooks*, ed. Q. Hoare and
    G. N. Smith. London: Lawrence & Wishart.

HALL, S. 1988. 'The Toad in the Garden: Thatcherism among the Theorists',
    in Nelson and Grossberg, eds., *Marxism and the Interpretation of Culture*.

HARVEY, D. 1992. *The Condition of Postmodernity*. Oxford: Blackwell.

JAMESON, F. 1991. *Postmodernism: Or, The Cultural Logic of Late Capitalism*.
    London: Verso.

JOHNSON, R. W. 1996. 'On the Way to First Base'. *London Review of Books*.
    17. October.

MCGRATH, M. and A. WHITEFORD. 1994. *Distribution of Income in South Africa*.
    Pretoria: Human Sciences Research Council.

MOUFFE, C. 1988. 'Hegemony and New Political Subjects: Towards a New
    Concept of Democracy', in Nelson and Grossberg, eds., *Marxism and the
    Interpretation of Culture*.

NELSON, C. and GROSSBERG, L., eds. 1988. *Marxism and the Interpretation of Culture*.
    London: Macmillan.

Magazines

Bona. Durban: Republican Press.

Drum. Cape Town: National Magazines.

Ebony South Africa. Johannesburg: EBCO & Johnson Publishing Co.

Pace. Johannesburg: Caxton Publishers.

Thandi. Durban: Republican Press.

Tribune. Johannesburg: Penta Publications.

True Love. Johannesburg: National Magazines.

15 African languages as European scripts: the shaping of communal memory

CALTEAUX, K. 1996. *Standard and Non-standard Language Varieties in the Urban
    Areas of South Africa*. Pretoria: Human Social Sciences Research Council.

CAMERON, D. 1995. *Verbal Hygiene*. London: Routledge.

CONNERTON, P. 1989. *How Societies Remember*. Cambridge: Cambridge University Press.

FARDON, R and G. FURNISS. 1994. *African Languages Development and the State*. London and New York: Routledge.

GILROY, P. 1987. *'There Ain't No Black in the Union Jack': The Cultural Politics of Race and Nation*. Chicago: University of Chicago Press.

HARRIES, P. 1995. 'Discovering Languages: The Historical Origins of Standard Tsonga in Southern Africa', in Mesthrie, ed., *Language and Social History*.

HERBERT, R. K. 1992. *Language and Society in Africa: Theory and Practice*. Johannesburg: Wits University Press.

HOFMEYR, I. 1993. *'We Spend Our Years as a Tale That is Told': Oral Historical Narratives in a South African Chiefdom*. Johannesburg: Wits University Press.

JEATER, D. 1994. '"The Way You Tell Them": Ideology and Development Policy in Southern Africa'. Paper delivered at 'Paradigms Lost, Paradigms Regained', *Journal of Southern African Studies* Twentieth Anniversary Conference, University of York.

LE PAGE, R. and A. TABOURET-KELLER. 1985. *Acts of Identity*. Cambridge: Cambridge University Press.

— 1982. 'Models and Stereotypes of Ethnicity and Language'. *Journal of Multilingual and Multicultural Development* 3 (3).

MALIMBE, R. M. 1990. 'The Influence of Non-Standard Varieties on the Standard Setswana of High School Pupils'. MA thesis. Rand Afrikaans University, Johannesburg.

MESTHRIE, R., ed. 1995. *Language and Social History: Studies in Southern African Sociolinguistics*. Cape Town: David Philip.

NTSHANGASE, D. K. 1995. '"Indaba yami-i-straight": Language practices in Soweto', in Mesthrie, ed., *Language and Social History*.

PENNYCOOK, A. 1994. *The Cultural Politics of English as a National Language*. London and New York: Longman.

RAMPTON, M. B. 1990. 'Displacing the Native Speaker: Expertise, Affiliation and Inheritance'. *English Language Teaching Journal* 44 (20).

RANGER, T. 1989. 'Missionaries, Migrants and Manyikas: The Invention of Ethnicity in Zimbabwe', in *The Creation of Tribalism in Southern Africa*, ed. L. Vail. London/Berkeley and Los Angeles: James Currey/University of California Press.

STREET, B. 1984. *Literacy Theory and Practice*. Cambridge: Cambridge University Press.

— 1993. 'Culture Is a Verb Anthropological: Aspects of Language and Cultural Processes in Language and Culture'. *British Studies in Applied Linguistics* 7.

ZUNGU, P. 1995. 'Language Variation in Zulu: A Case Study of Contemporary Codes and Registers in the Greater Durban Area'. M.Phil thesis. University of Durban–Westville, Durban.

16 The constitutional entrenchment of memory

ALEXANDER, N. 1989. *Language Policy and National Unity in South Africa/Azania*. Cape Town: Buchu.

BAILEY, R. 1995. 'The Bantu Languages of South Africa' in Mesthrie, ed., *Language and Social History*.

BASSON, D. 1994. *South Africa's Interim Constitution: Text and Notes*. Cape Town: Juta.

CHASKALSON, M., J. KENTRIDGE, J. KLAAREN, G. MARCUS, D. SPITZ, and S. WOOLMAN, eds. 1996. *Constitutional Law of South Africa*. Cape Town: Juta.

COCKRELL, A. 1993. '"Can you paradigm?" – Another Perspective on the Public Law/Private Law Divide'. *Acta Juridica*.

— 1996. 'The Law of Persons and the Bill of Rights', *Bill of Rights Compendium*. Durban: Butterworths.

CORDER, H. 1994. 'Towards a South African Constitution'. *Modern Law Review* 57.

COULMAS, F. 1992. *Language and Economy*. Oxford: Blackwell.

DAVIS, D. 1992. 'The Case against the Inclusion of Socio-economic Demands in a Bill of Rights Except as Directive Principles'. *South African Journal on Human Rights* 8.

DE VILLIERS, B. 1994. 'Social and Economic Rights', in Van Wyk et al., eds., *Rights and Constitutionalism*.

DU PLESSIS, L. 1994. 'The Genesis of the Provisions concerned with the Application and Interpretation of the Chapter on Fundamental Rights in South Africa's Transitional Constitution'. *Tydskrif vir Suid-Afrikaanse Reg*.

DU PLESSIS, L. and H. CORDER. 1994. *Understanding South Africa's Transitional Bill of Rights*. Cape Town: Juta.

DUGARD, J. 1978. *Human Rights and the South African Legal Order*. Princeton: Princeton University Press.

DWORKIN, R. 1987. 'What is Equality? Part 4 – Political Equality'. *University of San Francisco Law Review* 22.

GELLNER, E. 1983. *Nations and Nationalism*. Ithaca: Cornell University Press.

GRIN, F. 1996. 'The Economics of Language: Survey, Assessment and Prospects'. *International Journal of the Sociology of Language* 121.

HAYSOM, N. 1992. 'Constitutionalism, Majoritarian Democracy and Socio-economic Rights'. *South African Journal on Human Rights* 8.

HENKIN, L. 1962. '*Shelley vs Kraemer*: Notes for a Revised Opinion'. *University of Pennsylvania Law Review* 110.

KENTRIDGE, J. and D. SPITZ. 1996. 'Interpretation', in Chaskalson et al., eds., *Constitutional Law of South Africa*.

KLUG, H. 1996. 'Historical Background', in Chaskalson et al., eds., *Constitutional Law of South Africa*.

MALHERBE, S. 1995. 'Dealing with Social Welfare in the South African Constitution'. Unpublished paper.

MESTHRIE, R., ed. 1995. *Language and Social History: Studies in South African Sociolinguistics*. Cape Town: David Philip.

MUREINIK, E. 1992. 'Beyond a Charter of Luxuries: Economic Rights in the Constitution'. *South African Journal on Human Rights* 8.

ROUX, T. 1995a. 'Commenting on the Property Clause in the Interim Constitution'. Unpublished paper.

— 1995b. *Constitutional Review of Social Reform Legislation in South Africa: A 'Civil Society' Model*. Cape Town: UCT Press.

SACHS, A. 1990. *Protecting Human Rights in a New South Africa*. Cape Town: Oxford University Press.

SCOTT, C. and P. MACKLEM. 1992. 'Constitutional Ropes of Sand or Justiciable Guarantees? Social Rights in a New South African Constitution'. *University of Pennsylvania Law Review* 141.

SOUTH AFRICAN LAW COMMISSION. 1991. *Project 58: Group and Human Rights*. Interim report.

SPROULL, A. 1996. 'Regional Economic Development and Minority Language Use: The Case of Gaelic Scotland'. *International Journal of the Sociology of Language* 121.

TRAILL, A. 'The Khoisan Languages of South Africa', in Mesthrie,. ed., *Language and Social History*.

Transcript for the proceedings of the mini-conference on Social and Economic Rights held on 21 June 1995 in the Good Hope Chamber, Parliament, Cape Town, under the auspices of the Institute for Democracy in South Africa.

TRIBE, L. 1988. *American Constitutional Law*, 2nd edn. Mineola: Foundation Press.

VAN WYK, D. 1994. 'Introduction to the South African Constitution', in Van Wyk et al, eds., *Rights and Constitutionalism*.

VAN WYK, D., J. DUGARD, B. DE VILLIERS and D. DAVIS, eds. 1994. *Rights and Constitutionalism: The New South African Legal Order*. Cape Town: Juta.

WECHSLER, H. 1959. 'Toward Neutral Principles of Constitutional Law'. *Harvard Law Review* 73.

WOOLMAN, S. 1996. 'Application', in Chakalson et al., eds., *Constitutional Law of South Africa*.

WOOLMAN, S. and D. DAVIS. 1996. 'The Last Laugh: *Du Plessis v. De Klerk*, Classical Liberalism, Creole Liberalism and the Application of Fundamental Rights under the Interim and Final Constitutions'. *South African Journal on Human Rights* 12.

Index